AN INCONVENIENT COP

AN INCONVENIENT COP

MY FIGHT TO CHANGE POLICING IN AMERICA

Edwin Raymond

WITH JON STERNFELD

VIKING

VIKING
An imprint of Penguin Random House LLC
penguinrandomhouse.com

Library of Congress Cataloging-in-Publication Data

Names: Raymond, Edwin, 1986– author. | Sternfeld, Jon, author.
Title: An inconvenient cop : my fight to change policing in America / Lt.
Edwin Raymond (Ret.), NYPD, with Jon Sternfeld.
Description: New York : Viking, [2023] | Includes bibliographical references.
Identifiers: LCCN 2023022720 (print) | LCCN 2023022721 (ebook) |
ISBN 9780593653166 (hardcover) | ISBN 9780593653173 (ebook)
Subjects: LCSH: Raymond, Edwin, 1986– | New York (N.Y.). Police
Department—Officials and employees—Biography. |
Police—New York (State)—New York—Biography. |
Whistle blowers—New York (State)—New
York—Biography. | Police misconduct—New York (State)—New York. |
Police—United States.
Classification: LCC HV7911.R396 A3 2023 (print) |
LCC HV7911.R396 (ebook) | DDC 363.209747—dc23/eng/20230621
LC record available at https://lccn.loc.gov/2023022720
LC ebook record available at https://lccn.loc.gov/2023022721

Printed in the United States of America
1st Printing

Designed by Amanda Dewey

Some names and identifying characteristics have been changed to
protect the privacy of the individuals involved.

To both the well-known and unknown
who have made great sacrifices for the masses

Early in life, I had learned that if you want something, you had better make some noise.

—MALCOLM X

CONTENTS

INTRODUCTION

N o role in society is more divisive than that of the cop. Feared and re- spected, insulted and embraced, viewed as both the glue keeping it all together and the force breaking it all apart, the heart of our civiliza- tion and the soul of its disruption. He is both uniter and divider, torn by allegiances, recognized as the cure and the disease itself.

The police officer occupies a central role in our society, but he's pulled in two directions—by the people he ostensibly serves and the sys- tem that provides for him. And he can't serve both. If he is true to him- self and to his job, his center cannot hold. I wake up every morning feeling this tension in my bones.

These days a Black cop may seem oxymoronic, like that Jean-Michel Basquiat painting *Irony of Negro Policeman*. The painting captures the conflict, the reality of the limbo that I'm in. The irony of being on the receiving end of oppression while donning the uniform of the oppressor. Basquiat himself was a downtown graffiti artist of Haitian descent whose provocative and renegade genius was embraced and then com- modified by the uptown elite. He knew from ironies. The double life of someone who sees himself one way and is seen by the public in another.

I'm a police officer, but it's not my identity. I'm a man who *became* a cop. At one time, I saw becoming a police officer as a way to serve my community. But when I got into uniform, got a look at things from the inside, I saw something that I couldn't ignore. Despite my aspirations and inspirations, I wasn't in a position to fix anything. In trying to rectify the issues, I was mocked, insulted, gaslit, elbowed aside, set up, lied about, retaliated against, and treated as the problem.

There are eighteen thousand law enforcement agencies in the country. Because of New York City's claim as this country's safest big city and its influence across the nation, its policing model has been packaged, marketed, and sold across the United States and even to cities overseas.

So when I speak of the ills inside the NYPD, I am speaking of all U.S. policing. New York City is the headwaters of the behavior infecting modern police departments, the red-hot center of the problem. Fourteen years behind that curtain have opened my eyes to the yawning gap between the police's ideal potential and the stark reality of its failures.

The police force is not a benevolent, well-meaning but merely misunderstood institution. The brass will insist it is unfairly treated; they will claim its reputation has been tainted by so-called bad apples. This is a convenient fiction maintained to insulate the leadership and the department itself from criticism. The academy churns out cops who are indoctrinated in the myth of the heroic policeman (this is especially true for the vaunted NYPD), his selfless courage and honor, his central role as the protector of public safety, his precarious presence as the dam preventing the rushing wave of crime from engulfing us all, the thin blue line keeping us from chaos.

Under the banner of public safety, the police force incentivizes its officers to maintain the racial and social order. They are the most visible organization tasked with America's subjugation of its minority citizens. Cops who won't engage in this behavior, who want to be valuable contributors to the neighborhood, who want to help the community instead of harass it, are kept knocking around the bottom where they cannot threaten it. The institution has a violent, visceral reaction, like a gag reflex, to anyone who resists the program. These "problem cops" often get chewed up and spit out.

That's what usually happens. That's what the institution's defenses are trained to do. But they didn't plan for someone like me.

IN 2014, Eric Garner died from a banned police chokehold after being suspected of selling loose cigarettes. Six years later, George Floyd was suffocated to death after allegedly passing a counterfeit twenty-dollar bill. *Elijah McClain. Philando Castile. Walter Scott. Terence Crutcher. Tamir Rice. Tyre Nichols.* When we speak of the police who killed these innocent people, we're not talking about bad apples anymore. It's time we start talking about the barrel. Or, even further back in its creation, what I call "the soil."

Police reform has been on the public agenda for years, but well-meaning activists, politicians, and experts keep missing the big picture. They're focused on accountability for the individual officer when things go terribly wrong. These incidents are tragedies, but nothing about them—from the initial encounter to the fatal final decision—happens in a vacuum.

We need to bring change to the day-to-day police behavior that is ravaging communities. We must root out the rank-and-file harassment that doesn't appear on the news but that most men, women, and even children of color can tell you stories about. The persecution of citizens of color spreads like a toxin through my city, through every city. By the time someone ends up dead, that's just the final breath, the last gasp of air.

We have to focus on the meticulous and deliberate poisoning of the soil. What are cops being taught? How are they rewarded for policing?

Which type of officer is getting ahead and which is passed over? Cops are created by a system, function in a system, and are *rewarded* by a system that sees Black men as threats. Harassing men of color is not an offshoot of the job, or a side effect of the job. *It is the job.*

I experienced this treatment as a Black teenager in East Flatbush, Brooklyn, and I've seen it throughout my nearly fifteen years on the force. The police, as they currently behave, are not doing the best they can to solve the problems they are dealt. In fact, they are at the root of the problem itself.

THROUGH RACIST, unlawful quotas and its harassment of residents of color for low-level offenses, the NYPD raises revenue for the city and salaries for itself on the backs of Black and Brown residents. Citizens' lives are being squeezed in a modernized convict-lease system. Today's police force is the kin of the slave patrols of the nineteenth century and the Black Codes of the Jim Crow South. Anyone who knows their history understands that it's no exaggeration to draw a straight line from there to here. The NYPD model has been packaged and sold by politicians and top cops in New York who have made millions off it. The policing born in New York City continues to spread like a poison through America's cities. Until we get a groundswell of police, public servants, activists, and civically minded residents pushing this issue, we will never be able to address the damage it has done and continues to do.

A police officer's job is to address certain conditions by protecting, facilitating, and sometimes enforcing things in his community—but focusing on enforcement to the exception of all else is like a teacher whose only job is to flunk students. As an incentive to keep his job, to advance in his job, he begins to look only for reasons to fail them. Pretty soon, that's *all* he sees. Even if it is against his better judgment, that's what he's paid to see, so he adapts accordingly. A cop who does this isn't a bad apple; according to the strictures of the system, he's exactly the kind of apple they're trying to grow.

All the best-intentioned efforts to get cops to stop policing this way are futile because *they think this is what policing is.* From the rank and file all the way to the top, this is the job to them. They don't see the larger harm they're doing to communities by throwing people into the system because of their skin color, because of their address. Cops don't even realize they're doing it for those reasons; they've convinced themselves they're increasing public safety.

Petty arrests, the bread and butter of the NYPD and departments across the country, further disenfranchise the already marginalized. Arrests follow people throughout their lives, pushing them away from mainstream society. Once they enter the system, their job prospects, housing opportunities, finances, relationships, and family security are irrevocably affected. From what we know about how disenfranchisement leads people into illicit activity and how prison encourages criminal behavior, the conclusion smacks us in the face: police are at the heart of the very problem they are supposedly trying to solve.

And it's been upside down like this for so long no one knows any other way—not the chiefs in power who were brought up in this system nor the new recruits being churned out every six months who get inculcated in it. They are all blind to the damage because it reads to them as success.

But I see it. Everywhere I turn, I see it. And before becoming a cop, I knew it from the other side of that line. I lived it.

As a child of immigrant parents in the poor Black neighborhood of East Flatbush, born in the eighties and coming of age in the nineties, I regularly dealt with aggressive policing. Over time, I felt the effect it had on me, my friends, and my community. I saw how it increased the very crime it was ostensibly looking to stop by marginalizing people for the smallest things. I recognized how it severed any potential bridges between the neighborhood and police. Cooperation between communities and police would serve both parties, but the negative cycle runs on its own momentum. And no one on the inside wants to gum up the works.

Idealistic but not naive, I became a police officer at twenty-two in an effort to try to right the wrongs the criminal justice system imposes on members of my community. I opted to be the kind of cop who could help, support, and lift up my people. I assumed that all it took for me to police this way was the desire to do so.

I could not have been more wrong.

I have faced harassment, threats, isolation, and punishment in service of that mission. But all of that led me to believe I'm onto something; it made me dig in my heels more firmly.

While writing this book, I was the highest-ranking active whistleblower in the history of the NYPD, sickened by what I had seen, by what the police force thinks is its job. I won't participate in it and I refuse to quietly bear witness.

When I began to speak out against racially motivated quotas and harassment policing, the retaliation came swift and direct. First with my assignments. Then by being passed over for promotions even though I was more than qualified, with test scores in the highest percentile. Then I was set up by fellow cops while libel about me appeared in the news media.

Prior to going public, I sought out other whistleblowers and joined eleven fellow officers in a civil suit against the police department and the City of New York for pushing illegal quotas and punishing officers of color who refused to participate. I became the face of the NYPD 12 lawsuit, got put on the cover of *The New York Times Magazine*, was featured in the award-winning film *Crime + Punishment*, and stood with activists such as Colin Kaepernick—all of which brought me even more threats and retaliation.

I HAVE BEGUN to accept that I now stand for something larger than myself. It has threatened my well-being, my career, and my sanity, but it has also fortified my life. Purpose will do that to you. Growing up in poverty, losing a parent at a very young age and watching the other slip away, I have known suffering too intimately to stand down. So I've kept fighting—even as the threats grew worse. Frank Serpico, the most famous whistleblower in police history, who has become a confidant of mine, says that his father once told him, "Never run when you're right."

I know that if the soil is prepared properly, the right seeds planted and allowed to grow high into the ranks of the department, then the same power that has made the police force such a poison can be the source of positive change. The department has never been able to take self-corrective action; it typically happens in response to monumental lawsuits, public embarrassments, and massive protests. I hope this book will open people's eyes, start a conversation, accelerate a movement, and push to move that needle. We can't afford another generation scarred by this kind of policing.

The NYPD is the seventh-largest armed force in the world. There are enough people who want to change it, but they're rarely in a position to do so. But I blew the whistle and still rose through the ranks. I subjected myself to danger and heavy scrutiny and was forced to watch my back. In my fourteen years with the department, I learned that the problem is not localized. It's a cancer that has spread into every corner of policing across the country.

I hope to shed light on the ways in which we can bridge the gap between law enforcement and the communities they are sworn to protect.

The extremes, the two loudest sides, have shouted out that middle. What's missing in today's conversation about police are justice-minded officers who sensibly stake out the middle ground, who work within the system yet are still able to see its faults. Police who aren't blinded by tribalism. Due to their unique position, they should be part of any decisions made to remedy issues in the criminal justice system.

We exist. We push our way to the front and then lay ourselves down. Not because we are giving up, but because we are the bridge.

Edwin Raymond
Brooklyn, NY
April 2023

PART I

Men who are in earnest are not afraid of consequences.

—Marcus Garvey

One

The Line

2008

When I was a teenager, my dad used to say to me, with the confidence of someone who knew best: *You know, Edwin, I think you should join the police force. You'd be a great cop.*

To put it bluntly, this sounded crazy. At the time, I didn't know a single cop, and the ones I interacted with in East Flatbush weren't exactly role models. Since the first hairs sprouted on my chin, they had been on me—up against the wall, harassing, you-must-be-doing-something-wrong-even-if-it's-not-now kind of stuff. But Dad came from Haiti, where police hold a respected, elevated position in society. Maybe he saw that for me. Maybe he just didn't want me to struggle the way he had.

I was an artsy kid who loved drawing comic book characters, and I once thought of becoming an architect, designing magnificent buildings to beautify the hood or help restore my Haitian homeland. Later, after I'd encountered Malcolm X, I thought of maybe opening a Black business in my neighborhood to help generate wealth for my people.

But a cop? What young Black man wants to be a cop?

But there I was, in the passenger seat of a white Lincoln Town Car on my way to be sworn in to the police academy. Taking the oath was the first thing you did, not the last, which meant I'd technically be a police officer that afternoon. Mr. Faustin, the father of my childhood friend Nemo, offered to drive me out to Queens College for the ceremony. Dark-skinned with a thin, serious mouth and a close haircut, Mr. Faustin was proper and classy, always in dress shirts and slacks. He drove a gypsy cab around Flatbush and Crown Heights, a job that was to Caribbean men what being a home health aide was to Caribbean women: the engine keeping the community running.

Touched by the offer, not being familiar with Queens, and lacking anyone in my family able to take me, I accepted.

"Don't fidget so much," he said in the car. "Especially once you get there. They'll be watching you."

"I know, I know." Cops had to be able to be still. That I knew. Stillness is how you see what others can't. I kept shifting and resetting my body, not comfortable in the skin of my three-piece suit. I had just gotten it the day before in Midtown Manhattan, the most expensive thing I'd ever purchased. But I needed something that fit properly, made me look like I belonged. And that's what it costs to fit in. People will pay good money to look the part; whether they feel it or not, that's something else.

"I'm proud of you, Edwin," Mr. Faustin said in his heavily accented English, a trace of Creole in his rounded vowels. "Making something of yourself."

"Thank you, sir."

"You know . . . ," he started, and then stopped. His tone lowered though it was just the two of us. "I know your dad wishes he could be doing this. Taking you. Any father would."

"I know it, Mr. Faustin."

"I'm sure he's very proud of you."

"Yeah," I said.

Smoothing out the fine linen pants that rustled on the leather seats, I kept my eyes fixed out the window. I was twenty-two years old, no longer a kid, but as a child of East Flatbush, the world felt small to me. Even going the twenty minutes from Brooklyn to Queens was a glimpse at the majestic size of the world. Out the window on the Jackie Robinson Parkway, with Mr. Faustin taking those S turns as slowly as possible, the glistening metal of Manhattan skyscrapers rising in the distance, I got a sense of how far out there the horizon really was.

"I tell you, Edwin, you know you're every immigrant father's dream," Mr. Faustin continued, patting my shoulder. "*This* is our dream. Coming to the United States and our children being better than us."

Mr. Faustin's words gave me a sense of pride but also connection. I was like his child too. His own son had fallen hard into the streets, and my father was slowly disappearing in a hospital bed. It was like Mr. Faustin and I were re-creating a parental bond out of the survivors.

It had been a long process to even get to that day—two years of background checks, interviews, tests. An entire institution with a long history and a proud tradition deciding if I was worthy of wearing the uniform. Were they going to judge me based on my character? Or on what kind of cop I would become? And where did those two things meet?

ON THE CAMPUS of Queens College, in the hazy sunshine, a sea of overwhelmingly white men in suits stretched across the auditorium. Every six months, another eleven hundred or so came through the academy, mostly white, mostly suburban. The demographics of who became a cop had been steady for some time; it was practically a conveyor belt, churning out the same type year after year. I had a lurking sense that I was entering hostile territory, a place that would not welcome me with open arms. I straightened my shoulders, pushed out one big breath, and got in line.

It was scorching that morning, and I sweated into my vest and jacket, staring at well-dressed backs in a line that stayed stubbornly still. The local media was there, trucks and camera tripods and reporters, as well as security details for Mayor Michael Bloomberg and Commissioner Ray Kelly, conspicuously coming in and out of rooms. The bustle important people create in their wake.

Mr. Faustin was right. In line, the academy staff was already starting boot camp, scrutinizing us up and down, left and right. A female recruit was reading a book while she stood in the unmoving queue. An instructor got up in her face and said, "Recruit! Do we bore you? Are we boring you here?" They were looking for any reason to mess with us, and they seemed to be watching me particularly. I knew why: my dreadlocks. They kept staring me down, going over it in their heads, trying to understand: *What's this guy doing here?*

It was a good question.

Two

My Mother's Face

1988

I remember being not quite three years old, playing on the floor of the living room with my brother Ronald, who was four. The bedroom door was cracked open enough for us to see Mom lying in there. She was completely still, more object than person, on the bed in her burgundy gown. It was a deep red color that made me think of blood, but also God. Around her sleeping body stood people from the church, praying over her. They sang hymns, and the occasional voice spoke low and private, but the whispers barely traveled outside the door. I couldn't hear what they were saying.

Mom was there, but not there.

When I went into the bedroom, she didn't move or respond when I called her name. "Mom," I said. "Ma." But she didn't even turn or open her eyes. I climbed on top of her still body, wanting to get as close to her as possible. At first she didn't react, but then she pinched me really hard on my upper arm. It hurt so much I started crying—at the pain as well as the cruelty. But she didn't know what she was doing; she didn't even know who I was. When your mother doesn't recognize you, especially at that age, you doubt who you are. It's like you don't exist at all.

It was so quick, the decline. A year earlier, she had been making electronic parts at Omega Heater out on Long Island. One afternoon, punching out at the end of her shift, she bent down to tie her boots and just collapsed there on the hard floor. She was rushed to the local hospital, where doctors ran a load of tests and discovered the brain tumor. After being transferred to Kings County Hospital in Brooklyn, she had to undergo three different surgeries. They removed what they could of the cancer, which also excised parts of her memory. Because your memory is who you are, it was like Mom was gone before she was really gone.

Not too long after she came out of the hospital, I was sitting in the living room watching cartoons when cops came to the door. I remember the crackling of police radios as Dad spoke to them low at the end of the long hallway. It was the first time I had ever seen police up close; they took up so much space in the house, in their dark uniforms, their heavy utility belts, their radios carrying signals across the city. They seemed gigantic and serious but also powerful, helpful, heroic. My only comparison: Batman.

Dad had called them because my mother was missing. She wasn't in her room or in the hallway or anywhere outside the building. He had called her name, loud and constant, and she didn't reply. The police took down his answers to their questions, which they wrote in their little pads, and then left. Not too long after, my dad threw back the shower curtain in the bathroom and there she was. Sitting in the bathtub with a frozen look on her face. She hadn't responded to her name when he had been calling, probably because she didn't recognize it.

Eugenie.

That was her name. Eugenie. When I look at her face in photos, I see my own. Dark and round, full lips, high cheekbones. It's startling how much of me is in there.

———————

THIRTEEN DAYS AFTER I turned three, my mother was gone. Thirty-five years old. I am older now than she ever was, which doesn't make sense to me. It is like a glitch in the universe, time bending back on itself.

Ronald and I weren't allowed at the funeral, which my dad probably thought was the right thing to do: all that death, all that crying—it was no place for children. Or maybe he knew he'd be carrying as much as he could already handle that day. But all it did was compound my confusion. Seeing everyone gather, speak over her, watch her be buried might have helped me understand what was going on. So she looms like an unfinished sentence, just dangling there.

Mom was excised out of our lives. I was too young to know that, no matter how much time passed, the hole would never close up. It would always be part of my makeup, and I would grow up around it, like a tooth coming in crooked or a branch curving around a fence post, my direction off from the start.

A mother protects you in the world when no one else will. I enviously watched tired kids on the subway just lean on their moms' bodies and close their eyes. It seemed so comforting, just knowing that you could put your weight on this person and safely let go like that, that you had a home base out in the world.

Manman mwen. It is this presence that hangs over me, like a ghost. This missing thing. Manman mwen. *My mother.*

MY FATHER WAS STRONG and resourceful, willful and self-educated, but he couldn't carry the weight of being a single parent. He was fifty-one when she died, older than any dad I knew. He was left alone with two young boys, and he had no idea what to do.

When my father first met my mother, he already had four children by three different women. I found out in later years that he was abusive to his first wife, but that my mother had a soothing effect on his temper. He'd come home from work, angry at the world, and she'd take his hand. "Okay, Lenord," she'd say, "but you're home now. I am here." That would calm him down. She was like a buffer between him and his struggles, him and his temper. When she was gone, he had nothing to protect him from himself.

Dad had to fight for what little he had. In the Haiti of his youth, America was this mythical land of opportunity; he'd hear stories of Caribbean immigrants who found ways off the island and built a life in this land of plenty. In the late 1960s, after living for decades under the dictatorial rule of François "Papa Doc" Duvalier and then his son, my father made plans to move to the United States, which had just opened its gates. But America didn't want everyone, especially not dark Haitians. It wanted those it had use for—skilled laborers, those with a trade. The first set of visas after the passage of the Immigration and Nationality Act of 1965 spelled that out.* For centuries, Europeans could arrive on these shores with a ball of lint in their pockets and no English and slip right in. Take part in the dream like it was designed with them in mind—which it was. But the dark-skinned need to fight, to force themselves through. They have to prove their worth to be allowed in, so my dad did.

Dad was a jeweler and watch repairman, could fix Rolexes and Movados, understood the intricacies of pallet bridges and barrel drums. He had the tools and knowledge to take something dead and make it run. In Williamsburg, Brooklyn, he ran a watch and jewelry business, which was frequented by Mafia guys. At some point they asked him to move drugs through the business, and he refused. They offered him good money, but my dad wanted nothing to do with it. Soon afterward, the

---

* It replaced an overtly racist immigration policy favoring Europeans that had been in place for decades.

business got broken into—windows smashed and watches stolen. He couldn't prove it, but he knew it was punishment for not playing ball and an implicit threat about saying no. Dad didn't think he could ever get out from under them, these white men with power who'd been there for generations, whose every word carried the air of violence. He decided to shut down the store and got a job on the line in a paper factory.

A FEW MONTHS after my mother's passing, our father dropped us off with Samantha, my mother's best friend, and left without explanation. This was standard for Dad, who rarely told us what was going on. Samantha had two older kids and beat us all as a matter of course. That was just part of the culture. Rather than a lesson or explanation, adults went for the belt. I had friends beaten to learn times tables, beaten to read. It was just considered parenting.

When Dad visited, I jumped on him the minute he came through the door, climbed all over him as he ate a plate of green bananas, plantains, and fish. I wouldn't let go of his hand, like I could make sure he never left again. When he was done eating, he stood up and patted his stomach. "Mwen pral fè yon ti dòmi," he said in Creole. *I'm going to go take a little nap.*

He went into Samantha's bedroom to lie down. Even though I knew the kids were not allowed in there, definitely not allowed on the bed, I followed him in and fell asleep next to him. The moment my father was gone, Samantha took out her martinet, a whip with a wooden handle and leather straps, and beat me good across my torso and limbs. *Thwap.*

"Didn't I tell you not to go on my bed!" she screamed. *Thwap.* I understood it was not a question to answer. "What did I tell you?" *Thwap.* It was just a few lashes but they stung badly, leaving raised welts on my body. That night, when I pressed down on the bruises on my legs, I saw the color go in and out as the blood rushed away.

After one too many beatings, I grabbed a serrated knife from the kitchen and cut a few of the lashes off. I did this little by little over time, until only two lashes remained. Then I threw what was left of it behind the refrigerator.

"I WANNA GO HOME."

A few days later I built up my nerve and told Samantha, my voice nervous and scratchy. I braced myself, ready for her to beat me.

Her face clouded over and she bent down to my level. I flinched like I was going to get hit, but she was more surprised than anything. "You want to go home?"

I nodded. It was the first time I had ever spoken up for myself. Samantha terrified me, but my desire to go home was stronger.

"Okay," she said.

I was shocked at how a few words altered my situation. *That's all I had to do? Just say something?* I got a brief glimpse of my own power. It struck me as a type of magic.

I was too young to understand what my father was going through. In my mind he was still Superman, picking me up with the left arm, Ronald with the right, and not even breaking a sweat. Of course I knew parents could be taken away, but my father seemed invincible, more than human. I wonder now if I *had* to think this way, to make sure he could never leave us.

One evening the summer before first grade, when my older brother Lemy was living with us, my dad was cooking clams at the stove. I stayed as far away as I could from the kitchen, in my room with the door closed. That salty ocean smell made me sick. Dad never ate healthy, puts mounds of salt on everything, smoked and drank all the time.

Suddenly I heard a loud thump, which shook the floor, and Lemy yelling, "Papi! Papi!" When I came in, Dad was on the ground, a puddle of vomit by his head. Lemy ran to call 911. The whole scene was a shock, mostly because it was the first time I realized my father was mortal. Up until then, I had figured that nothing could touch him. Thinking that way made me feel safe because then nothing could touch me. But once Dad hit the ground, that illusion came crashing down with him.

Three

The Academy

2008

That first week, I got suspicious looks during my commutes to the academy: side-eyes, stares, and surprised glances. In my standard gray shirt and navy blue trousers, holding my black duffel bag, I looked the part: an NYPD recruit in training. Sometimes the looks were from elders, subtle glints of admiration and pride. Other times I'd have to pretend not to hear being called things like "coon" and "sellout." There'd also be this confusion, a young dark-skinned man with long dreads who for some reason had chosen to become a New York City cop.

Built in the 1960s, the police academy on East Twentieth Street in Manhattan was once a state-of-the-art facility with well-lit linoleum hallways, wooden desks, and scrubbed blackboards. It carried the air of a very clean but dated high school. The thirty of us in my company did everything as a group: class, physical training, meal, back to class. The academy was run like boot camp, a reminder that the police department is a paramilitary organization, with the structure, chain of command, and war footing that this phrase implies.

As in the military, we had to muster in formation. It was a physical manifestation of how our behavior needed to be: in lockstep, obedient, automatic. This wasn't difficult for me, as I had always been a rule follower. Our platoon commander, Lieutenant Cheng, was a muscular Asian man with a shaved head and deep voice. He would inspect every element of our dress, posture, and grooming, and I always felt he and others assessed me with much more scrutiny. It was a sign of things to come.

For instance, in the patrol guide, an officer's hair was explicitly required to be "off the collar." My dreads were tied back in a style that kept them off my collar, but the "fry hat," the tented cap recruits wore that resembled a fast food cook's, sat high and awkward on my head. One instructor mocked me for looking like a "jack in the box." Others made a point of calling me out.

"Recruit!"

"Yes, sir!"

"Take a look around!"

I froze, thinking this was a trick. We were at attention: feet together, head forward, and arms in fists at our sides. At attention, we were not allowed to move, not even to wipe sweat or scratch our noses. If we moved, it was automatic push-ups, sometimes for everyone.

I knew at attention I couldn't look anywhere but straight ahead. So I stalled, hoping he'd realize his mistake and command me to switch to "parade rest." We stood there in silence staring at each other. Then I watched his eyes shift imperceptibly as the thought reached his brain.

"Recruit!"

"Yes, sir."

"Parade rest."

Like loosening a strap, I switched to the more relaxed position: feet shoulder-width apart, hands behind my back, palms facing outward with thumbs crossed.

"Look around," he said.

I scanned my eyes across the room.

"Recruit, *look around.*"

I turned my head deliberately to look at both sides of the line.

"Do you not see how everyone else is squared away?" he asked. "Do you not see how your hat is not fitting how everyone else's fits?"

"I understand, sir."

"You say that, Raymond, but what are you going to do about it? If you can't fix it, can't your mom do something about it?"

It was like grade school all over again. It was a weird thing to say to a grown man, whether my mother was alive or not.

"I'll see what I can do, sir."

After going through this routine a few more times, I pleaded my case to the Office of Equal Employment Opportunity. Since my hairstyle represented my spiritual beliefs, it was therefore protected. They mostly left me alone after that, though the fact that I went to EEO at all was frowned upon. That office threatened the power of the white boys' club.

At the police academy you learn the basics—tactics, defense, police science. You learn about the dark periods of the NYPD and the efforts to clean it up—the Knapp Commission in 1970 after whistleblower Frank Serpico made them all look corrupt, the Mollen Commission in 1992 after disgraced officer Michael Dowd made them all look criminal. In fact, the first trimester focuses heavily on the NYPD's black eyes. It goes all the way back to the Lexow Committee and Tammany Hall around the turn of the twentieth century, up through the infamously corrupt "Buddy Boys" of Crown Heights' Seventy-Seventh Precinct and the "Dirty Thirty" precinct in Harlem in the late 1980s and early 1990s.

Incredibly, Serpico himself is never named in the curriculum, though he's the entire reason the Knapp Commission existed. We were taught that period as though Mayor John Lindsay just woke up one day in 1970 and decided to investigate the police department. I had to learn about Serpico's heroic crusade on my own after our instructor mentioned his name in passing. Even though he was the most revolutionary figure in the modern NYPD, there was still resistance from within to glorify him: *A whistleblower. A rat. A turncoat.* They were trying to celebrate themselves for the clean and upright institution they believed they had become but refused to name the person who got them there. That tells you all you need to know.

On my own, I learned about Serpico, understood he was a hero. As his biographer noted, "He had broken an unwritten code that in effect put policemen above the law, that said a cop could not turn in other cops."[1] That weekend I watched the film in which Al Pacino plays Serpico and was blown away. I couldn't believe such blatant corruption was just a normal part of how the police department operated. Serpico literally risked his life—he was shot in the face and survived—to change things. He proved that one person could spark a movement.

I give the department some credit for teaching this history; not all institutions focus on their own black eyes in such detail. Unfortunately, while the facts of the scandals may have been correct, the perspective was all wrong. And history is all about perspective. The instructors made it seem as though this was all *merely* history, a dead thing in a book. They taught us about these ugly periods so they could put them behind us and separate them from the present. They didn't address the DNA of those problems, the systemic issues, catalysts, and feedback loops that made those dark periods come about. That would require them to go deeper than they were comfortable doing.

They wouldn't go deep enough to cut. It was all surface. For instance, as part of his deal, Michael Dowd spoke honestly to the court about how, when he first got on the force, he was arresting crack dealers with more money in their pockets than he'd see in months. He used to get free cups of coffee and reached a point where he wondered what else he could get away with. That was the rabbit hole. Before it was all over, Dowd was dealing stolen cocaine and pulling down eight thousand dollars a week.

But the lesson that the chiefs took from Dowd and his compatriots' rampant corruption? The lesson they took from so many other cops knowing about it and looking away? To this day, police are not allowed to accept free cups of coffee. That was the department's conclusion; this is the kind of institution we're dealing with here. It takes a type of will-ful blindness to see things so narrowly.

At the academy you learn what they teach you, but most lessons come outside the classroom. For one, you learn about other cops. Or cops-to-be. You meet your peers, your future colleagues. You learn how they think. How they talk. How they see you, as a Black man. Even with a badge and the force of the state behind you, you are still only a Black man. And because you are entering an institution with historical antago-nism to your people, you are seen at best as an oddity. At worst, as an object of suspicion, scorn, derision. It comes down to this: you can't be trusted.

As a Black man it's rare to have so many white people as peers. They are often figures of authority: bosses, landlords, principals, someone who has power over you. But at the academy, most of the white people were my equal. In the cafeteria, I sat at the long folding table with white recruits on benches on each side. They told me to have a seat, munching on their PB&J sandwiches wrapped by their mothers in Long Island homes, cultural light-years from the communities they would be polic-ing. They talked sports, complained about Manhattan prices, and shared Black jokes.

What's the difference between a Black man and a pizza?
What do you call a Black woman who had an abortion?
Then they said, "Okay, Raymond. Your turn."
But I had nothing to offer them. I didn't know what they meant.

"Yeah," they said. "Ray, tell us a white joke."

A white joke? What's a white joke? It was too much of a thicket, so I just smiled. I defused. I passed it off. When I didn't join in, they all looked mortified. By not engaging, I had thrown off the balance.

"Oh shit," one of them said. "Sorry, we're not racist, Ray. It's just jokes."

"It's cool," I said. "It is what it is."

The irony is they all loved hip-hop, openly and ecstatically. I marveled at how those two forces coexisted in their minds: appreciating Black culture but thinking so little of the people who made it, whose lives it reflected. This was one of the things I learned at the academy.

I thought about how I once knew these guys—not these exact ones, but versions of them—a decade ago in junior high, in the flow of adolescence. Back then, their opinions about who they were and who I was hadn't yet hardened into place. We played ball together, drew superheroes, talked girls. And then we separated—traveled through our respective pipes. I went to a diverse high school and they went to a homogeneously white one and in that time a change happened. When they came out the other end, it was like they'd been injected with something. While I had some peers who picked up guns or started selling crack, these guys were going through something too: a type of education. In *Caste*, historian Isabel Wilkerson writes about the "toxins...absorbed from the polluted and inescapable air of social instruction we receive from childhood."[2] This is what my white peers had breathed in: lazy stereotypes and the worst kinds of assumptions about Black people. They developed eyes that couldn't see me for who I was, eyes that unsaw anyone who looked like me.

This was in the fall of 2008 when a young Black senator with multicultural roots and an African-sounding name was about to become president. America was busy patting itself on the back about how far it had come. But no one told these guys. The strongest forces of racism in this country are the ones that deny such a thing even exists. They'll swear up and down that you're making the whole thing up.

They said: *Black people are in the position they're in because they don't have the merit to work hard for what they want. We're leaving our comfortable neighborhoods to keep them safe and they don't even appreciate us.*

They said: *Democrats give Black people handouts, tell them their problems are because of racism, to keep them from doing for themselves and instead to feel they're victims. They leech off the system, and in return the Democrats get the votes.*

These guys were ignorant of basic history. They were clueless about Black Codes, Jim Crow, the KKK, race riots, Wilmington, Black Wall Street, restrictive covenants, and redlining. Even those who knew that history thought it was simply a remnant of the past, a dusty daguerreotype. Too many thought historical racism had no lasting effects, that the past has nothing to do with the present.

They thought East Flatbush looked different from Suffolk County because Black people *decided* to live in shit.

What they didn't know and chose not to see was going to affect the kind of police they would become. It influenced the systems that paid their checks and the minds that set their policy. That ignorance isn't a closed system. It doesn't just sit there and fester. It rises to the top and then trickles down, serving on oversight panels and promotion boards and every other check and balance on the system. It will never correct itself because it doesn't see the need for correction. If you just see inherently violent and lazy people shooting one another, if you think you're saving them from themselves, how in the world are you going to see *yourself* as a problem?

I was troubled that some of the guys in my academy class had made it this far. I remembered the battery of interviews and tests and background checks I had to go through just to be there. In less than six months, each of these guys was going to have a badge and gun and the authority of New York City behind them. They were going to be walking the streets, canvassing the subway stations, inspecting the building hallways, responding to the calls, driving the avenues, entering the homes— responsible for me and my community. I got a good look at the whole assembly line, churning out another class of eleven hundred cops, less than one in five of whom were Black.

It scared the shit out of me.

"MAN, FUCK RODNEY KING," they said when our instructor brought in a documentary on the 1991 beating and its fallout.

"Savages," they murmured when we watched footage of the LA riots in the wake of the cops' acquittal.

"Animals," they said. "Destroying their own neighborhoods."

"Now," our instructor asked, "where did the police go wrong?"

I remembered as a six-year-old watching footage of Rodney King's beating at the hands of four LAPD officers on television. My only frame of reference at the time was pro wrestling: when the other guy was staying down, it was over. You won. It seemed as obvious as one plus one equals two.

When my fellow recruits were kids, they inherited their racialized views—from their fathers, uncles, grandfathers, mothers, friends, neighbors, and media outlets. Some were raised in cop homes among cop blood. Their racist perspectives were like family heirlooms, passed down, toxically seeping into their worldview.

"Where did the police go wrong?" the female instructor asked again. I knew that "by beating Rodney King senseless" was not the answer she was looking for. So I stayed silent. She meant: How did the LAPD lose the city? I remembered reading that when the supervisor at the scene,

Sergeant Stacey Koon, first heard the King arrest had been videotaped, he thought it would make for a good training film.[3]

I didn't respond to my peers' Rodney King comments just like I didn't respond to their Black jokes. Malcolm X taught that you should let people reveal who they are. Staying silent gave me the advantage because then they would show me their hand. If I reacted to everything, it just told others to be careful around me, to hide who they were. This is how we have white supremacists in law enforcement, in the legislature: they have learned to hide themselves.

But I wanted to hear what else my fellow recruits had to say. That was their truth, so I should learn what I was dealing with. You give people enough rope, they'll do their own hanging. You don't even have to say a word.

I wasn't cocky enough to think I'd be the best cop, but I thought I could at least be a counterweight. I hoped to become an antidote to racially motivated policing by those who didn't understand the neighborhood, speak the language, respect the culture, or care about the people. In short: I wanted to be a different kind of cop. Nowhere in my mind did I think it would be easy.

But I still didn't have any idea of what I was up against. If you had told me at the time what I'd have to go through, I wouldn't even have believed it. I would have assumed you were telling tales to scare me away. Even though I don't scare easily. Even though I never did.

Four

The 2 Train to Florida

1991

After passing out in the kitchen that summer, Dad was in the hospital for two weeks and diagnosed with hypertension. But that was just the tip of an iceberg that went very deep. When my father buried my mother, he buried part of himself. The man who was left was in no position to raise us. He couldn't figure out how to fix us, so he did what he once did with objects put in his care: he took us apart.

Dad sent us to live with his brother's family in Florida. I was only six, too young to know how far apart things were, how big the world was, so I thought you could take the 2 train from the Newkirk Avenue subway station to South Florida. We got on one train, then another, a nap, a warm crushed sandwich, a pee stop. I put my head up against the cold window and watched farmland, plantations, oceans, highways, mountains, then blue water stretching past the horizon. Florida opened before me in bright, dazzling colors, unfolding like a new planet.

My aunt and uncle had teenage kids, a big house near the beach with high ceilings, smooth vacuumed carpet, and a glistening pool that reflected sunlight like diamonds. They had a farm where they grew most everything we ate: coconuts, beans, watermelon, oranges, apples. I didn't even know those things grew out of the ground; I had never seen it happen.

Dad stayed for a week and on his way out the door, he was crying, something I had never seen him do before. I was too young to understand the pain it must've brought him to leave his children, to turn his back on his family like that.

I felt safe there, in this place that felt like the inside of one of my TV shows. My aunt's elaborate Haitian meals turned dinner into a production. School was much cleaner: bright pastel colors, reflected light, whiter faces. I picked up on what my teenage cousins were learning in school: times tables and division, photosynthesis and evaporation, the Constitution and the Civil War. After dinner every night, I translated the evening news into Creole for my uncle, so the world seeped into my mind that way as well.

Ronald and I did chores around the house, like vacuuming, but were also put to actual work—though my cousins never lifted a finger. We spent hours in the hot sun shelling peas, piling them in buckets, getting grossed out by the worms that burrowed in. In Haiti there was a tradition called restavek* where poor families sent their kids to wealthier families who could pay for their school. The trade-off was that the kids were made to work as a form of payment.

Most of what I experienced in Florida came through the television, especially movies on cable. One night we were watching the film *Ghost*, where Patrick Swayze is killed and comes back to warn his girlfriend, Demi Moore, that people are trying to hurt her. At the end, when the gates of heaven open up and Demi Moore can finally see Patrick Swayze again, it was the first time I was presented with the idea of an afterlife. Ronald

---

* Literally translated as "stay with."

and I got right up to the screen to look for Mom. Swayze is surrounded by angels waiting to take him to heaven, and I assumed Mom had to be back there among them. Every time that part was on, we'd be inches from the screen. "You're not looking hard enough!" I'd yell at Ronald when we couldn't find her. But it was comforting to think that she was at least somewhere, that she hadn't just disappeared.

While we were in Florida, Dad stopped working, so his money ran out. Ultimately my dad and uncle got into a fight over it and my brother Abner came to take us back home.

After the long train ride to New York and then the subway ride to Brooklyn, we trudged up the four flights to our apartment, clomping footsteps on the cracked linoleum. When we reached our landing, Abner pushed the door hard with his shoulder, pressing all his body weight against it. A padlock and slack chain appeared on the inside, which he reached in and removed. I was confused by the lock and chain and was going to ask him about it when we caught sight of my father.

I was stunned.

In those two years, he had aged a lifetime. Dad was unshaven, wearing briefs and a dingy T-shirt with a stretched neckline. He was a shell of his old self, his body sagging on its frame. We took our luggage to the back of our apartment, turned on the light, and saw the kitchen walls covered in roaches. It was like a coat of black paint until they scattered, revealing that mustard color of the wall. The apartment was filthy, with a thick stale smell in the air, papers and unopened mail overflowing out of drawers, on the coffee table, and covering the floor. It was not how we left it. It was not how we left him.

Before we went to Florida, Dad had still been going to work, putting on his coat and tie, with its perfect symmetrical knot like a tiny fist. But underneath, something had been dying inside. While we were over a thousand miles away, it was easier for him to let go. Once he dropped that last tether to the world—us—his grief just dragged him down to the bottom.

BACK IN BROOKLYN, Ronald and I had to adjust to a new reality. We never had much money before, but now we had nothing. Dad couldn't work and complained, "Tèt mwen toujou ap vire." *My head is always spinning.* He'd go see Dr. Michel, one of the two doctors in the area who spoke Creole and had a monopoly on the community. He worked out of a residential brownstone where the living room overflowed into the hallway and a visit took half the day. A lean dark man in a white coat, Dr. Michel insisted all Dad had was hypertension.

Even as a third grader, I could tell Dad's problems went deeper. He carried himself like a haggard old man. At the time, mental health was not something discussed or addressed in the Black community, especially among those from the Caribbean. Some of it was cultural, a resigned philosophy that island life is hard on the body and soul. Dad had been a parent to six children but was not used to parenting any of them. He had relied on the women in his life to raise his kids while he worked to put food on the table. With Mom gone, it never clicked for him that he had to take over certain responsibilities.

Usually, Dad was off in his own world, watching TV or listening to the stereo, which had a special chip in it so he could get Haitian political radio. When I walked into the apartment, I would see him down the narrow hallway, in his bedroom, which doubled as the living room, with an eight-track player and his collection of broken radios. In an armchair by the window, he watched nature documentaries, historical programs on PBS, and—religiously—*Jeopardy!* There was no way his English was good enough to follow it, but he liked to bathe himself in all the knowledge drilling out rapid-fire from the small TV screen.

On the streets, Ronald and I played tag and manhunt with

friends, our sneakers slapping on concrete, hiding in alleys and hopping fences. When the streetlights came on and our friends' mothers called them back for dinner, they all went home, but Ronald and I didn't. We knew there was nothing to eat there. When we came in after dark, we tried to go to sleep as soon as we could just to escape the aching hunger, the hollow pits in our stomachs. Sometimes it worked, but our starved bodies would often wake us up early or in the middle of the night.

The weekend was the roughest because we wouldn't even get free school meals. Watching Saturday morning cartoons, I'd become dizzy in front of the screen. Dad would sometimes give us potato chips or vanilla wafers, which hurt my stomach after a while. By afternoon, I'd get these pressing headaches that made it hard to concentrate. Ronald and I got into the habit of splitting up and spending dinnertime at alternating friends' houses. Everyone from the islands was poor; they might not have two plates to share, but they always had one. I went to Romain and Herby's house and Ronald was at Billy and Melissa's house and then we switched. Ashley's mom sometimes had two plates for us, but she worked nonstop and her husband was abusive so we avoided their apartment in the evening.

Billy was one of my best friends, younger and shorter than I was, with puffy cheeks, lighter skin, and curly hair in a mini-Afro. We sat on his front stoop watching the older Haitian guys playing dominoes on foldout tables, trying to talk to the girls skipping rope. Across Newkirk Avenue someone strung up a whole sound system and played music for the block.

"Yo, Mommy Florise coming!" someone yelled, which meant playtime was over.

Billy's mother was a dark-skinned Haitian woman, less than five feet tall with hard eyes. His father had left them when he was one and Mommy Florise carried a look of fatigue that acted like a weight on her scant frame. She made her way down the block from the bus stop after work, leaning slightly to balance the thrift shop bags in her opposite hand. Like many women in the community, Billy's mom worked as a home health aide, and since many mothers had to spend the night sleeping at their clients' homes, it was grandmothers and aunts who did a lot of the raising. Kids called their grandmothers "mom," and up to a certain age, they didn't even know the difference. Many island immigrants came to America for a better life only to flip to the other side of society. Some of those who grew up with servants in Haiti essentially became servants here in order to survive. It's one of those things I noticed before I knew why or what it meant.

No matter how much Mommy Florise struggled, she never let me and Ronald go without. Under their Christmas tree every year, there was a wrapped gift marked "Edwin" and one marked "Ronald." This showed her heart more than anything because it wasn't even a necessity; it just made us feel like regular kids. I never believed in Santa because I knew those presents came from a parent who spent money to buy them. We couldn't afford school supplies either, so Dad gave us oxidized paper from his time at the factory. It was yellowed, sickly looking, and we had to hole-punch it ourselves to make loose-leaf paper. Whenever I pulled it out in class, the kids whispered and laughed. Even poor people noticed how poor we were.

We got up super early to get free breakfast at school, PS 269. On our way out the door, we went into Dad's room to get a quarter each, which he kept in a big jar next to his bed. At first, we spent them on gumballs or cheap toys at vending machines, but then we saved up to bring them to the Chinese restaurant on Fridays. We emptied our pockets and slapped down the piles of quarters for fried rice and chicken wings. At home, we'd eat on our beds watching *Family Matters*, laughing at a world where everyone's problems were funny.

In East Flatbush, the Haitians were treated like the bottom of the status barrel—seen as the poorest and the dirtiest. A Jamaican girl in my class, Mareena, popular and beautiful with lighter caramel skin and bright eyes, made fun of me more than anyone else.

Once, a kid named Akeem came up to me after class. "Can I call you for help with these fractions?"

"Sure," I said.

"What's your number?"

Mareena's eyes dropped down on me. "Ed don't got no phone," she said, as loud as possible. "What are you *talking* about?"

"Of course I got a phone!" I protested, embarrassed. "Who doesn't have a phone?"

Mareena crinkled up her face like she thought I was lying. The phone might have gotten shut off sometimes, but it was always there. Dad's money came from Mom's Social Security checks, so it was like musical chairs in our apartment. He had to decide which utility we could do without: some months it was the phone, others it was electric or gas. Once in a while there was no power and we had to bridge it from a neighbor using an extension cord that ran through the hallway, a favor we would return to the other floor.

Haitians were ridiculed, ostracized, and treated as "other"—even by Brooklyn's Caribbean diaspora. Unlike the Trinidadians, Bahamians, and Jamaicans, who had English in common, or the Puerto Ricans and Dominicans who shared Spanish with the other Hispanics, the Haitians were alone. There was one nanny all the Haitians went to, one doctor, one lawyer, one mechanic. Because Haitian kids were picked on, adults started their own "cheese bus" service to keep them safe and shuttle them around. There was a hierarchy of immigrants and, as dark Haitians, we were at the bottom. I wondered if I was cursed.

Back when he was learning opposites—up/down, left/right—Ronald asked me, "Edwin, what's the opposite of Haitian?"

"American," I said.

RIDING BIKES IN THE STREET on Newkirk, I saw ragged men pushing shopping carts or baby strollers, plastic bags full of bottles and cans piled high and spilling out. Five cents a bottle, I started calculating, meant twenty bottles was a dollar.

On a hot Saturday morning, with not a crumb in our bellies, Ronald and I hit the streets. We'd dig through the recycling bins in front of our building—piles of bins mixed with torn and pungent leaking garbage bags. Newkirk Avenue was mostly large apartment buildings, where the garbage piled and sat for days, so we went to the cross streets like East Twenty-Fifth Street, where there were single-family homes, early twentieth century clapboard houses. We hit each blue bin, our bags clinking along our thighs as we made our way down the block. At sundown we turned in our bounty to the soda place on Avenue D and collected around thirteen dollars, enough for a few dinners for both of us.

We'd get shooed away by neighbors, cross paths with crack addicts, participate in the underground economy of glass collectors. But our feelings of pride—*we're making money off this!*—eventually gave way to something else: shame. Shame about what we had to do to eat. Our desperation hung on us like a smell, like a presence. At some point, it made us feel so bad about our situation that we stopped. It just didn't seem worth it anymore.

The hierarchy that existed in Brooklyn because of skin color, because of money, was like oxygen and gravity to me. Just there. But slowly, I learned about the history. Every Wednesday morning in third grade, a teacher named Ms. Brown took over to teach "multicultural studies." Short with salt-and-pepper Jheri-curled hair and skin dark as night, she taught about the civil rights movement with great pride, sharing first-person accounts of what she experienced down south as a teenager. It opened my eyes to how certain things I saw as normal shouldn't be taken for granted. The next year, during Black History Month, we learned about Dr. King from a Jewish teacher named Mr. Block. One of the kids raised his hand. "What about Malcolm X? How come we don't talk about him?"

"Ah, the violent one," Mr. Block said.

When someone asked about Spike Lee's Malcolm X movie, which was scheduled to air on TV, I saw Mr. Block's discomfort, a fear behind the eyes. *Oh, I gotta watch this movie,* I thought. Dad and I watched it in two parts, me translating it into Creole for him. Through that TV, whether it was news or movies, the outside world seeped in. It got me asking questions and, fortunately, my father was game to answer them.

My consciousness about who I was and where I came from began with Dad. When we saw images of kids with swollen bellies in Africa, he got serious. "Edwin," my father said, pointing to the screen, "you know that's you, right?"

He leaned toward me, seeing my confusion.

"Look at them," he said, gesturing. "They don't look like you by coincidence."

"No?" I had no idea what he meant.

"They look like you because they *are* you. That's you. You did nothing to be in a better position than them. All you did is you were born in the United States. And I'm the reason you're born in the United States. You did not earn your position in this part of the world, where everyone would love to be. So never forget these people."

No matter how much he struggled in his own life, Dad taught me to always look out for those less fortunate. He explained that because I was blessed enough to be able to look out for others, I had to. There's no saying no, because God put you in that position for a reason. That idea stuck to me, hung on me like an appendage. I carried it with me wherever I went.

Five

Immaculate Perception

2008

At the academy we ran. We ran every day. We ran in the gymnasium in maddening circles until we were panting, dog-tired, and dripping pools of sweat. The department's Job Standard Test (JST) required us to throw on weighted vests and run up portable stairs and climb over miniature walls, drag a heavy dummy fifty feet, and then pull a resistant trigger over and over again. Some recruits struggled with the obstacle course, but I played manhunt and jumped fences and climbed walls all throughout my childhood. When we changed out of our gym shirts in the locker room, I'd be drenched. Though I had never been hefty, as the months wore on, I lost a ton of weight.

After running was tactics: boxing, grappling, cuffing, and take-downs. We'd pair up and use each other's bodies for training. We learned how to survey a scene, approach a suspect, where to stand and position ourselves if someone pulled a gun on us: a cop should create a triangle so his partner was never in the line of fire. They drilled into us to always think about what's *beyond* the target we were shooting at. Something they don't show you on television: most bullets *miss*. Well, they miss the target, but they have to hit something. One instructor from the firing range told us, "Two things you can never take back are words from your mouth and bullets from your gun."

The use-of-force lessons at the academy washed all that TV cop fiction out of our minds. Like a lot of people, almost everything I thought about police came from Hollywood. The NYPD was often depicted using the latest tech, but what we actually found were typewriters, ribbon, carbon paper, and Polaroids. That first trimester at the academy, we came up hard against the cognitive dissonance between what we thought we could do as cops and what was allowed or realistic out there. Hollywood had shown us cops firing warning shots in the air (banned in New York City), cops shooting a car's tires (not part of training), shooting to wound a suspect (against *all* gun training), and shooting at a moving vehicle (forbidden in almost all cases). Even if a vehicle is being used as a weapon against you, you can't shoot at it: you have to get out of the way. The whole class was in an uproar about that one. We'd seen enough movies where the driver is shot point-blank through the windshield and the car comes to a halt. But that's not what happens. If there's weight on the pedal, then you have an out-of-control vehicle, an errant missile in a densely populated area.* The constant use of guns was also a fiction. A huge percentage of cops go their whole careers without ever firing their weapon. If and when they do, they won't see that gun for months while they're in the office pushing papers and the entire incident is investigated.

Television is responsible for the single most common misconception about police, even from those like attorneys who should know better: the Miranda warning ("You have the right to remain silent . . ."). The warning is to be read only to a suspect who is in custody, about to be

---

* An exception was made in 2017 after someone used a truck to ram people on a bike path along the Hudson River. Now, if someone is using the vehicle as a deadly weapon in an act of terrorism, you can shoot at it.

officially interrogated. Miranda warnings are never read on the street, as the cuffs are being slapped on. But that is what universally happens on television, and that misuse has become the expectation in reality.

The problem, I'd later learn, is that elected officials, activists, and organizations that legislate, battle, and work with the police get a great deal of their perspective from fictitious cops. And the discrepancy between what's real and what they think is real is pronounced. No one watches *Grey's Anatomy* and then makes suggestions in the operating room, but that's been happening to police for decades. A lot of recommendations about how cops should behave—things like shooting a fleeing suspect in the foot or an armed suspect in the hand—are fantasy. Anyone who suggests such a thing has never picked up a gun. When shooting at an armed suspect, the best way to stop the adversary—to use the gun for what it's for—is to aim center mass.

Some of these suggestions actually get recommended and then turn into police policy. Then the department is forced to implement practices that were designed in a room by people with no knowledge of what policing actually entails and too often without the willingness to learn.

OUR OFFICIAL COMPANY INSTRUCTOR (OCI) was a piece a work. Wide-eyed with a high-pitched voice that pierced into your brain, she brought that boot-camp energy from day one. "I am not your friend!" she would bellow, and we believed her. Our OCI sternly explained that we were a unit and if one of us messed up, the entire company would be punished. This is an intentional part of training, to get us accustomed to being judged for the actions of others. But Black people don't need that lesson. Black men are always having to answer for negative things that other Black men have done. We live that every day; that's the burden.

Our team leader, Sergeant Tam, would periodically visit his officers—our instructors—and randomly quiz us on things. One day he dropped by and told us about a RAND Corporation study regarding stop, question, and frisk, the infamous practice that was being challenged in federal court at the time. The study showed that 92 percent of those stopped in New York City were Black, even in Staten Island, which is mostly white.

"Does anyone know why this would be?" the sergeant asked. "Ninety-two percent of stop, question, and frisks are for a population that is less than twenty-five percent of the city?"

Immediately I thought: *Because of racial profiling.* No one said a word so I raised my hand.

He nodded at me. "Recruit?"

"Racial profiling."

"Oh shit," someone said under their breath. Tittering from other corners of the room.

Tam's face pinched tight. "Excuse me?"

"Racial profiling," I said, turning to look at my classmates, who I assumed would agree.

"Oh yeah, so that's what you believe?"

"Well, isn't it—"

"You know what, Raymond? Now you better score a one hundred on the two-fifty* exam since you know so much." Then he moved on, never responding to my answer.

If the conversation with Sergeant Tam had continued, he would have argued race essentialism—stereotypes. He would've claimed that the statistics are skewed toward Blacks not because of targeting, but—due to the race of a high percentage of gun perpetrators—because *Black people are the problem.*

"You're crazy, Raymond," one of the other Black officers said to me after class.

"Why? I'm just telling the truth."

---

* Police code for stop, question, and frisk.

Racial profiling was never mentioned, which baffled me. The reason I answered Tam's question so confidently was because I'd been waiting for the topic to come up. I'd just assumed racial profiling was part of the training. It can't be a coincidence that city cops harass the young Black and Brown people as a matter of course. The behavior was so blatant and so rampant that it was inconceivable to me that they didn't actually teach it.

But in my six months in the academy, that brief exchange was one of the only times it ever came up (and, tellingly, I was the one who brought it up). Race was practically taboo in the academy. The instructors spent maybe half a day on "cultural competency," but that was a joke. It was things like how Haitians are usually very loud, but it doesn't mean they're fighting. Rastafarians might give you a closed-fisted hand bump—"a pound"—instead of a handshake as a greeting. Laughable stuff.

There was nothing about implicit bias and how it accounts for a person's thinking and decisions. Even though it's been proven that "well-intentioned actors can overcome automatic or implicit biases . . . when they are made aware of [them], have the cognitive capacity to self-correct, and are motivated to do so."[1] Knowing and accounting for one's bias was a key factor in being effective in the job. But it was nowhere to be found at the academy. There was little about how to treat the community respectfully, how that benefits both the police and the community. My only lessons on bias came from eating lunch with my white peers.

Profiling based on race was this mysterious lesson cops were just absorbing. I couldn't make the correlation between what we were taught and what I'd seen with my own eyes in the streets. There was a gap, a chasm. A gigantic missing link. What was happening? Just like my white middle school peers were getting indoctrinated into a belief system, something was happening to cops between their graduation from the academy and when they hit the streets. What produced the type of policing that I knew existed? It couldn't just immaculately appear fully formed in cops' minds and behaviors.

If it was not taught in the academy, then where was it coming from?

THERE WAS NOTHING HEROIC about it; it was just instinct. I saw something and I reacted. My peers reacted too—but their reaction was, *Let's get the fuck out of here.*

One day after our workout, my company was on a lunch break at the pizza place around the corner on Second Avenue. As we were all sitting down with our trays of food, there was a rumbling in the air, that noticeable vibe where you could tell something was happening. Then, beyond the front window a mass of people emerged from the bar next door, with two people fighting in the center. All the other recruits started putting their fry hats back on, zipping up their jackets, and hightailing it out of there.

I didn't judge them for taking off. As a recruit you're watched so carefully and even the slightest mistake could hurt you. But none of that factored into my decision: I was a cop. I met eyes with the other recruit still sitting there. Bolivar, a former marine of Peruvian descent, had jet-black hair, hard eyes, and the discipline that the military breeds into you. The two of us spoke without speaking: *We got this.*

We had no guns, but we had our batons, most of our training, and handcuffs, which we had just learned to use a few days before. When we got out onto the sidewalk, we pushed to the middle of the circle, where one young white guy was hitting another with a metal pipe. I ran from behind the attacker and timed it so that when he put the pipe up to go back down, I grabbed it. Then I used that momentum to pin him while Bolivar cuffed him.

A young white woman ran up to us. "This guy's drunk," she told me through tears and running eye makeup, "and disrespecting me, and he was just defending my honor!" The beaten guy was bloody and dazed, his face a mess, and he and his girlfriend waited for an ambulance. Bolivar and I stayed with the attacker until the crowd dispersed and the responding officers appeared. Even after everyone had left, I felt this quick beating in my chest. It was the first time I was able to use my authority in a physical way and my body *reacted* to it, instinctively. It let me know I was going to be okay on the job.

As officers involved in an arrest, we had to go back to the Thirteenth Precinct to put down our testimony, voucher the metal pipe, and document the incident in our activity logs. Everything seemed to be leading to Bolivar and me actually processing the arrest—getting credit for it—but one of the responding cops stepped in. "No, no," he said, "you guys are just recruits. Plus, I need a collar for this month."

Need a collar for this month? The sentence didn't make sense to me, but I didn't ask. I was just a recruit pulled into real police work for a moment. But it was my introduction to the cancer of quotas in the NYPD.

Back in class, we got a standing ovation from our peers, looks of admiration, and even the instructor—who had been giving me a hard time—seemed impressed. The next day Bolivar and I had breakfast with the chief of training, who asked us to tell him the story. After we did, he complimented our courage—stepping up while "in gray" and with no guns. Then he gave each of us a challenge coin, an important symbol in military and police culture. Again, I felt like I was cut out for this job, would be an asset and, hopefully, appreciated as one.

TWO WEEKS BEFORE GRADUATION, we had our internal ceremony where we got our guns and shields, officially becoming cops. From then on, we wore blue like everyone else. The distinction between instructors and recruits faded, the military discipline loosened. They'd combine companies and other instructors would come in and drop some knowledge on us.

One sergeant, Sullivan,* was a chubby Irish American, stoic and down-to-earth. He came into the class to talk freely about things we could expect on the job. "Remember to use your training from the gym out there," he said. "If you see a Black guy or a Spanish guy, and they have a gun, don't just pull out your gun and start blasting. Find cover, yell out some commands, try to get the situation under control. Remember, the department is getting more and more diverse so we're starting to look more and more *like perps.*"

I looked around the room and realized I was the only one who caught it. *We're starting to look more like perps?*

He was trying to warn us against being victims of implicit bias, but he was using implicit bias to do so! It demonstrated how ubiquitous and omnipresent that kind of bias is; even the well-meaning are operating from that foundation.† Experts who have studied implicit bias believe that it is more central to racial profiling than egregious bias,[2] partly because it slips in unnoticed.

"RAYMOND, LISTEN," my OCI told me during my final evaluation, "you're very intelligent, very disciplined. You can be a true asset. But I have to be straight with you . . ."

I got nervous because I had no idea what she was going to say, but I kept my poker face.

"I cannot have you going to your command talking about the things

---

* Not his real name.
† "When these implicit biases are imposed on top of the training of police officers to be hypersuspicious, differential policing outcomes are a natural result." (Renée McDonald Hutchins, "Racial Profiling: The Law, the Policy, and the Practice," in *Policing the Black Man: Arrest, Prosecution, and Imprisonment,* ed. Angela J. Davis [New York: Pantheon, 2017], 109.)

you've been talking about in here. You're going to stick out, get black-balled."

I was a little stunned.

"Look, you made it," she said. "Coming from immigrants, losing your mother, your father sick, you work your ass off. Don't give that up. Don't jeopardize your career because we're not in a space where people are ready to hear it. I'm a Black woman—you don't think I understand what you mean? You don't think the other Black recruits understand what you're talking about?"

"Sure," I said, nodding my head. "I understand." I appreciated her looking out, but I had no intention of keeping quiet. I just couldn't do it. Because I could intelligently make my argument, it didn't occur to me that it was going to cause a problem.

This was my first of countless "play the game" conversations, but I tuned it out. I had hope that people on both sides of the line would listen to me. I thought I could operate as a link between the communities most affected by police and the police themselves. One of the reasons cops don't listen to our community is because of insular thinking: *They're not cops so they couldn't possibly understand what we face.* I figured by becoming a cop the brass would be open to what I had to bring. This was the optimism I carried as I left the academy.

At graduation at Madison Square Garden, finishing in the top ten of my class, I was given a Commanding Officer's Award for exceptional police duty for breaking up that bar fight, was invited to walk across the stage, and shook hands with Mayor Bloomberg and Police Commissioner Kelly. Later, I did my first interview for the *Daily News*, though I didn't stick around for the picture. I was nervous about being a new officer, and I already got the sense that sticking out wouldn't be appreciated—even for something supposedly good.

When the ceremony was over, I watched as my peers ran to waiting family and friends, sharing their moment with loved ones. My father had been felled by a stroke in 2003 and had been in a nursing home for years. I shrugged it off; it was an absence that defined me as much as anything. I'd been through it for so long, I barely knew another way. That hole was in me and I accepted it as part of who I was. It was like the sound of my voice, the shape of my nose, the color of my skin—just part of what made me who I was.

Six

Black Boys

Black boys don't get a long boyhood. It ends
where white fear begins.

—Brian Broome[1]

1995

My East Flatbush neighborhood could be rough, but it still burst with life: the savory smells of Caribbean food in the air, reggae and dancehall music out of car windows, firecrackers and fireflies on summer nights, walks with my dad and Ronald down Flatbush Avenue to the barbershop and Geronimo Records, a drive in his blue Ford out to Sheepshead Bay, the bottom of Brooklyn, where the water stretched out past our sight line and disappeared on the horizon.

As a child, I didn't know much about the outside world, what I thought of as the white world. But in fifth grade, some of it slipped through the cracks, giving me my first peek at how that world saw things differently from mine. My teacher, Mrs. Cross, was a Jamaican woman with a slight British accent. She was discipline oriented, always lecturing us about our behavior and our futures. Though the class groaned when she did it, I soaked it all up, especially her lessons about being Black in America.

"Remember, you have to be twice as good for half of the recognition," she told us, which was the first time I heard this adage. She explained that though it's unfair, we carried the weight of the entire race with us: when someone did something negative it would be treated as typical of Blacks. But when we accomplished positive things, we were all of a sudden individuals again—outliers.

One afternoon, Ms. Pierre, another teacher, ran into the class. Her eyes were glassy like she'd been crying, but her face didn't match. She crossed the room and whispered into Mrs. Cross's ear. Mrs. Cross nodded and smirked before Ms. Pierre ran back out. We'd never seen our teachers humanized like that. Our curiosity was lit:

"What was that?"

"What'd she say?"

"Tell us what Ms. Pierre just told you!"

Mrs. Cross had a smile behind her eyes. "You'll know when you get home," she said, turning us back toward our lesson.

That night I was translating the local evening news for my dad when I realized what my teachers were whispering about: O. J. Simpson had been acquitted. On the TV, there was a white bar down the middle of the screen and they were showing the different reactions in white and Black neighborhoods. It gave me a visual understanding of the divisions in the country that I hadn't been able to see so plainly before. White people were shocked and appalled, while in the streets of Harlem people were honking and cheering. While the white world saw a man getting away with murder, the Black community saw one of their own finally beating the system.

Activist and author Tim Wise wrote that the O.J. verdict was the first time white America—as a whole—ever questioned the judicial system, ever had a reason to. It was made stark for them that there was something inherently broken about justice in this country. Black America knew this intimately. The cheering was not for O.J., it was for us: something finally fell in our favor. Underneath those cheers was a long history of pain, and misguided or not, the collective release we felt that day was real.

THE BROOKLYN OF MY YOUTH was a dangerous place. Crack had landed like a tornado, hollowing out the neighborhood, and violence rushed in to fill that hole. They called the intersection a few blocks from our apartment building at Foster and Nostrand "Front Page" because of all the murders there that ended up in the paper.

The drug game happened out in the open, right on my stoop. The dealers were only a few years older than we were. I saw handshakes, exchanges, negotiations all happening under the beat of Tupac and Biggie blasting out of stereos, but it took a while to figure out what exactly I was seeing. A customer ("custie") walked up the stoop, mumbled something, and the dealer went with him or her inside the building and reached into a mailbox. The exchange was made quick, palm to palm, and the custie moved on. No one ever had enough money to buy a lot, so they always came back soon after. When a cop car approached from down the block or what appeared to be an unmarked car slowed down in front, a younger lookout would call out, somehow both loud and quiet, "Yo, the boys. The boys." Then the dealer took off. Sometime later, it started up again, like someone hit the reset button.

I also witnessed street robberies in broad daylight, often perpetrated by the young drug dealers who were just flexing to make a point. Some of my friends began to emulate the dealers' fashion, their slang, their mannerisms. Although just a few years older than we were, the dealers seemed to be adults, especially since the actual adults were afraid of them.

The luxury of being young was that I didn't really understand what I was swimming in. We heard gunshots and ran for cover, but when they stopped, we got back to playing. They were like thunderstorms we had to wait out.

Ronald and I were watching TV one night when the sound of gunshots cut through the evening outside our window.

"Seven," I said.

"Eight," he responded.

"Nah, seven."

We called Billy and Melissa. "Yo, Billy, how many gunshots was that?"

"Seven," he said.

"I told you it was seven," I said to Ronald.

This was as normal to us as our lessons in school, as watching our TV shows. A kid can absorb anything. I saw shootings, stabbings, fights, and heard about ten times as many. There'd be excitement around it—"Did you see that fight over on Newkirk?" "Did you hear Maurice got stabbed?" It was so normalized that it felt like gossip or entertainment. Then one night, it landed right on my doorstep.

After dark, I was leaving Billy and Melissa's and heading around the corner back home. The drug dealers were busy, but kids my age were still lingering around—a mix of the hangout and the grind. It was like a split screen: my group talking about Michael Jordan and Busta Rhymes while the dudes a few years older were handling custies, orchestrating handoffs, playing dice, and counting money. We coexisted, but there was this invisible line.

Right as I got to my steps, I saw a blur out of the side of my eye and then the *rata-tat, rata-tat* of a semiautomatic and the high-pitched sound of metal plinking off the concrete. Then a car door slammed, someone yelled, "Yo, bounce! Bounce!" and the screech of tires pierced the air. Everyone on the stoop booked it inside, tripping over one another to get up those four flights to my door. We all streamed past my dad in the doorway, the panic and momentum pushing us in. Dad stood there in the messy apartment in his briefs and dingy shirt, but I didn't sweat it like I normally would. My heart was in my throat.

"What's going on?" he asked in Creole. "Edwin, what's happening?"

"Someone just shot up the block," I said, catching my breath.

"Yo, yo! Deedee's hit," someone said. Deedee, one of the older gang members, was sitting in a chair holding his right arm, the blood flowing out. I quickly grabbed a polo shirt, ripped it up, and tied it around his shoulder like a tourniquet. Someone called 911, and when we heard the ambulance pull in, we brought Deedee back downstairs.

I watched Deedee sitting at the back of the ambulance, getting his wound treated, my breath heavy and my heart pounding. As the adrenaline flowed fierce, I played everything back in my mind, how easily it could've been me. The gushing red liquid, the blinking red lights, the fear in his eyes—it stayed with me. That protective wall had come crashing down. Now I was in it.

WHEN IT WAS time to choose a junior high school, I scanned the choices until I landed on what I was looking for: Marine Park.

Not too long before, I hadn't even heard of it. A year earlier I had gone over to Billy and Melissa's and they weren't home, nor were any of the other kids and older men who would sit on the veranda. Later, all the cars started pulling up, guys hopping out in their soccer gear. "Where'd you all go?" I asked Billy.

"Marine Park," he said.

"What the hell is Marine Park?"

The next time I saw the Haitian men in their cleats with their cooler and soccer balls, I just hopped in one of their cars, squeezing in like a piece of cargo. The ride was short, but when we got out, it was like we'd gone through a magic portal.

The park itself was massive, with freshly painted playgrounds, intact fences, and clean bathrooms. The air was clean and because I could actually breathe, there was this strange open feeling in my chest that I didn't know was normal. The rolling park had blooming flowers, lined and mowed fields, snack bars, and golf courses that took up miles of that green. Compared to parks in the hood, it was Disney World. We were not even three miles away. But in New York City that's enough to take you to a distant world.

Marine Park Junior High was not at all like grade school. I was separated from most of my friends and put in the advanced classes, one of six Black kids out of thirty. The lower-performing classes had the bulk of Black and Latino students, which included friends like Eddie and my brother. Across the lunchroom, I watched them roughhousing and laughing while I sat with the white kids, whose home lives, free time, and even sense of self were so different. I understood that this put me on a promising path, but the separation didn't sit right with me.

I started to question things even more. I knew life in Florida felt different, but that was half a country away. Marine Park was only a handful of bus stops from our apartment. Why was it so different out here? It sure wasn't the intelligence of the people; I could see that for myself. The discrepancy planted the seed of my racial consciousness but also grew my self-esteem. When you don't have access to white folks early in life, and the world revolves around them, you assume they're better. You imagine they're brilliant and worthy of all that praise and attention. That lie creates an inferiority complex among Black people that can last for generations.

I started to understand the fictions about white people, but things like economics, class, and resources were very real. When we had to write about what we did for the summer, Pasquale told the class he went to Italy. I didn't even know you *could* go to Italy; he might as well have gone to the moon. Too embarrassed to write about what I actually did—splashed in the open fire hydrant—I lied that I went to Florida, which was easy to fake.

Early in the year my class got an assignment to write a book report on a famous monument and make a model of it. I'd always been the artist in the class, but I had no money, supplies, or access to adult help like my peers did. Ms. Cologna was a young white woman with blond hair, the focus of a lot of boys' crushes. She meant well, but she didn't consider socioeconomics, didn't really get the Black kids from Crown Heights and East Flatbush. "If you're struggling with this," she said, "go home and ask your mom to help you."

But my mom was gone and my dad didn't even speak English. My friend Cliff, one of the only other Black kids in the class, was also poor, smart, and Haitian. At Marine Park, we were surrounded by white kids who seemed to have all these advantages. When it was time to present our monuments, our peers came in with professional-level stuff, properly finished and painted projects made out of balsa wood, created with their parents in basements and garages. My Parthenon's base and roof were made out of a cereal box, its columns rolled-up pieces of loose-leaf paper. The kids struggled to hold in their laughter, which was humiliating but also unfair. If I'd had the tools or materials they had, I could make their jaws drop. But I wasn't even given the chance.

When I rode the B41 bus home every day, traveling out of the green suburbs of Marine Park into the hood, I felt the change in the people's energy. The calmness and beautiful homes shifted into the high-stress, low-wage hustles of darker people crammed on top of one another in run-down apartment buildings. *What is going on here?* I wondered. *Why are things like this?*

IN SEVENTH GRADE, our history teacher was Mr. Schoenwetter, a tall white man with glasses, salt-and-pepper hair, and a matching thick mustache. We were learning about the Louisiana Purchase, how it expanded the size of America, when Mr. Schoenwetter made a left turn off the curriculum to explain why Napoleon made that sale.

"It's because of *Haiti*," he said. My ears perked up. I had never heard the word in school unless it was connected to an insult. Mr. Schoenwetter explained that the Battle of Vertières—part of the Haitian Revolution, the first successful slave revolt in history—solidified the island's eventual victory over Napoleon. The defeat damaged Napoleon so badly that he was forced to raise funds for the Napoleonic Wars across Europe by selling all of the Louisiana territory—two-thirds of United States' eventual continental landmass—for an affordable price. "So that's why America looks the way it does," he said. "Because of that Haitian victory."

I was stunned. My people changed the course of U.S. history, the Western Hemisphere, and the world. For the rest of the day, I was beaming, electric. I bounded off the bus on Flatbush and Foster, zigzagging home—one block, two streets—running up the flights of stairs and going on and on to my dad about it.

"They're just teaching you that now?" Dad asked. "What's wrong with the American school system?" He learned Haitian history his first year of grade school.

"This isn't Haiti, Dad," I said.

He made a face that said, *You don't think I know that?*

From that day forward, I read everything I could find about my homeland, scanning indexes of any book at the library and copying down whole pages. Haiti was not beaten down because it was weak; it was beaten down because *it was strong*. That strength was intimately connected to why it was treated harshly by the white nations that controlled the world order.

Compared to all other colonies in the Caribbean and West Indies, Haiti was independent far earlier. While our peers in the region were heavily influenced by European colonization up until the 1960s, Haiti was on its own in 1804, not too long after America. That independence—and the racism that it engendered among world powers—affected Haiti's ability to thrive in the international community, where the rest of the Black populace (with the notable exception of Ethiopia) continued to be enslaved and colonized. The last thing colonial powers wanted was for the world to see a successful slave revolution and a thriving country as a result, so they made us pay.

I started to embrace my heritage, which lifted me up, connected me to something larger, offered me pride in a place that had often been connected to shame for me. The story that I had told myself about who I was was a lie.

Before the Haitian revolution's leader, General Toussaint Louverture, died in a cold French dungeon, he wrote in one of his last letters that got smuggled out, "In overthrowing me, you have cut only the trunk of the tree of liberty. It will spring up again for its roots are numerous and deep!"

People were taught to demonize Haiti because the system depended on its isolation. Slave labor became the backbone of European and U.S. economies. The white world didn't want enslaved people thinking they had rights or power or potential. They couldn't afford to have such ideas take off and spread. They knew that freedom, in all its forms, is a contagious thing.

Seven

Racist Math

2009

In the academy every recruit got a "dream sheet"—a chance to choose the top three boroughs in the city where they wanted to work. "Don't get your hopes up. Nothing is guaranteed," they told us. "That's why it's called a dream sheet." Some recruits had connections, phone calls to higher-ups that helped grease the wheels. A "hook" is when you know a captain or inspector, a "crane" is knowing a chief. Hooks and cranes have far more pull than outsiders realize. So much of the internal dynamics of the department are based on whom you know and who is pulling for you.

As a medal winner, I got to choose the specific command I wanted, so I picked Transit District 30 in Brooklyn. A mentor of mine had worked the subways and it felt like the right place to start. I had enough horrible memories of various robberies, assaults, and general mayhem riding those trains. New York City is an enormous and unwieldy place, but I liked the idea of a contained space where I could have an impact— to aid and address issues.

The NYPD Transit Bureau polices the 850 miles of New York City subway tracks that function as its major arteries. Much of getting around in New York happens underground. For residents, cars are impractical, cabs are expensive, and gridlock is just part of life. The New York City subway system is the country's largest and busiest: it carries 5.5 million a day on over six thousand trains, through thirty-six lines and 472 stations. It's an underground collection of tunnels, booths, ticket machines, platforms, and trains that keeps the city running, while also functioning as its own realm beneath the city itself, a world under the world.

It's like a science experiment down there, a supercollider, tossing New Yorkers of all stripes—the busy, the aimless, commuters, tourists, students, homeless, performers, and panhandlers—into a deafening, unventilated space. It all creates the manic chaos you'd expect but also the beautiful flow of urban traffic, like ants that know where to go by smell. I've witnessed the aftermath of suicides, train surfing, and accidental electrocutions but also weddings, the No Pants Subway Ride, and the most talented singers, musicians, and dancers I've ever seen. It's the ugliness and beauty of New York all in one place.

At Transit orientation, about two hundred rookies filed into an auditorium at a Metropolitan Transportation Authority (MTA) training facility on Coney Island. Among the sea of blue, I saw only a handful of Black and Brown faces. The union delegate in charge of Transit spoke, as did Richard Green, a Crown Heights community leader. Green had long graying dreadlocks, a beard, and serious professorial eyes behind glasses. He looked like an aging sixties radical, which is what he was, except he was also a decorated marine who had served in Vietnam.

I was shocked to see a conscious Black man (with dreads!) given a prominent role there. He had amassed enough wisdom to know that having a relationship with the cops was better than not having one. Green gave a powerful speech about the police's role in the community and reminded us that there is a way to do our jobs that respects that.

The main speaker was the chief of Transit, James Hall, a tall, skinny white guy with a bald pate, bright teeth, and intense blue eyes. He explained that the Transit rookies were part of Operation Impact, a unit that flooded into high-crime areas, whose hours—1130 to 2005 (11:30 a.m. to 8:05 p.m.)—reflected when most transit crimes take place: after school, rush hour, and after work.

He gave us a pep talk, telling us that officers in Impact excel at identifying people from wanted posters. "Those posters go up in every Transit district, but you guys are the best at actually getting the collars from them, closing out the most warrants, and the most I-Cards."* The group seemed to eat it up, but I was suspicious of this psychological priming—telling us what we were good at before we even started. I had no idea if it was intentional, but Hall was increasing buy-in to the culture by acting as if we already had done it. It was a manipulation: if you're already successful at something, why would you question it?

After he spoke his prepared remarks, Chief Hall spotted me in one of the front rows with a glint of recognition. "Hey," he said, pointing at me from the stage. "I remember you coming up onstage at graduation for an award, right?"

"Yes, sir."

"Yeah, yeah, I remember you. What'd you get your award for?"

"I actually—" My voice came out scratchy and I cleared my throat. "I actually made a collar in the academy, during meal break."

"Right, right. Great. So you're going to be one of my hammers," he said. "Hammer" was police jargon for a heavy arrest machine. "I'm expecting you to make the first arrest Wednesday when you guys start," he said with a little bit of a laugh.

"Yes, sir, I'll do my best," I said uncomfortably, though I just smiled along.

---

* I-Cards are not warrants, but it means the detective or investigative unit is looking for someone. Sometimes it's a suspect, sometimes a witness.

"First arrest" seemed a strange thing to hope for, especially coming from the man in charge. Of course, some people need to be arrested, but the chief must know that there's so much more to being a police officer than arresting people. I just ignored it, chalking it up to motivational talk. We heard Mr. Green speaking about our responsibility to the community and then our boss came out treating arrests like trophies. It was as if the problem and the solution were sitting in the same room, not recognizing each other.

AT THE COMMAND in downtown Brooklyn, for roll call, we filed into the muster room, a tight standing-room-only space with a large corkboard and lectern. The walls were plastered with those wanted posters rookies were always so good with, alongside informational bulletins on tests, meetings, and team-building events like Yankees games.

They didn't have enough lockers for us yet, so I had my duffel bag with all my gear at my feet. The full uniform ("bag") I'd go out in was an eight-pointed hat, a navy blue coat, a navy blue collared shirt, navy blue cargo pants, thermals for the brutal winter, black work boots, and a bullet-resistant vest—a stuffy thing that felt like the world's heaviest life preserver. The belt had a 9mm Glock 19 (with two extra fifteen-round magazines), handcuffs, flashlight, OC (pepper) spray, expandable baton, whistle, work keys, and a radio. Attached to my left leg was my escape hood, which would give me twenty minutes of filtered air in the event of a biological terror attack. Walking around under all that gear took some getting used to—your body and posture have an unnatural way of moving, almost like being in a space suit.

"Welcome, new guys," Lieutenant Meglio said from the lectern. He was a white dude with a flat face, chubby cheeks, and the mean eyes of a pro wrestler. "We're technically a citywide unit, but you guys are the

Brooklyn team. The chief loves you guys, loves Impact, because you get the collars."

There it was again—the priming.

"Right now, we'll be rotating people around, putting two of you with a veteran cop, who'll show you how we do things around here." "Veteran" was something of a joke—these were cops who had graduated in the class before us, six months earlier. "And remember: We're an enforcement unit."

An enforcement unit? Didn't all police enforce? I didn't say a thing. My "veteran"—Gorsky* —was a bald guy with a thick eastern European accent, friendly but dispassionate and strictly business on shift.

"We're headed to Bedford and Nostrand?" I asked him on the train.

"Yeah," he said. "We're going to go into the rooms, play from the rooms."

I just nodded, having no idea what he meant. Being in full uniform on the train—seeing the way people looked at me now—drove it home: I was suddenly in charge. I respected it as an immense power, not something to be taken lightly or abused. That was my mindset on that train, headed into my first shift. And I was about to collide with the reality.

When we got off the train at the Bedford-Nostrand station, I followed Gorsky up to the clerk, who sat on a stool in an enclosed booth behind streaked plexiglass.

"You guys are already in there," the clerk yelled through the speaker, pointing over to the left.

"Oh, they're in there already," Gorsky said.

"Where?" I asked, but the question got sucked up by the sounds of squealing and screeching metal braking to a stop. Your own voice only travels about five feet in the subway before getting drowned out.

---

* Not his real name.

We walked toward one of those mysterious off-white side doors that dot every subway station, a portal among the unwashed tile. The door had a square window vent at eye level; before we reached it, a cop on the other side opened it like he saw us coming.

"Get in here, Gorsky, you dumb Russian fuck," he joked.

"Eat my shit, Burns," Gorsky said, approximating American slang.

Inside was a large supply closet–type room filled with boxes of garbage bags, spray bottles, brooms, dustpans, mop buckets, and three other cops. The officer who had let us in closed the door and put his face to the vent, looking out. He *had* seen us coming, right through that vent. Two other cops lingered in there, looking at their phones, making the occasional comment to each other.

"What are we doing here?" I asked Gorsky quietly.

"It's the best angle," Gorsky said.

"For what?"

"TOS." He gestured with his head. *Theft of service.* Turnstile jumpers.

"Burns, let Raymond take a look," Gorsky said. The cop at the door got out of the way and motioned for me to look through the vent. It was a small square one at eye level, which offered a clear view to the turnstiles, the bank of metal entrances where passengers swipe their subway card to pay for the ride and enter the platform.

"When they hop the turnstile," Burns said, "or double up, or use the door without cargo or a handicap, wait till they hit the platform. Then we grab them, run their name; if you're lucky, they pop and you get a collar. We rotate."

While Burns peeked through the vent, we all just sat there, quiet for a while.

"Ah . . . fuck," one of the cops sitting on a box of paper towels said.

"What?" Gorsky said.

"Lost my guy," he muttered.

I was alarmed until he turned his phone around to us to show it was a game he was playing.

Maybe twenty minutes in, Burns broke the monotony. "Let's go," he said, opening the door. Everyone hopped up and followed him out, like gangbusters. Six police officers, all for one fare evasion.

A subway ride cost two dollars, so it seemed bananas we were going through all this trouble just to catch one TOS. I didn't protest right away, figuring that maybe it was a first-day thing. Maybe this was a type of training exercise, like they were going to manufacture this situation, so when I arrested someone organically, I'd know about the procedure and paperwork.

Here's how it would go down: Once the officer spotted a TOS, he waited a beat for them to pass onto the platform, because he didn't want to give away his hiding position. Then the officer approached them and said, "I need to see your ID."

Sometimes they argued. "What do you need to see my ID for?"

"You didn't pay your fare."

"Yeah, I did, what are you talking about?" They were baffled because they hadn't seen the officer, so they assumed he couldn't have seen them.

Once they handed over their ID, the cop got on the radio: "Central, can I have a seventy-five William?"—code for a warrant check.

Then it came back staticky and quick: "Proceed with your William."

The cop read: "Last name: David, Ocean, Edward. First name: Jon, Ocean, Henry, Norah. July twenty-eight, 1977."

If it came back "ten-eighteen," it meant they had a warrant.

"I'm going to have to put you under arrest," the cop explained.

"What for?" they asked.

"You have a warrant," he said, cuffing and searching them. Every now and then the person had a gun—the holy grail—and that officer became the most popular cop for the week.

But most of the time, the perpetrator didn't pop—no warrant—so the radio came back with "ten-nineteen." Then the cop either gave a warning or wrote the summons—a ticket to pay a fine—and handed them a copy. There are different rules and procedures depending on the infraction and the person, but that's the general framework. A C-summons was a criminal court summons, which meant they had to show up to see the judge and then pay the fine. And if they didn't, they became arrestable—which triggered a warrant. That's the cycle.

Later that day Gorsky and I moved on to the Myrtle-Willoughby station in Bedford-Stuyvesant and repeated the whole process. The secret room, the vents, the turnstile jumpers, the warrant checks. School had just gotten out and we spotted a sixteen-year-old girl using an orange student MetroCard, which is for grade school. She told us the card was her little sister's, and I issued her a summons.

Then Gorsky told me I had to confiscate the card. I hesitated. "Yeah, but if we take the card," I said, "how does her sister get to school?"

Gorsky shrugged. "Not our problem. Just take it."

The indifference bothered me: Who was being served by that decision? But again, I was new, so I did as I was told.

At roll call and in private conversations, our lieutenant was clear: the goal for Impact was a monthly quota of arrests, summonses, and stop and frisks.* At the time, in 2009, quotas had been illegal for decades, but there were loopholes on the books that the department exploited.[†] The numbers were given to us plain as day: four arrests, ten summonses, and ten stop and frisks every month. No matter what we saw out there, that's the minimum we had to produce. And "produce" is the operative word. The average citizen may not realize how difficult those numbers are to

* Actually known as stop, *question*, and frisk. The common omission of that middle word tells you a lot about the problems with that practice.
† Those loopholes would be entirely closed the next year, though this did nothing to lessen the practice. Supervisors just became more careful with their language.

achieve. It comes out to about one arrest or summons a shift, which is not as easy as it sounds. It requires the cop to get super technical and petty in a way he'd never be in white neighborhoods; it also encourages the cop to hide in order to lure the behavior he is then rewarded for spotting.

If a cop stood in plain sight, at the turnstile, he'd deter the behavior, which is supposed to be a good thing. Isn't that what the community wants? Isn't that what we as cops should want? But deterrence is not valued. Problem-solving is not valued. What's valued is the number. Discretion goes out the window, the larger picture is ignored, and the community gets harassed because of cops' adherence to their own incentives. Hiding cops are spending time on petty things, and by remaining out of sight they're not in position to stop or even see serious crimes.

I was baffled by all this. Isn't the point of having a police presence so that the public can find you? Don't we show our faces to *prevent* crime? Weren't we now sitting around hiding just so we could encourage minor infractions and then get credit for stopping them?

When our lieutenant said we were an "enforcement unit," he meant that we concentrated on racking up numbers all day. It was so single-minded that when certain calls came over the radio—a medical emergency, an EDP (emotionally disturbed person), a missing kid—we were incentivized to ignore them. Those calls gave up our location, took up time, and hurt our chances of hitting our arrest and summons quotas. "Don't worry about that," Gorsky would say. "Let the regular district cops handle that." Gorsky was no monster—he was just responding to his training and incentives. So was everyone.

Transit cops were always hiding, peeking through those vents, huddling in mold- and rat-infested storage rooms, musty locker rooms, damp bathrooms. Transit staff would come in to use the toilet and then leave us there trapped with the smell. It seemed beneath the job to hide in the bowels of a decaying century-old system, cramming into these tight spaces in my bulky uniform and gear, avoiding puddles and leaks of unidentified liquid of indeterminate color, all to sneak up on a citizen who was avoiding paying two dollars. I went to the academy and took an oath for this?

In my first week, it seemed like I was the only one who hadn't gotten an arrest. I went back to the station at the end of the day and saw who was dressed down, gun belt off, doing paperwork—which meant they were processing an arrest.

For the first six days at roll call I had to hear Lieutenant Meglio congratulate all my peers.

"Raymond?"

"Here."

"McLean?

"Here."

"By the way," Meglio said, "McLean got an arrest yesterday for TOS. Everybody: one gym clap." Everyone would then clap once simultaneously, a ritual from physical training at the academy. I knew I was doing my job properly, but even I was not immune to the forces of normative social behavior, free from the desire to please my bosses.

My first arrest came on my seventh day, at Rockaway Avenue station in Brownsville. I saw a man urinating in the subway from an elevated platform. "C'mon man," I said, "someone could be walking down there and get a face full of piss." When I ran his name, I saw he had a warrant for doing the same thing three months earlier, so I arrested him.

The next day at roll call, I was called out by the lieutenant and got my gym clap. I felt relieved, which demonstrates the problem. I knew we had a job to do, but applause for locking someone up for petty stuff? This wasn't playful competition or just bragging rights. There was a pervasive and destructive ugliness lurking underneath all this. And wherever I turned, I kept finding it.

RACIST MATH

THERE WAS ONE other thing we learned at the academy that colors all that I saw in Transit and beyond. The NYPD subscribes to a version of recent history that goes something like this: the once crime-ridden city of New York had become "the safest big city in America" because of a revolution in its policing. In reality, there was a confluence of reasons—political, economic, social, judicial—that New York City became safer in the mid-1990s and onward, along with the rest of the country. But that complexity was lost on the NYPD. Inside the department, it all melted away into one reason: broken-windows theory.

Here's how it started: In 1982, public safety expert George Kelling and social scientist James Wilson wrote a hugely influential paper that studied the Newark Police Department's increase of officers on foot patrol. Those cops were tasked with focusing on so-called quality-of-life policing: vandalism, blocking the sidewalk, public drinking, marijuana possession, and other low-level infractions. Their hypothesis was that crime was attracted to crime. If someone sees a broken window, they're more likely to break another window, or jump a turnstile, or steal a car. A broken window is supposedly a sign of apathy about public safety, making it more attractive to criminals. In Kelling and Wilson's words, "Disorder and crime are usually inextricably linked."[1]

Ultimately, though the crime rate in Newark did not drop during the period of the study, something else did happen: a portion of Newark residents—especially older ones—*felt* safer because everywhere they turned, cops were arresting someone. Public perception was that cops were doing more.

Enter Bill Bratton, an ambitious and academically minded cop out of Boston, who fell in love with the broken-windows theory and rode it up the career ladder. When he became chief of the New York City Transit Police in 1990, Bratton brought broken windows with him. He took

over Transit at a time of high crime in New York City, when the subway was a legitimately dangerous place with frequent muggings, assaults, and worse. It was also a free-for-all of graffiti, pissing, and turnstile jumping. Bratton instructed Transit officers to *overly* enforce low-level offenses in the subway stations and on trains in the hopes that it would do two things: one, have a broken-windows-type effect on serious crime; and two, round up a number of actual criminals walking around with arrest warrants and guns.

At first, it somewhat worked. Because the NYPD had never before focused on enforcing these minor infractions, that first push turned up a huge number of guns and felony warrants. Bratton was hailed as a conquering hero, the man who cleaned up the subways; a few years later, in 1994, he was made New York City police commissioner.

With Bratton at the helm of the NYPD, broken windows went topside and citywide. Bratton and new mayor Rudolph Giuliani went all in on "quality-of-life" policing, which was incorrectly getting all the credit for the drop in crime.* The NYPD got caught in a self-perpetuating game of limbo, where the commanders had to find ways to keep getting the crime rate lower. And if they couldn't, they had to at least show they were *trying* to get it lower. How do you show you're trying to stop crime? According to the powers that be, you had to show general "activity"— arrests, summonses, stop and frisks—in high-crime areas. Not arrests for serious crimes, mind you. Arrests in high-crime *areas*, which could be for anything. And they often were.

It didn't take too long for the spike of success from broken windows to flatten out. A few years in, violent criminals adjusted to the new environment. People who were armed or carrying an outstanding felony warrant weren't jumping turnstiles anymore, not in the numbers they once

---

* The crime drop was nationwide. Cities like Atlanta that didn't implement broken windows *also* saw a dramatic decrease in crime starting in the mid-1990s. Because broken windows happened at the same time in New York City—and it benefited the mayor and the commissioner to connect the two—it got the credit. But as they teach in science: correlation does not imply causation.

had. So aggressively summonsing everyone spitting on the tracks or littering was doing nothing useful to stop serious crime. It was just harassing residents in certain minority neighborhoods and putting people in the system for barely any reason at all. The ripple effects were profound.

In the Black and Hispanic neighborhoods, where broken-windows policing was the norm, working people who couldn't make a court date and struggling people who couldn't pay a fine were now getting locked up. Being arrested—even for something small—isn't just a brief inconvenience. They're in the system now. They have a record. The next time they have a police interaction, they're more likely to go back to jail, which affects their job and housing prospects, their schooling, their finances, their families, their futures. That's why it's called a system: it turns you into a number and you can get lost in it. That arrest also affects innocent people in their orbit, including their children. This just perpetuates the cycle as "studies suggest that children with an incarcerated parent are six times more likely to end up incarcerated themselves . . . They're also more likely to suffer from emotional and behavior problems."[2]

Even though broken windows eventually lost whatever cogency it once had, it had made too many careers. It was gospel, traveling down the chain of command to the exclusion of commonsense policing that served the citizenry. Broken windows also further polluted the relationship between cops and the communities to the point where many residents didn't talk to police even when they needed them. Certain citizens, especially the Black and male, were so used to getting bothered by cops that they would enter any interaction defensively or aggressively. That's what they had been conditioned to do from a young age. As law professor Kristin Henning writes, "Early encounters with the police—both personal and vicarious—have an enduring impact on the way young black males respond to the law and law enforcement as they transition into adulthood . . . Over time, negative police interactions with black boys have cascading consequences for public safety, officer safety, and ultimately the mortality of black boys and men."[3]

The cops didn't care about the collateral damage of their harassment, and the residents lost respect for the police, which made the cops care even less. Officers simply completed their tasks as though they were part of a blind assembly line, failing to understand the cumulative sum of their individual contributions. Policing became a repetitive action without context, disconnected from the final product. The feedback loop had been going on for many years by the time I got to Transit. Barely anyone bothered to question it. It was just a feature of the city's landscape.

Broken windows is actually part of a two-headed monster. The first head is what and who cops are hunting. The other head is *how* they track and respond to serious crime. Enter CompStat, a hyperspecific system of locating where major crime is happening in a city. A computerized map of index crimes* (also known as the seven majors) was produced weekly, and commanders would then have to go in front of the chiefs and get grilled about their numbers (projected on giant screens throughout the conference room), their precinct's "activity," and what they were doing to stop crime in their area.

Some cracked under the pressure of being scolded in front of their peers. If the brass didn't like what they heard, the commanders were put on notice; if improvements weren't made, they were relieved of their command. This sent a shock through the system, running all the way down to the rank and file, who learned quickly what the new game was. After all, shit travels downhill. Activity became the order of the day. Quotas now ensured that officers got in line.

What CompStat led to was a type of theater. Commanders up on that podium had to show police presence in high-crime areas, along with

* Index crimes are the seven major crimes, which every department has to report to the FBI: murder, rape, robbery, aggravated assault, burglary, larceny, and motor vehicle theft. They are the Dow Jones of American policing and the numbers used to determine the safest U.S. cities. The index numbers are wrapped up not only in law and justice, but economics, tourism, real estate, politics, taxes, education, and just about everything else that matters in America.

arrests, summonses, and stop and frisks from those cops. But the two aren't even connected. An increase in theft-of-service arrests at a single subway station isn't doing anything to address a spike of robberies around the corner. It's nonsensical. But in the world of CompStat, cops just have to show general "activity" in the area: summonses and arrests for *unrelated* things. A murder on one block will lead to a slew of littering and blocking-the-sidewalk summonses in that spot days or weeks later. Cops know it's a charade, but they need to do it. It's called "paying the rent."

When I was in Transit, there was a murder on Newkirk and Nostrand right outside the subway. That next week, the precinct commander called our Transit commander asking for "some help over at Newkirk." Transit police were then forced to get as much activity from Newkirk train station as possible. The sergeant was pushing for us to heavily enforce "unsafe riding"—moving between subway cars using the end door, which is a minor offense. We were actually instructed to pull the offenders out at the Newkirk stop so we could show activity there. *Even if they commit unsafe riding three stops ahead, don't pull them out until they get to Newkirk.* That way Newkirk gets the number. This is what runs the largest police department in the country. Everything comes back to the single cop trying to get his numbers because that is what he's measured by.

A good cop is like a Swiss Army knife. Depending on the situation, he has to protect, assist, mediate, communicate, connect, encourage, monitor, discourage, respond, de-escalate, facilitate, prevent, and sometimes enforce. With an array of options and a variety of situations, it doesn't make sense to use only one tool. A cop's effectiveness at stopping crime doesn't always track as a number. Sometimes his presence—appearing in the station rather than hiding in a room—prevents the crime from happening at all. But that's not measured, so it's not incentivized. And because it's not incentivized, it's not done.

In 1994, the first academy class who graduated knew nothing but broken windows. By the time I got to Transit, those graduates had become the chiefs and commanders who indoctrinated their beliefs into every rookie. Broken windows is now in the institution's bloodstream. It *is* the institution's bloodstream.

The racial element of broken windows is a feature, not a bug. Officers in white neighborhoods (Midtown, the Upper West Side, Park Slope) aren't expected to fulfill their quota in the same way. Broken windows criminalizes entire zip codes for innocuous infractions, some of which—like substance-related issues—actually occurred at higher rates in white neighborhoods.* I found that in a fully residential white area, with no commercial strip or transient population, the quota was essentially nonexistent. In white residential areas that had people from other neighborhoods moving through, the police were expected to fulfill their quotas on the backs of transient people of color, *not* the white residents.

In Transit, sometimes we got sent to South Brooklyn to help out in the subway stations at school dismissal. It was a predominantly white residential area (Sheepshead Bay Road, Brighton Beach, Ocean Parkway) where Black kids from other neighborhoods came to go to school. The number of open containers, bikes on the sidewalk, and turnstiles blocked by residents was just like in other neighborhoods, but not a single cop enforced it. According to broken windows, serious crime is supposedly tethered to these behaviors. But the biggest hammers in the command ignored the white guy from South Brooklyn as he passed between moving cars. It was like there was a silent contract not to railroad white people.

* "Between 2001 and 2013, black and Hispanic people were more than four times as likely as whites to receive summonses for minor violations, according to an analysis by the New York Civil Liberties Union" (Saki Knafo, "A Black Police Officer's Fight Against the NYPD," *New York Times Magazine*, February 18, 2016). Additionally, "African Americans were up to 30 times more likely than their white counterparts to be arrested for marijuana offenses." (Renée McDonald Hutchins, "Racial Profiling, The Law, The Policy, and the Practice," in *Policing the Black Man: Arrest, Prosecution, and Imprisonment*, ed. Angela J. Davis [New York: Pantheon, 2017], 96.)

The arrests were more frequent in Black communities because that's where more cops were placed and motivated to enforce the tiniest things. Put cops in any neighborhood and pressure them exactly the same way and that neighborhood would now have the highest arrest numbers. But the police operated according to a self-fulfilling prophecy. This was where the arrests were, so this was where the cops needed to be. But arrests aren't a naturally occurring phenomenon. The arrests were in these neighborhoods because this is where the cops were pressured to make them.

CompStat and broken windows were part of a data revolution that swept through various industries and institutions in the nineties: business, the stock market, sports, technology, entertainment, the internet. But the police department is not a business that answers to shareholders seeking dividends—it's a tax-funded public service. You can't just put people in the same line as profits as though they're part of a balance sheet. There are collateral consequences to every enforcement-related police-citizen interaction in the city. On the other side of every one of those petty arrest numbers is a person.

Additionally, petty arrests can actually breed crime because of the compounding factors. You get a petty arrest or two and pretty soon the system clamps down on you: you are closed off from society's benefits. A neighborhood where people are always getting locked up—for minor things—isn't safer. Those people get out of jail, and then what? They can't get jobs, they can't get housing, they lose their wives or kids: What do you think they turn to?

Broken windows, whose originators have since claimed it has been misapplied by police,[4] is no longer about stopping crime. It's about serving the numbers themselves. The brass demands the numbers, and the commanders produce them by pushing the patrol. In order to repeatedly satisfy that pressure, gray areas get manipulated and things are made to happen. The single officer looking to keep his job, and maybe move up and out, motivates the entire system.

So, this is how we got here. The cops are contributing to the very problem they are supposedly trying to solve. Once I saw it, I spotted it everywhere. I couldn't unsee it.

Eight

The Invisible Line

1997

D id you hear what they did to that guy?"

Outside one summer afternoon, Ti Lou, the butter-knife mechanic, and some other older Haitian cats were in a huddle playing dominoes. Ronald and I would play nearby, waiting for one of them to send us to the corner store because it always came with a tip.

As they spoke, their voices were low as they asked the question.

Growing up, I watched the TV show *Cops* with my dad, translating it for him into Creole. In the world of that show, the police officers were the good guys, kicking doors and ass, bringing in the bad guys. It was a superhero fantasy not too far removed from my comic books. With age and experience that picture faded away. A turning point for me—and the city—came in 1997, when I was eleven years old.

That evening, when I translated the local news for my dad, I pieced together what had happened. Abner Louima, a Haitian security guard from Flatbush, was in the crowd during a fight outside a club. One of the intervening cops claimed to have been punched during the ruckus, and when he turned around, he arrested the first person he saw—Louima, who had nothing to do with it.

"You people can't even talk English," the cop told him in the police car. "I'm going to teach you to respect a cop."[1] Whether the cop—Justin Volpe—was angry about getting hit or just using it as an excuse to go sadistic is a mystery. What happened next is not.

Louima was stripped naked, beaten, and then sodomized with a broomstick in the bathroom of the police station. I had difficulty explaining the full story in Creole to my dad; at the time, I didn't even know what sodomy was. We stared in shock at the images of Louima in a hospital gown, his busted lip, broken teeth, and swollen face driving home what cops did to him. *Cops.*

The beating and torture of Louima was a jolt to the entire community: this was what the cops can do to Black men, what some of them *wanted* to do. It was the first time I had a firm sense that police saw me as a problem, a threat, an enemy. I didn't have to do a thing to provoke it. My very existence was the provocation. That was a scary thing, especially to someone just figuring out the world. Soon after Louima's case faded from the newspapers, my father had "the talk" with me, a rite of passage for Black boys.

"You're getting older, Edwin," he said, "and the cops are going to start looking at you as a problem, and you have to make sure you stay calm, don't talk back rudely, answer their questions, make sure you have ID on you."

It didn't matter how good my grades were, how well behaved I was, how I couldn't even lie to my own father. I inhabited a young Black male body, and I needed to know how that was perceived, especially by law enforcement. I was taught how to respond to police, the danger implicit in any interaction with them, why they saw me the way they did. Dad painted the larger picture, the contradiction that we faced in the United States, the trade-off we made in living here.

"This is the land of opportunity, Edwin," he said. "Just keep your nose clean, get your education, and you will be able to do something for yourself. But remember: a Black man can never be president. That's something that can never happen. At the end of the day, we're still Black. This place won't let you forget it."

Two years later, a twenty-three-year-old Guinean immigrant named Amadou Diallo was shot nineteen times and killed in the vestibule of his apartment building by four New York City police officers after reaching for his wallet. Everyone in school the next day was talking about it. My eighth-grade English teacher, Mr. Gori, a conservative white man, heard us talking before class. "Now, now," he said. "Let's wait for the facts."

Even the white kids pushed back on that:

"The what?!"

"Forty-one shots, Mr. G!"

"Wait for what facts?!"

"It was a wallet, Mr. G!"

"What?" Mr. Gori responded, holding his hands out to calm us down. "You think there aren't guns that look like wallets? There are guns that look like cameras, there's guns that look like cellular phones."

Wait for the facts. Amadou being killed for no reason at all—shot at forty-one times—further upended my understanding of the world, of cause and effect, of the rudiments of justice and fairness. An African who came here to be a student, to achieve the American dream, killed just for being Black. I was old enough to be upset by his murder but still too young to process it.

Both the Louima and Diallo incidents stayed on my mind as I matured and became part of my rising consciousness and understanding of myself. Maybe if I looked closely enough at these incidents, turned them over in my head, and examined them from all angles, I could make sense of the incomprehensible.

DURING A SUMMER heat wave in New York, I was riding bicycles with some high school kids in the empty parking lot next to Sears. Zulu, the unofficial leader of our group, was a very dark Haitian, short with a muscular build. Already in high school, he got respect from everyone on the block, even though he mostly hung out with younger kids like me. "Yo, let's hit up the school," he said. "Wait on line for the free lunch."

"Nah, shit," Fat Cat said, "that line's gonna be crazy long right now."

"I don't want to wait on that shit," Chris said. "Not worth it for that raggedy-ass food."

They all started laughing, but I didn't say anything—I usually ate at the school, no complaints. A lot of days it was *all* I ate.

"Let's hit up the Haitian place, play some games," Chris said.

We all agreed.

The Haitian restaurant around the block had a few arcade machines in the front. I used the daily quarter Dad gave me to play a quick game of *Street Fighter II*, which lasted about two minutes. The technician sometimes gave us free credits, but he wasn't around, so I went from machine to machine to watch friends play *Mortal Kombat* and *Pac-Man*. Once in a while, they gave me a turn.

After about an hour, an employee walked past us holding a big brown bag and headed toward the back area where the tables were. Zulu ran up to us, his eyes opened wide.

"Yo! There's mad money in that bag!" Zulu half yelled, half whispered.

"Where?"

"Right over there!" he said, gesturing with his chin. "That table right on the other side there."

"For real?"

"Yo, I'm about to take that shit," Chris said.

72

"What? Chill, man," I said. "Don't you—"

"Shhh . . . is he coming?" Zulu said. "Check if the guy's coming back."

I tried to protest. "What are you guys—"

"Edwin, man, shut up," Fat Cat said.

There was no talk for a while, and I thought they'd dropped it, but before I knew what was happening, Zulu jetted out of the restaurant with a brown bag in his hand, the dull thumping of the rolled coins smacking together. Everyone dashed out after him. I hesitated but quickly realized that if I stayed, I'd be the one in trouble. I already knew that this was how justice operated.

Out on the street, I followed them to the regular meet-up spot: the roof of my building.

When I got there, they were already sitting on the black tar-paper ground, the rolls of quarters spilled out. Fat Cat and Chris were breaking the rolls on the stone ledge, and Zulu was counting out the quarters into piles, the coins gleaming in the summer sun.

"Edwin, come get some of this," Zulu said. He was passing out the rolls like he was dealing cards.

"Nah, I'm good," I said, staying outside the circle. "I don't want any of that shit." My friends just shrugged, like I was weird for not taking it. They knew I was poorer than all of them. But I was thinking about how the woman who ran the counter there was always nice to us, how the technician gave us free plays, how we'd never be able to go back there now.

As my friends and I came of age, and we got into what city kids get into, I was saved by two things. The first is that, from a very young age, I had a concept of delayed gratification. I understood decisions made in the present would impact my future. Maybe it was because I was forced to grow up so quickly, but I just knew that one day I'd be an adult and all of this would matter. My friends didn't think in advance about how they couldn't go back to the arcade now, but I had. They mostly lived for the day, seeing only as far as that afternoon or maybe the release of the next pair of Air Jordans.

None of my friends could afford to stay on top of the fashions, so they started turning to other things for money. We knew teenagers who were already making six figures in the drug game, way more than any adult in the community. They were too young to own cars or property, but they had bodies on which they could flex: jewelry, clothing, sneakers. It was not just about the items themselves, but the fact that they could afford them. It sent the message that they had power.

The second thing that kept me out of trouble started when I was twelve. One day, I was playing video games at Eddie's when our friend Oliver called. "Yo, I got us a job," he said, "but y'all gotta get there quick. The new Food County Supermarket on Nostrand."

I hopped on my bike and Eddie threw on his Rollerblades, grabbing the back of my seat. We coasted down Rogers Avenue the thirteen blocks to Nostrand and Lenox, navigating parked cars, bikes heading the other way, motorcycles kicking up smoke, bulky buses, the whole mad-ass ballet of Brooklyn. At Food County we met the owners, four Palestinian brothers who chain-smoked and pounded coffee all day. They were looking for cheap labor to distribute circulars, thin newspaper pamphlets with deal notices and coupons. For one Saturday's work I came home with twenty-five dollars, a fortune to me.

When we came back to the block with cash in our pockets, we got everyone's attention. "Yo, how'd you all get that money?"

"Doing the circulars," I said, glad I'd found something less embarrassing than digging through garbage.

"Can we do that?"

Every Saturday some new kids from the block came to work at Food County, but—as was the pattern—they rarely went back. We pushed shopping carts around Flatbush, dropping off circulars in mailboxes and lobbies, which by hour five was boring and exhausting. Your feet burned, your legs turned to jelly, and you sweated through your clothes. Manual labor was for suckers, they thought; there were easier ways to make twenty-five dollars.

One other kid who stayed with it at Food County was a younger Haitian whom I knew only by his street name: Buffett, like the billionaire. He spoke no English but was very talkative in Creole, confidently throwing himself into any conversation and making jokes. All the signs of being new to the country and poor were there. His hair was barely combed, he didn't seem to care much about his appearance, and he hadn't yet absorbed that desire for name-brand clothes. I could tell he was still taking it all in, wide-eyed and energized by being in a big American city. He loved watching all the girls walk by but sometimes said too much, forgetting that there were other Creole speakers around. After about a year at Food County, he quit and started hustling, selling crack. I'd visit him and the others on his block every now and then, and every time I ran into him, he had absorbed a little more of the environment. One day I passed by his block and was told that both he and his brother had been deported. I figured his new job had finally caught up with him.

I stuck with Food County every weekend and the summers, and just like that, I was no longer hungry. As time went by, I could afford real school supplies, money for the mall, and, eventually, name-brand clothes.

Even Mareena, the Jamaican girl who used to make fun of me, noticed. One day, she saw me dressed in a polo shirt and Guess jeans with new Jordans. "Ed, you win the lottery or something?" she asked in that acid voice of hers. I just smiled.

The money gave me a sense of independence but also power, especially when it came to my father. I grew more vocal about how dysfunctional our situation was. "You know, you're supposed to be doing this stuff, Papi," I said to him after grabbing another dinner for me and Ronald. "We're just kids. We're not supposed to be feeding ourselves all the time." Dad never tolerated when I talked like that and sometimes the fights got loud.

One afternoon, I brought friends over, including a girl we all had crushes on—Jaira. We were watching music videos in my brother Lemy's room, when Dad stormed in. "You all being too loud!"

"No, we're not," I said. "We just got here. You're just looking to start something."

Dad left and came back with his brown leather belt, partly wrapped tight around his wrist.

Oh hell no, I thought, *not in front of Jaira.*

I grabbed the hanging part of the belt, wrapping it around my own forearm. We tugged at it until Dad, seeing he was losing, hit me in the face with his other hand. After that, he left, embarrassed.

Later that evening he was on the phone for hours to friends and family members. "Edwin tried to fight me! His father!" he said, exaggerating to a comical degree. "I raised him on my own, and now he's hitting me!"

"What are you talking about?" I yelled from down the hall. "I didn't try to fight you!" I had just stopped him from hitting me. But that was enough for him. *If I want to hit you, you have to let me hit you. Don't be rude.*

He was hurt, feeling his power over his children slipping away, the only power he had left in the world. He never tried to hit me again after that.

A few weeks later, after he saw me working hard to make my own money, he sat me down. I was afraid he was going to light into me, but he said, "Listen, Edwin, I'm proud of you. I know you and your brother will be all right now if something happens to me."

Working a steady job from a young age set me off on the right path before other influences could settle in. It was not just the money; I had a place to be, which kept me away from my peer group right at the time when they were discovering things to lure them into the streets.

One summer afternoon, I came back on the block after work and I couldn't find any of my friends: no manhunt, no tag, no flirting with girls on the corner. Then I spotted them all coming down from my building's roof, veiny red eyes, high as kites, the pungent smell wafting off their clothes. For a while smoking weed on the roof was the thing but pretty soon they'd just do it in the open, on stoops, the sidewalk, anywhere.

The next summer their behavior became much less innocuous. Up on the roof, I found them all sitting up against the stucco walls in the sun, huddled around Leroy, with his cornrows and high-pitched voice. Leroy was an athlete and a magnet for girls, who would flood in from other neighborhoods just to be in his orbit. He was holding a nickel-plated .25-caliber pistol with a brown wooden handle—a Saturday night special. I recognized it right away, though I'd never seen a real one up close.

I tried to ask what it was for, where they got it, but I was drowned out by everyone else. They were enamored with it, admiring it, each trying to hold it like it conferred something on them.

"Yo, let me see that shit."

"Can I hold it?"

"Nah, you're doing it wrong, bro."

"Stop grabbing at it like that, damn!"

I was shocked but not entirely surprised. For a year they had been saying, "We need ratchets. We need ratchets." There was a sense that we weren't safe without one. Our radius was expanding outside our comfort zone: parties, the skating rink on Empire Boulevard, new neighborhoods with their own pre-gang types. Stepping to people for no reason was a currency, a way to get your street credibility up. If you had a gun, even better; plus, they might have one too, so it was a type of insurance. There was a ritual dance going on among Black teenagers in Brooklyn, a contest over machismo, a battle of egos. Everyone was trying to look tough while working to hide that they were really terrified. You hid your true feelings so no one saw you as an easy target and tried you. But then you started living out that caricature, and before you knew it, you were unrecognizable. Perceptions became reality.

The gun began as protection and a status symbol, but then it became this tool to get what they wanted. On the roof, they were setting up their robbery routes on Flatbush Avenue. *Wait, when did we decide to start robbing people?* I thought. *Weren't we just playing* Mario Kart *last week?*

The job at the supermarket kept me at a certain distance from them. I was not around when they were making the poor decisions. I showed up after the decision was made, and it always stood out to me. A frog slowly boiling in water doesn't notice it. But I came home from work and dipped my toe in the scorching liquid and was like, *What the fuck?* The street life was like a cauldron that my friends had adapted to. They had changed, right there but far away, now on the other side of that invisible line.

I tried to talk sense into them. "Yo, why are you all doing this?"

They looked at me like the answer was obvious. There were things they wanted: *How else were they going to get them?*

As I came of age, the gangs mostly left me alone. The cops didn't.

I got harassed by police all the time, usually a plainclothes unit, officially known as Anti-Crime, but we all called them "the Dees" (short for Detectives). Two years earlier I was invisible to them. Then, one day, I couldn't help but set off their radar. I knew I wasn't doing anything different, except now I had filled out a little and sprouted slight hairs on my chin, which alerted them to my presence. They never once handled me professionally. Their bullying was prevalent and unprovoked—the cost of simply going outside.

"Yo," I complained to a cop blocking the subway stairs. "I'm just trying to get home."

"Yeah," he said. "Where's that?" He was eyeing me like he'd caught me in a lie.

"Newkirk, it's two stops."

"What are you doing all the way over here?" he asked.

"I just got off work," I said. "I'm just trying to get home."

"Well, slow down. You got some ID?"

I never hated police as a whole, even when individual ones were harassing me, stopping and frisking me on my way home from work. I didn't blame them all when I was held up just trying to get on the subway to do my homework. I simply thought there was a disproportionate level of racist cops in New York City.

I was on my block with friends when another cop stopped us. "Where they selling drugs at?" he asked me. "Over there?" He pointed to my building. "I know they're selling drugs up in there, right?" The cop was a burly white guy with a mustache and broad shoulders. He asked us where the drugs were being sold like he was asking for directions.

"I don't know," I said. "I know nothing about that. I just live there."

"Shit, please," the cop said. "I bet all of you have been locked up already."

"What?" I asked. "What are you talking about?" I'd been hanging out with a group of other kids from the block, none of whom were in the street. The cop was making an assumption based on our color and addresses.

"Come down to the precinct," he said, "and we'll run all your names. Shit, I bet you all have records."

Bet, I thought. We had nothing better to do, so later that day we all flooded into the local precinct. We asked for the officer by name, excited to show him we were squeaky-clean. All the other cops at their desks or on phones were eyeing us. Teenagers—especially Black ones—didn't voluntarily come into the police station, and we clearly made them uneasy.

When our cop came out to greet us, he had transformed into a completely different person. "Hey, guys, thanks for stopping by," he said nervously.

"Yeah, so, we're here," I said. "We just wanted for you to look up our names—"

"Your names?" he asked, not sure what we meant. "Oh, I was just play-ing with you guys. It's good to see you got good heads on your shoulders. Stay out of trouble." He led us all out the door. "Have a good day, boys."

I walked away mystified.

"WHAT'RE YOU DOING?" uniformed cops would ask me. "Where you heading?" I tried to remember what my dad told me about being re-spectful, but it got frustrating. The plainclothes cops were even worse—rougher and ruder than the rest. I was disturbed but also curious: What the heck was going on here? Why did this keep happening?

I'd be walking along and plainclothes cops would jump out of an un-marked car and start randomly searching me. It didn't make any sense. Nothing triggered it but basic movement—going and coming from work and school. I felt like I wasn't free because I got stopped just for being outside. It went from annoying to something more nefarious. I started to get nervous for no reason.

"Hold up, hold up," a plainclothes officer said. "Where are you going?"

"I'm going to work," I replied, already irritated.

"You work? Where do you work?"

"Uh, I work at the supermarket. Over there," I said, pointing down the street. I tried not to react, not to give them a reason to escalate. It was in their eyes—they wanted me to talk back. They wanted to make it more than it was. They also had watched too much TV.

"Okay, you have anything on you you're not supposed to have?"

"Uh, no."

As he was asking, he was moving forward into my space, then frisk-ing my front and back pockets. He then asked me to lift my shirt so he could check my waistband. Instinctively, I froze and put my hands up as he patted down other areas of my body, private ones. People on the street were now looking at me. They stopped what they were doing to stare and whisper; sometimes it was community elders, friends' parents. They knew I was a good kid but they were still watching. The police had the power to make anyone look guilty.

The cop then left, like it was nothing. He moved on but I stayed, the experience hovering like something poisonous in the air. I was standing there collecting my thoughts and my things, which had been tossed onto the ground. I picked up my wallet and my keys, feeling eyes on my back, my good mood extinguished. It was humiliating. I felt like a criminal, a prisoner in my own neighborhood.

In Manhattan, I attended the High School of Art and Design. My plan was to become an architect, get some money and stability, and then come up with durable but inexpensive homes that could be replicated across the island of Haiti. When I saw pictures of those zinc roofs and shanty homes, my heart broke, and I wanted to contribute.

My friends in high school all came from different neighborhoods, but they had the same issues with cops wherever they went. At the lunch table I vented about getting stopped and my friend Alan from Harlem jumped in. "Yo, you too? Saturday I was with my man and the cops just hopped out and violated us. They made me empty out all my pockets and searched my bag, and I told them I had to head to SoHo to meet Ashli. I ended up being late from missing the train."

Another Black friend from Jamaica, Queens: "Damn, me too. Yo, let me tell you, man, on my block . . ."

"Shit, on my street, every time . . . ," a friend from Staten Island chimed in. We'd all been experiencing it, all corners of the five boroughs. The only common factor was our skin color.

It was my first look at the inner workings of the police department. But the explanation, the easy go-to, was the racism of individual cops. *The NYPD must hire a lot of bigots,* I thought. *Why else would they bother all of us?*

Nine

High School with Guns

2009

Yo, what the fuck are we doing here?"

Privately, I would suss out other cops who came up with me in the academy. I'd ask them about the quotas, the harassment, the blatant racial profiling. Some of these cops—especially the ones of color—came from the same communities I had and were now perpetuating the same problems they had recently faced. But they didn't see that cycle. All of them were just coming to work, clocking in and out, and getting paid to feed off this low-level harassment. It had little to do with crime and everything to do with self-interest. It wasn't necessarily out of malice or anger or even personal prejudice, though systemic racism was baked into it all. They were just doing their job, trying not to piss off their bosses, looking to get paid and to get ahead.

In the locker room, an old TV blasted out Fox News like a bugle call. Cops got changed on wooden benches among rows of rusted gray lockers laid out like tombstones, paint curling off the walls. The difference between the clean, well-lit academy and the run-down precinct started to feel like a symbol of something larger. What we learned in class was not what was going on here.

Cops joked around, pulled pranks like flipping rookies' lockers or hanging up someone's failed shooting-range silhouette. The police department was not what I thought it would be. It was high school with guns.

"What do you mean?" a Black officer asked.

"This hiding in the broom closet shit." Each week, each shift, brought new lows. I watched officers harass and ticket a mother who crawled under the turnstile with her child because she didn't have fare money, a student using the electrical outlet in the station nabbed for "theft" (stealing city electricity), more than one person of color stopped for dropping their MetroCard receipt on the ground (littering).

"Yeah, I know. It's bullshit," he said, resigned. "But what are we gonna do?"

"This is the same shit we were up against in the streets just a year or two ago," I said. "Before we were cops."

"Yeah, it's fucked up. But this is just how it is," he said, pushing his bag into his locker and closing it.

They couldn't defend it, but they were still going to go along with it. Beyond the fact that rookies were cheap labor, units like Impact were filled with brand-new cops because they were far more malleable and impressionable. They were eager to work, not yet burned-out, and unwilling to speak up. Supervisors were quick to remind them that they still had eighteen months of probation left after completing the academy. Impact cops were trusted to act like zombies, mindlessly feeding on the status quo.

Few cared, but even those who did care didn't want to cause problems. They just wanted to be promoted out of Patrol, to get off the hamster wheel. These officers didn't join the police department to change it. That was the farthest thing from their minds. They were looking for that cushy job, or that detective shield, so they didn't have to hide in cramped rooms or chase the radio all day. And it was pretty clear that producing numbers—literally *producing* them—was the way to get there.

There were things they wanted: How else were they going to get them?

My regular partner got pregnant, so she was put on administrative duties and I started bouncing around to different partners. I was working with people I'd known in the academy, men and women with good hearts and sharp minds. But in order to become cops, they had to leave those qualities behind. There was no use for them in the New York City Police Department.

At first, I was mad at my fellow officers of color. They were not just fulfilling quotas; some of the Black cops were the *worst* harassers. It reminded me of the house-slave mentality: not wanting to rock the boat and upset the masters. I thought about Marcus Mosiah Garvey, a hero from Jamaica and leader of the Pan-African movement. In the early twentieth century, when he tried to get Black people all over the world to join together and see that they each counted as much as any white person, they all thought he was crazy. They were stuck in the house-slave mentality too. Garvey blew open the complacency that Black people had about being second-class citizens. He pushed the idea that being free from physical enslavement wasn't enough. There was *mental* slavery too.*

The idea that Blacks had the right to live as well as anyone else was a foreign concept to a lot of them. Every seed that later grew into the civil rights movement was first planted by Garvey; he vitalized millions of Black people a generation before by making them believe they were worthy of more.

One day I was partnered with an African American woman whom I knew from the academy to be a genuine sweetheart. She was a short and dark-skinned West Indian with an infectious smile. We used to grab a

---

* The famous Bob Marley lyric is actually a Garvey quote.

drink and talk about her young son or carnival season back home in the islands. During one shift we were in the filthy transit facility room that was used to store cleaning equipment. Her face was pressed against the vent.

"How many collars you got this month, Ray?" she asked.

"Oh, just one."

"Really?" she said, turning around to face me. "Damn, I already got four. I'm good for the month, so if we collar up today, you take it so you could get on the board."

"Oh, I don't really care about that," I said. "It doesn't matter to me."

The look she gave me was unmistakable: it was like I was an alien.

In Williamsburg, we watched a group of white teenagers jump the turnstile on the opposite platform. We went up and around the other side to stop them. They were respectful, but they had this nonchalant air, like they didn't take it seriously. I'd noticed that Black kids of that age were always worried when we stopped them.

"Hey," I said, "why didn't you guys pay your fare?"

"Oh," one of them said, casually, "we don't have MetroCards."

"We have money," another one said, making a show of reaching toward his back pocket.

They were young—around sixteen—so I wasn't looking to bust them. But I had to make sure there were no warrants, so I started running all their names. There were seven of them so it took a while, but my partner started prematurely writing out the summonses before their names came back 10-19.

I walked over to her, puzzled. Maybe she knew these kids. Maybe she'd run their names recently. "Yo, what's going on?"

"Oh, they're good, Raymond."

"How do you know?" I asked, genuinely confused. "Central didn't come back yet." I held out my radio.

"Trust me, they're good," she said. "They're good."

"Yeah, but *how* do you know?"

"Trust me."

"But how?" It was like an Abbott and Costello routine.

"Because *they* don't do anything," she said.

She meant white people. I was speechless. Here was a personable and kind woman, generous and smart. She was one of the cops who invited people out after shift, tried to keep other cops' morale high. The institution had already gotten to her, infected her like a virus.

Later, we were back in the storeroom when she spotted a pair of Black teens doubling up through the turnstile. We let them get to the platform downstairs and then approached. After running their names, we got back 10-19—no warrants. After we wrote their summonses, they went on their way.

As we headed back to the room, she was annoyed. "Shit, I was sure one them was going to pop," she said. "Especially that taller one."

I looked over at her in shock. A young Black mother was upset that a Black kid had a clean record? That she *didn't* get to put him in a cage for the night? She was completely sucked into what the leadership had incentivized. Whatever value the NYPD and the city could've gotten from her life experiences would never manifest. The department's culture bulldozed over all of it in the interest of one thing: numbers.

She was a stark example of how the system denigrates character, overtakes it in the name of "activity," which is ultimately just about keeping people's jobs and the status quo in the streets. There are only so many times this happens before it begins to seem like a plan, built into the American structure to keep certain people and certain neighborhoods in their place.

"REMEMBER, GUYS, this is an enforcement unit," Lieutenant Meglio reminded us one morning at roll call. "We have OT available, but if you're not active you're not gonna get any. There are others who actually want to work." This type of overtime was officially called "spike," meaning it was given in response to a spike in crime. It was unofficially called "blood money" because of what had to be done once you got it. Meglio equated work with collars—it was just common sense to him, to all of them. He was all about the numbers because those above him were all about the numbers. The more I saw it, the less I blamed him. What choice did he even have?

When the individual cops weren't meeting their quotas, there were consequences. They were denied requested days off, not selected for overtime, reprimanded for things that their peers did with impunity, punished with grunt work like transporting or guarding hospitalized prisoners. At the same time, Meglio tried to incentivize us to hit our quotas like we were salesmen aiming for quarterly goals or factory workers on a deadline. There was never a discussion or understanding of the effect of this kind of policing. It was like these weren't even people we were locking up.

For those who surpassed their quotas, he'd dangle things like medals, high evaluations, and the possibility of being selected for "Impact Plus." Impact Plus consisted of rookies who worked exclusively in plainclothes and got to pretend that they were action-chasing cops in the Anti-Crime Unit. In cop culture, working topside in plainclothes is coveted—that's what the guys on TV do—but it normally takes around five years just to get the training. In Transit, however, you get that training immediately following the academy because plainclothes is just a tactic there, a type of hiding in plain sight. Transit plainclothes can tell their friends they're Anti-Crime cops, though they just stand around all day waiting for someone to beat their fare or walk between train cars.

The first police shooting that I responded to happened a few months into my time in Impact. My partner and I were two stations away at Saratoga Avenue when "Ten-thirteen, shots fired" came over the radio.

We looked at each other, our faces screwed up like we weren't quite sure if we heard right. It happened at the Utica Avenue train station, and we couldn't get there because it was a crime scene: no trains could pull in. We ran out at Sutter Avenue and stopped an unlicensed cab to take us to the scene. (We are not trained to do this; I had just seen so many TV cops stop a car and commandeer it during an emergency that I did this on instinct. The fact that I thought this was what was done shows how influential those TV cops are, even to cops.)

When we arrived, the yellow crime-scene tape was up, and it was a madhouse: all sorts of detectives, chiefs, and media members were already there. I could still smell the gunpowder in the air and noticed a round of 9mm ammunition on the ground. It turned out the officer's gun had jammed. My partner and I were quickly reassigned to help with crowd control right outside the subway entrance steps. It had been a "good" shooting—meaning justifiable—because the cop, who was in plainclothes, got stabbed with a screwdriver. Luckily the vest underneath prevented it from doing much damage.

As I made my way through the flood of other cops, a gaggle of video cameras and microphones awaited a press conference from department leaders. I noticed all the other cops on their cell phones.

"Yeah, Ma, I'm fine."

"Hi, Mom, I'm okay."

"Just got your message, Mom, thanks. I'm fine."

Most of the cops were young, but even the older ones had moms checking in on them. It felt like everyone got a call except me. In the chaos, with the adrenaline flowing, I felt this emptiness. The deafening silence of my phone not ringing. I could tell my dad about it when I saw him, but it wasn't the same. He might not even understand what I told him.

After the attack, Commissioner Ray Kelly was on the news talking about the stabbed cop being part of a specialized unit looking for pickpockets. He was just trying to make it sound more glamorous than it was. These were guys out of uniform looking to sneak up on turnstile jumpers. There are lots of units that work the subway that have cool-sounding names—Gang Squad, Vandal Squad, Anti-Terrorism Unit— but over 90 percent of their job is theft-of-service enforcement.

Kelly's version of events was my first indication that the department would say anything publicly to make the police look like something they weren't. Residents want to picture their cops wrestling down murderers and rapists, not aggressively enforcing littering and fare beating, though that's what they mostly do. Insulating the department from public view, making sure outsiders didn't see what was really going on in there, was clearly a top priority. I made a note of it.

In the academy, we all knew about the starting salary—around $36,000 a year at the time;* it was one of the things recruits bonded over complaining about.

"Listen, I know it sucks," one of our instructors had told us, "but when you get to your command, you will know how to make money. Don't worry about that salary. You will learn how to *make money*," he repeated. It was like this reassurance he kept giving without any specifics. When I got to Transit, I understood what he was talking about. I saw it everywhere. "Learning how to make money" was code for finding ways to use overtime pay (which was time and a half) in your favor. Among cops, it's a racket known as "collars for dollars."

There's two ways to use overtime. The first is producing enough numbers to get your sergeant or lieutenant to like you—your numbers reflect on him, after all—so he picks you for assigned overtime. Once

* In that same year—2008—starting salaries had been raised from a paltry $25,100, though they took away ten vacation days in order to get to that figure (Reuven Blau, "It's NYPD 'Green' for Cops," *New York Post*, August 22, 2008, https://nypost.com/2008/08/22/its-nypd-green-for-cops.)

you get chosen, you want to stay in that superior's good graces, so you make sure you "produce" during that overtime. If cops don't get activity early in the month, they get extremely petty and engage in what they call "ice picking."

One of the most egregious forms of ice picking I saw in Transit involved the emergency exit. People exit the subway through the same type of turnstiles they enter through, but there are also two doors: a service exit, which the toll clerk controls with a button—for strollers, wheelchairs, etc.—and an emergency exit, which has a panic bar. When cops are ice picking they will stand right outside that emergency gate and pick off the Black and Brown males for exiting through that door. Again, they are *exiting* the subway, meaning there's no fare to pay. What tends to happen is that one person will push the emergency exit and then a flood of people will pass through it, like water finding an opening. Among the crowd, the cop will grab someone for "failing to obey a sign," a technicality used just to run their name. A sergeant I later worked with was known to do this anytime he was getting pressure from his lieutenant to raise his squad's numbers. At Franklin Avenue, he would stand near a pillar at the emergency exit, grab people, and run names until he got a warrant. Then he would get on the radio and call over someone from his squad—"ten-two me at Franklin"—to give them an "assigned arrest."

In order to catch TOS, I've even seen cops tie that emergency exit door open with a piece of string and wait in the storage room to catch people walking through, just to run their names. When I confronted officers at Utica Avenue station about it, calling it entrapment, they responded, "It's not technically entrapment. We're just providing the opportunity, not *telling* them to go through."

The second type of collars for dollars has to do with timing: cops purposely wait until the end of their shift to grab someone for an infraction they might have ignored earlier so that the processing and paperwork of the arrest takes them past the end of their shift into overtime. This type of overtime also gets their superior paid, because in certain units like Impact, the sergeant has to stay late if any of his officers do. This practice is rampant throughout the department.

As a shift winds down, cops start hunting, looking like hawks for anything that could get them a collar, sometimes even escalating an interaction so it becomes an arrest. The really "active" cops try to combine both types of overtime by extending the hours of the assigned overtime with a late arrest, banking even more money. Cops who are known as "hard workers" know how to manipulate the system to get their yearly pay far past the base salary, racking it all up through overtime. It's hard for officers on a low salary to resist just getting with the program. Cops are inculcated into a system that doesn't reward them for doing good for the community but incentivizes them to do well for themselves.

Since the days when Frank Serpico blew the whistle on corrupt officers in the early 1970s, and especially since the time Michael Dowd got busted in the early 1990s, old-school dirty cops have had a harder time existing. Few would dare try to make extra cash through outright bribery and stealing. It has become too risky. The days of beat cops picking up cash envelopes has largely passed. But the drive to get paid hasn't gone away. Cops don't make money anymore by bucking the system; they do it by *leaning in* to the system, milking it for money. They can hide naked financial self-interest behind just doing what their supervisors want.

At 10:00 p.m. on a shift ending at 11:35 p.m., I'd see cops getting agitated, excited, hyperalert. "Yo, man," they'd say. "It's time to start looking. I'm gonna take my sweet time vouching property too." On train patrol, in heavily policed stations like Rockaway Avenue in Brownsville, we'd periodically run into other cops in Impact. I'd be in plain sight and then get a text from one of the other units: *GTFO of the station. We're trying to get some OT.* They'd be "playing" in one of the maintenance rooms, and my presence was hurting their shot at overtime.

While I was changing out of uniform, I saw those same cops riding those overtime hours, processing their arrests as slowly as possible. Some did it every now and then if they had a vacation coming up or had to pay for something like a new deck (both real examples I've witnessed). Others lived for it. It was those cops who got on the favored list for overtime. Their sergeant appreciated them hooking him up with overtime pay, so he'd pick them for overtime again and again, continuing the feedback loop. It was all about helping one another get fed, which is why most of the shifts were spent in those rooms. Six cops at a station and none were visible, which hindered actual police work. They weren't staking out a criminal organization or sneaking up on a serial killer; they were jumping on teenagers for skipping out on fares and littering. It was pathetic.

In those rooms, cops could see the bank of turnstiles but not the whole station. I started to protest: What if someone was mugged or attacked on the platform? When it did happen, I'd be enraged. "We're right here!" I said. "If we were visible, it wouldn't have gone down like that" or "We could've caught the perp if we were out there." We'd be stuck getting a victim or witness statement after the perp was long gone.

Cops weren't in position to stop the criminals because they weren't visible. I thought this was the whole point of being a cop, but few others did. The average person was not going to commit a crime in front of a cop, so why didn't we simply show ourselves? Shouldn't preventing crime be the objective? But then the officer doesn't get the arrest, the number, the overtime, the money. Safety itself is not valued because it's not quantified. If you stand at the turnstile, you're not going to get the collar because no one is going to jump the turnstile. Okay, I'd argue, we don't get that collar, but we also don't get robberies—and which is more important? What actually benefits and protects the public?

More cops don't mean less crime—especially if they're hiding; it means more *arrests* because each cop at work needs one. It's a toxic, self-serving system that incentivizes the cops to make money for themselves. The irony is that broken windows was designed to make people feel safer, but by cops hiding, they're making them less so. Everyone took the wrong lesson from that original study. Now it's mutated into a single-minded focus on numbers. Numbers that don't signify anything but themselves.

I could tell Lieutenant Meglio wasn't thrilled with my numbers, but I didn't have to deal with any direct blowback—not yet. My direct superior, the squad sergeant, had nearly two decades of experience and was one of the few who wasn't sold on broken windows. Sergeant Hughes was a tall Irish guy, a true prototype of a TV cop. He told me I was "ballsy" for speaking out and often threw jabs at cops who thought they were doing God's work with low-level arrests. On Sundays when the lieutenant wasn't in, Hughes did roll call and warned us not to stop and frisk people who stood around turnstiles asking people to swipe them in— something Meglio had specifically instructed us to do. Hughes stressed that this wasn't proper reasonable suspicion, the legal threshold to do a stop, question, and frisk. Hughes drove home to me that the dividing line between good and bad cops wasn't necessarily based on their color.*

I came into the police force under the impression that individual cops had autonomy. I thought they trained you, gave you a badge and gun, and then you went out and did police work as you saw fit. That didn't mean there weren't times we had to get tough, control rough areas and situations. But a good cop knows when to do that and when that's just making it worse.

Based on my own experience as a Black teenager, I assumed the race-based harassment in the NYPD was a reflection of the *personal* values of individual cops. Consequently, I assumed I had control over the kind of officer I would be. This was one of the reasons I became a cop in the first place: to police the way my community needed, be the kind of cop that I wish I had encountered as a civilian. But once I was exposed to how the department was really run, I saw that this wasn't possible. You don't bring your identity to the uniform; the uniform *is* the identity.

---

* After I became a whistleblower, Hughes would always joke when I saw him: "Wait, they haven't fired you yet?"

THERE ARE THREE LEVELS of infractions: violations, misdemeanors, and felonies. Violations are for petty things, usually enforceable with a summons. Misdemeanors can get someone up to a year in jail. Felonies can get you anything over a year of jail time. Impact wasn't going to hand me any opportunities to help my community. And though I enforced what I saw, I knew there were other ways to contribute while in uniform. I tried to make a difference where I could, because it sure wasn't going to happen in those storage rooms.

One summer morning, before a detail shift for the Puerto Rican Day parade, I was killing time and went to the juvenile room, which was rarely occupied. Right as I was about to walk in an officer said, "Yo, Ray, you gotta check your firearm."

"Why?"

"There's a perp in there."

I checked my gun and went in, spotting a lone skinny, dark-skinned boy handcuffed to the bench. I took a seat next to him at a desk where his paperwork was stacked.

"Hey. What's your name?" Everything was written down in front of me, but I wanted to get him talking. He looked prepubescent to me, around twelve, but his file said he was fifteen. He muttered something under his breath, though I could barely hear him.

"Sorry," I said, leaning in. "I didn't catch that."

"Jacob," he said, meeting my eyes. He seemed scared.

"Hey, Jacob. I'm Officer Edwin Raymond."

He just looked through me in the way kids do.

"What are you here for?" I asked.

Jacob didn't respond, so I glanced down at the paperwork, which said "robbery."

"Robbery? C'mon. You've been arrested before?"

He nodded.

"How many times?" I asked.

His voice came out scratchy, high-pitched. "Three times."

"For what?"

"Robbery."

"Wait, wait. You're fifteen with four felonies?"

He didn't respond, but he shrugged in a way that said, *I guess.*

"Let me tell you, man. Where we live, one felony can derail your whole life. And you're fifteen with four felonies? What're you taking, iPhones?"

"Yeah," he said, fidgeting in his seat.

People were always staring at their phones on the subway, not paying attention, so he'd grab one, sometimes get into a scuffle, and run through the crowd as the doors were closing. But he was caught on cameras and the detectives tracked him down.

"Where do you live?" I asked him.

"Crown Heights."

"Oh yeah? I'm in East Flatbush, out by Newkirk."

He nodded.

"And where's your family from?"

"Guyana."

I saw my way in. I started talking about the journey of our people. From being enslaved, to the Middle Passage, to being spread out all over the Western Hemisphere, to the foreign policy of industrialized nations destroying our homelands and hindering our progress. Then I talked about the few who were able to slip through and migrate to these powerful nations with the Immigration Act of 1965 that let my father through. "And you have the opportunity to be here," I told Jacob, "to be *born* here. You can't play around with that. You ever been to white neighborhoods?"

"Yeah."

"Don't you see a difference?"

He smirked: *Of course.* I shifted into talking about how he deserved better for his life and that the decisions he made now would impact the adult he becomes. "Look," I said, "it shouldn't be that your whole life can be dictated by a couple of bad decisions at sixteen, but this is the society we live in. But you, you still—"

A guy in my unit popped in and interrupted us. "Oh, Raymond, man," he said. "Don't even bother. We're just waiting for next year." Once Jacob turned sixteen, he could be tried as an adult in New York City. For now, he'd be released to his mom and get a family court date, but starting on his next birthday, he'd be on his way to Rikers for the same stuff.

I waited for the cop to get out of earshot.

"You see that right there?" I said, pointing at the door. "You see that?"

Jacob nodded.

"They think I'm wasting my time talking to you. They see a criminal. But I see my little brother. You're more than the crimes you've committed. I need you to understand that you're more than that." I looked into his eyes and saw something churning. "You tell me, am I wasting my time?"

He shook his head and then cleared his throat to say, "No."

"The only thing that determines whether I'm wasting my time right now is what you do with this conversation. You continue snatching phones, you continue wasting your opportunity to be here, then I am. Because people back in Georgetown would love to be here. We're second-generation Americans. Lucky, yeah, but not here to play games and waste our chance."

It was a version of the speeches my dad and Mrs. Cross once gave me. Their words had lived inside me and bloomed. Now I wanted to plant them elsewhere. I hoped with someone like Jacob, they would take root.

Ten

Being Seen

2002

After he started working at the Jamaican joint up near Rogers Avenue, everyone called my friend Chris "Jerk Chicken." A few years older than I was, Chris and I hung out a lot when we were younger, playing soccer and basketball, riding bikes, or playing arcade games at the Haitian place (until he and Zulu ran out with that bag of quarters). Chris was Jamaican, with caramel skin, a broad nose, and long hair usually braided in cornrows. We had these heated arguments about Haitian versus Jamaican food that I settled once and for all by bringing him some diri blan, sos pwa avek poul en sos;* he loved it so much he learned how to order it in Creole—a sure sign that I won. Chris seemed more dialed in to the larger world than other people on the block. In the middle of trivial teenage talk, he'd spark intelligent conversations with me about world issues and history.

In the winter of my junior year of high school, I ran into Chris on my

---

* White rice, puréed beans, and stewed chicken.

way home from work at KFC. I saw him across the street from my building, kicking the soccer ball in his thick Gore-Tex boots.

"Jerk Chicken!" I called as I walked up the sidewalk.

"Edwin! What's going on, man?"

"Work. What you been up to?"

"This," he said, rolling the soccer ball to the front of his foot and juggling it.

"How the heck do you get the ball up from your toe in those things?" I asked, gesturing at his boots.

"'Cause man have skills," he said in his Jamaican accent. We got to talking, reminiscing and laughing about waiting on line in the summer to get free lunches.

"What was that word you used last time we were talking out there?"

"When?"

"We were talking about Haiti and American colonialism and—"

"Hegemony?" I asked.

"Yeah. Yeah. *Hegemony*," he said, nodding. "How you spell that?"

After I spelled it for him, he took his attention back to his ball. "See, you smart, man. You're going to make it somewhere."

"Thanks, man. All right," I said, heading up the steps of my building. "See you later, Jerk Chicken."

I wish I could remember more from that conversation because it's the last one I ever had with him.

That April, a heat wave hit New York. When it gets hot in the hood, things get hot in the streets. Warm weather brings more people out, increasing the chance for conflicts; it creates the perfect storm of circumstances that can lead to violence. One evening I was on my way to pick up my paycheck from work when my cell phone rang.

"Yo," Eddie said. "Listen . . ." He paused. "Jerk Chicken got shot."

"Shot? What do you mean?" The words didn't get any purchase in my mind, wouldn't take hold. "Jerk Chicken doesn't even come on the block anymore." He had been working and was in and out of college at the time.

"Yeah, yeah, I know," Eddie said. He went quiet, like he was still processing it himself. "Listen, he's gone, man."

The next thing I remembered I was running to my corner, East Twenty-Fifth and Newkirk, like if I got there fast enough, I could stop it from happening. At the intersection, I saw the media vans with antennas going three stories high and the bright yellow crime-scene tape. The setup for something I'd seen in person and on TV hundreds of times, a quick hit on the evening news. *Black teen shot and killed.*

At the scene, Chris's best friend, Gerald, was crying on the ground, holding on to Chris's thick boots. The paramedics must have taken them off his feet, and there were swaths of blood all over them. Gerald was holding those boots tight, squeezing them to his chest, like the boots were Chris's body and he didn't want to let go. The whole scene played right in front of me, but it was distant, like through an old screen. As the shock wore off, I started crying, then took off down the street and up the stairs to my dad.

"What's going on, Edwin?" He was sitting in his chair by the window.

"My friend got shot. I . . . uh . . . I just saw him," I said, replaying that image of him juggling the soccer ball. "You remember Chris? We called him Jerk Chicken." I could hardly say the words. "He's dead."

I saw Dad was trying to remember Chris but couldn't place him. Since he didn't speak Creole, he was probably just a face among many to my father.

"I'm sorry, Edwin. Was he involved in drugs?"

"No, not at all," I said. That was the hardest part. He was just a bystander. "He didn't really even come on the block anymore." I kept repeating that, aloud and to myself, because it didn't make sense.

Here's what happened: An OG had gotten out of prison and took some of my friends under his wing, getting them to do robberies—far past the kind of street-level stuff they had been doing. This was around the time I started breaking away from that group, hanging with a different crowd. Chris also split from that group, refusing to go along with what the OG had the rest of them doing. The OG pushed back, once snatching Chris's gold necklace right off of his neck. After that, Chris didn't really come around anymore.

The OG had the young up-and-comers wrapped around his finger. He eventually got some of them to rob the local corner store on Rogers Avenue. This was a store we all grew up using, a place we went into with our parents, a place where the owner let our families buy things on credit. They had masks on, but the owner knew it was them—he had watched them grow up. After that, they couldn't go back in there anymore so they had to cross Flatbush Avenue to the other deli, which was a rival group's territory.

The day of Chris's death, two of the OG's protégés, Bop and Jared, crossed the line to buy blunts at the deli and got into it with a rival clique. In the scuffle, Jared pulled out a gun and everyone took off. Later that night, the crew from the other side came on our block to respond. They saw Bop with another kid, Flav, and started words. Then one of them punched Bop in the mouth, destroying his jaw. A fight broke out, and one of the guys from the other side pulled out a gun and shot three times, wounding Flav and a man named Shotta (who got hit rushing the shooter), and killing Chris.

EVERYONE IN THE NEIGHBORHOOD turned out for Chris's funeral; it was standing-room only, with every seat of every pew filled, family and friends lined up alongside the walls of the church, stacked side by side beneath the stained glass. I had been to funerals before, but for old people who were ill, those at the end of life. This felt like a mistake, a slip in the universe.

As the pastor dug deep to explain the unexplainable, I scanned the faces. Some of the toughest dudes on the block were there, and every single one was crying. They all knew Chris had nothing to do with that life, had no business being taken because of it. *The world is fucked up*, I thought.

They all seemed to nod back. *Damn right.*

When the pastor opened the casket, I slowly made my way toward the front. I got closer and closer until finally Chris's face came into view. Frozen in time like that, Chris didn't look like himself, except for his telltale big hair, picked out because he had been planning to get it braided on the last day of his life. He was there but not there, would never be there again. It was too much, something that I shouldn't have been allowed to see at sixteen.

As the years went by, I'd see it again and again.

WE KNEW PAIN, but in spite of that, maybe *because* of that, we embraced chances to soak in life's joy and beauty. Starting in my midteens, there was nothing I enjoyed more than a Jamaican dancehall party. They were usually held in basements or restaurants that became makeshift clubs at night. Teens and young adults mostly from East Flatbush and Crown Heights poured into a room with speakers stacked to the ceiling, loud enough for an outdoor venue. The DJ, set up near the wall, controlled the mood and crowd, shouting out in Jamaican patois. The DJ warmed up the crowd with classic reggae before eventually spinning dancehall hits, mixing and blending from one song to the other. Partyers would be showing off their practiced moves—Jamaican dances like the pepper seed and Jerry Springer, while couples danced intimately together in a style called rub-a-dub (or "dub"), where women gyrated their hips to the rhythm—"whining"—with the men in sync behind them.

When the party let up, I would be leaving unfamiliar neighborhoods in the wee hours, a dangerous proposition in the hood. While walking from one party at three a.m., I felt a sense of relief when I saw two rookie cops posted up on the corner, their radios spewing out static. But it was coupled with a low-level nervousness. I braced myself for the illegal search and harassment that I expected to happen. I simultaneously felt both safe and unsafe—from the same people. Eventually, cops became something to avoid. It was like I was trapped in skin they understood as dangerous, in a body they saw as threatening. Every time this happened, it just reinforced what I thought back then: racist people signed up to be cops. They must assume all Black men are up to something criminal.

Then something happened that shifted the whole paradigm for me.

Late one afternoon, I was leaving my friends Jeff and Habby's building on Newkirk Avenue, walking with my girlfriend to the subway, when I had a police interaction that would ultimately change my life. I was eighteen at the time, studying business and accounting in college. I had moved on from an interest in architecture; the plan was to learn business, save for a couple of years, and then pool my money with my friend Keny to open up an essential business in the hood for the locals, like a supermarket. I understood that it was difficult for Blacks to accumulate wealth, because we were left out of the ownership equation. I was hoping to do well for myself while also doing good for my community.

My girlfriend's mother didn't want her dating, so I was worried about passing in front of her building. "Maybe we should cut around another block," I said. "Go down East Twenty-Sixth."

"Nah," she said. "Mom's at work right now. Don't worry."

A dark sedan began to roll behind us in the street, then suddenly jolted forward in front of us, parking diagonally at the curb. The doors flung open and, in a breath, I was surrounded by three plainclothes cops: guns showing, shields dangling on chains from their necks, the bulk of bulletproof vests bulging under their sports jerseys. One put his forearm into my chest, like a hockey check, and pinned me to the fence. He started searching me, patting at my body hard and fast, and emptying my pockets. My body reacted before my brain did—there was something off about this, even more so than normal. It took a few seconds for me to place the extra discomfort, and then it clicked: the cop searching me was dark-skinned, as dark as I was.

"Hey, hey, where you headed?" the cop said. From the accent I could tell he was Dominican. He was with two white cops, one of whom was standing back like a supervisor.

"I'm going to the train," I said. "What's going on?"

"Hey! We're asking the questions here."

"Yeah," I said, "but you're stopping *me*." I met my girlfriend's gaze as she stood there, feet glued to the concrete.

He gave a deep squint and his eyes got hard. "That's right," he said, as though that answered every question. His hands were in the pockets of my jeans, lifting my shirt to check my waistband, patting around my lower back. "You carrying anything you're not supposed to? You have a gun?"

"No, I don't have a gun. What's this about?" I asked. "What's the reason for this?"

No response from the Dominican cop or his partners. His hands were doing all the talking.

My nervousness gave way to frustration, and then anger grew in its place. When cops first began stopping me, I figured maybe something must have just happened and I resembled the suspect. Not anymore. As quick as they arrived, they all piled back into the car and peeled off. As my girl stood there, I was embarrassed and livid. What else did I have to do? At what point did I get a pass?

But I already knew the answer: never. I'd never get a pass because I couldn't escape my skin.

For the rest of the day, then the week, I couldn't get my mind off it. People tried to talk to me and I tuned out. I sat in class and my mind wandered out the window. *What the hell was that?* It disrupted every-thing I thought I understood. I had been oversimplifying the situation— white cops hassling Black boys, police profiling me because of my skin color. But this cop was a dark-skinned Afro Latino behaving exactly the same as every white cop who'd ever stopped me. He was probably even rougher.

I was a college student with a sparkling record and a commitment to never participating in the street life. With the hand I was dealt, and surrounded by those who had chosen that life, I still had the discipline to avoid it. I said no to it over and over again, for years, when so many others in my circle were saying yes. Yet I was still being treated like a criminal.

During the search by the Dominican cop, I glanced across the street and saw a handful of young dudes who I knew were heavily in the streets watching me get manhandled. *Why couldn't the police tell the difference between them and me? Why were we the same in their eyes?* Because we were the same race? It didn't make sense. There's so much more nuance to who we were, if you paid attention, understood, or cared to try. The invisible line had been a feature of my life in East Flatbush since I was an eight-year-old hanging out on the stoop. But it didn't exist at all for these cops. It was *actually* invisible to them.

I had always processed police behavior as an individual thing, the product of a single person's raising, education, personality, race, socioeconomics, geography. After the stop by the Afro Latino cop, I was lost. I couldn't use my normal race-based assumptions about him and his behavior. My conception of racist cops didn't make sense in this context. Why did he see me as a problem?

It got me thinking about the police and how they operated. I started thinking less about the apples and more about the barrel. Then a second thing happened that year that pushed me closer to having a sense of mission.

On Haitian Flag Day, everyone in the neighborhood came out. It was a time to celebrate ourselves in a place that sometimes acted like it didn't want us. Nostrand Avenue was shut down and set up with a stage and display monitors on one end of the street. An MC and several artists performed while elected officials and other dignitaries came up to speak. Street vendors sold Haitian food as well as flags and other accessories to people from across the city who had descended on East Flatbush. In the mix of the celebratory crowd, socializing and dancing, I ran into a family friend who was like an uncle to me growing up.

Nickson was in his late thirties at the time, on the short side with a muscular build and a low haircut, a baldy.

"Edwin?"

"Oh shit, Nickson!" We hugged.

"You're getting big, my friend!"

"Ha, you know it," I said. As we broke from the embrace, I realized he was wearing a blue uniform. "Wait, you're a cop? What? What are you doing here?"

"Working," he said. "Yeah, I've been on the force a few years now."

"Working *this*?" I asked, gesturing out to the crowd.

"Yeah, they try to pull as many Haitian cops as possible to work it because of the language barrier."

Nickson and I caught up for a bit; he asked about school, my brother, and my father, who had just suffered a stroke. His health had started to fade a few years before and he was walking with a cane, but things had recently gotten worse. A few days earlier, he had woken up in the morning and couldn't get up. His entire left side wasn't moving but his face was fine, so we didn't immediately know what it could be.

"I'm sorry to hear that," he said. "He is a good man. What he went through . . ."

"Yeah, I know it," I said. There wasn't much to add; we both knew.

"I don't know if I ever told you this," he said, "but when I met your mom, being new to this country, it gave me hope, man."

"Really?" I'd known that they were close, especially when Nickson first got here as a teenager from Haiti.

"Yeah, I don't know," he said. "It's like you start to lose faith in people, but your mom, she gave me hope, like, there are still good people out there. She was an angel on earth."

When Nickson first arrived in America he worked for his uncle, who owned our building. Instead of mopping from top to bottom, as most do to use gravity, he would start at the bottom and end up on the top floor because my mother would then fix him a plate of food when he was done. I'd always seen him as something of a conduit to my mom, a trove of stories about her. There were things I knew about her only because of Nickson. Because of that, he occupied this important place in my history, and by extension, my heart.

But seeing Nickson in a police uniform was a shock. I was scoping out his uniform and all of the tools on his duty belt: silver gun, hand-cuffs, baton, some things I couldn't even identify. It was strange: I was standing close to him but not threatened. I had never known an NYPD officer personally, so cops had always been decidedly other to me. They were faceless bodies driving by or white boys from Long Island giving me a hard time about walking on my own street.

But I *knew* Nickson, I related to him; we came from the same place. I could talk to him, touch him, reminisce with him. Once the surprise wore off, I was hit with this sense of pride. He seemed important, central to the neighborhood. Young children were gathered around him, com-munity elders were seeking his help, and there was this cloud of love and respect hovering over him. It reframed for me what being police could mean—at a time when I thought it was only one thing.

I started hanging out with Nickson and his son, who was a few years younger than I was. I got a look at their large two-story house, with its long driveway, separate garage, and finished basement; it showed me the quality of life that being a cop offered. I saw that there could be a way to become a pillar of my community, to support my people while also mak-ing a good living for myself. It could bring me some resources and op-portunities for growth while also engaging me in the mission. In that time with Nickson, becoming a cop felt like it could be an answer to all these questions I had, maybe even be what I had been looking for.

I HAD WORKED at the supermarket for about six years before moving on; to KFC, Century 21, Kennedy Airport. My finances were unstable, so I tried to upgrade and get hired where my brother and my friends Romain and Herby worked. Young Adult Institute (YAI) was a nonprofit agency that provided living assistance to those who were developmentally disabled, with serious issues like autism or cerebral palsy. Even though he was struggling as well, my brother gave me forty dollars a week, which I stretched within an inch of its life on bus fare and Chinese food.

At nineteen, I finally got hired at YAI and was placed to work in a house for those who were "profound functioning," the lowest level. Clients there couldn't feed or wash themselves, and without our help would lie in their own waste. At the same time, my dad was dealing with the aftermath of his stroke. Working with the disabled helped me on a practical level, because I knew what questions to ask the nurses and caretakers when I visited my father. But it went the other way as well. Having my father in a similar position reminded me that each person I took care of was someone's loved one.

Working at YAI made me see people. Really *see* them. I assisted them with daily living: feeding them, taking them outside. They still had thoughts and behaviors, but it was like they were trapped inside their bodies. Unable to communicate, they would get frustrated and act out, break things, bite, slam their head into the wall. On my shift I worked with a Puerto Rican client named Tito, whom I took for walks outside on the grounds. He knew basic sign language, was something of a savant, in fact, and we became close.

During breaks, a colleague of mine at YAI, Bishme, would get talking to me about racial issues. He grew up with parents who were politically active, so he never really had to find his racial consciousness. It was in his blood, part of his makeup in the way that hunger was part of mine.

"You know what I realized the other day?" I asked him once during lunch.

"What?" he asked.

"You could spin a globe and wherever you planted your finger, if there were Black people there, they'd be the lowest status."

"The proletariat," Bishme said, nodding. "Damn straight." He often went into these explanations of class conflict, history, and politics. We discussed the macros and micros of the plight of people of African descent, "from Inglewood to a single hood in Botswana," as the rapper Common said.

"You know, Edwin," Bishme said, "the questions you're asking have been asked by people before you who've dedicated their life's work to turning things around." He pointed at me with a sly smile. "I knew I saw something in you."

Soon afterward, he put a book in my hand called *The Destruction of Black Civilization*. Even though I was not much of a reader at the time, I inhaled it. Up on the roof of my building, in a low beach chair or back to the ledge, I read after work and on the weekends. It educated me on how wide and how far back this race thing went. I learned how all these conflicts originated at one source: the subjugation of people of color by European powers through colonization, enslavement, or laws that kept them as second-class citizens.

Reading that book put me in conversation with my people, connected me to the larger story. I thought back to the young boy who flipped out when he learned that the Louisiana Purchase—America as we know it— existed because of Haiti, the son whose father taught him to see malnourished African boys on TV as his brothers. It sparked an awakening.

Then Bishme gave me *The Autobiography of Malcolm X*. I knew the basic outline of his life from the film: how he grew up poor, became a

Harlem hustler, and educated himself in prison and turned to Islam. But I hadn't ever had access to his rich mind before.

Malcolm also had confidence that people just hadn't *seen* in a Black man before. "All of us—who might have probed space, or cured cancer, or built industries," he wrote, "were instead black victims of the white man's American social system."[1] Later in life he came to understand that the problems went beyond individual racism, that "it's the American political, economic, and social *atmosphere* that automatically nourishes a racist psychology in the white man."[2] I didn't know a book could change someone's life—I'd hear people say that and not understand—but Malcolm's autobiography changed mine.

A larger racial consciousness, which had been seeded long ago, started to bloom in me. I grew my hair out and began wearing it in dreadlocks. It made me stand out, connected me to my heritage, and made white people uncomfortable. Most dark-skinned people have to find their confidence, and it's not just racism from others, but colorism—a bias against darker skin—within the Black community itself. As I embraced my identity, my Haitian roots, my African ancestry, the hair became a conscious decision, an external manifestation, a political act. A visual representation of unapologetic Blackness.

My eyes were also opened to white scholars and activists, which made me less dogmatic about who was fighting alongside us. My mind was expanding to include activist Tim Wise's books on housing and wealth inequality and especially Jane Elliott's famous experiment as a third-grade teacher in Iowa in 1968. She was so enraged by the assassination of Dr. Martin Luther King Jr. that, the next morning, she separated the class into brown-eyed and blue-eyed and created and reinforced a hierarchy for the day where one group was told they were superior, praised and rewarded, while the other group was treated as beneath them.*

---

* After explaining the purpose of the experiment, Elliott switched up the hierarchy. She later did the experiment with older kids, teachers, companies, the military, and the results were the same.

What stood out was not just the fact that the favored group acted superior to the unfavored group, but the way that the oppressed *internalized* the treatment. It affected their self-esteem, their behavior, their performance. She got to the heart of the relationship between Europe and Africa in the most direct way. She dug into how Black people in America are caught in a feedback loop that is generated by white institutions and white oppression.

Around this time, working at YAI, reading about race and history, I started toying with the possibility of applying to the police force. It could be a way for me to make an impact, be part of the larger story, and get my hands dirty with the work of lifting up my community and supporting my people. I sent in my application to the police academy, scheduled the tests, and took my first steps to get on the front line of people's lives. I assumed I could choose to be my own kind of cop and not just survive in the system but thrive in it.

I thought of Chris, lying in that box. I thought of Nickson, coming to this country and mopping floors, who was now a pillar of the community. I thought of my mom, who never got to know me. I thought of my dad, lying in a hospital bed, and what he thought I could be.

My YAI colleague Nikel, a big dude with a chubby face and Caesar haircut, knew I was looking to join the police department. We discussed it regularly, especially as my start date at the academy grew closer. Right before I left, he and his brother got stopped and frisked—again—based on nothing at all. "Yo, Ed, man," he said with pain and anger in his eyes. "Please get in there and do what you gotta do. I don't even dislike the cops. I know it's hot out here, but there's got to be a better way."

A better way. I decided to put my shoulder into it and work toward that very thing.

PART II

History, as nearly no one seems to know, is not merely something to be read. And it does not refer merely, or even principally, to the past. On the contrary, the great force of history comes from the fact that we carry it within us.

—JAMES BALDWIN

Eleven

Conditions

2009

In that first year in uniform, I would flash back to all those times when I got stopped on street corners or subway steps by cops, patted up and down, delayed on my way to work or school, interrogated as though I were a criminal. I thought of all the stories I heard from other innocent Black teenagers who had also gone through it—their exhaustion, their confusion, and their anger. Not just the hassle but the *indignity* of the thing.

Because I was still new to the force, I thought maybe Operation Impact was the problem. Six months in, during the summer of 2009, I transferred out to join seven other rookies in Transit District 32. I was placed in a unit called Conditions, covering the central and east Brooklyn subway lines. Every week those in charge took a close look at "crime conditions" in the district and we addressed them; at least, that's what our mandate was on paper. In reality, we had the same quota as Impact—mainly ticketing and arresting people for fare evasion, "unsafe riding" (walking from one moving train car to another using end doors), and being "outstretched" (taking up more than one seat).

In Conditions, I watched the entire cycle play out all over again: nab someone of color for a minor offense and hope they have a warrant so the officer could get the collar, hit the quota, and keep the boss happy—so he could keep *his* boss happy and all the way up. I again saw cops manipulating it into a money machine, clocking their arrests at the end of the shift so they could milk that time and a half. I again watched everyone making sure they got chosen for scheduled overtime by "producing." Moving from Impact to Conditions, I had gone absolutely nowhere.

Seeing the same problems replicated in a new unit gave me a sense of how far this thing stretched, like scanning across a panoramic photo. For every cop I watched in the dirty supply rooms or doing paperwork into overtime at the command, I multiplied them in my head, command by command, shift by shift, until I could see this vast operation across the city. What I saw at its center was not the individual racism of single officers. That existed—those cops I had lunch with at the academy were out there—but that's not what made things run.

The engine was the systemic racism of policing itself: not just the quotas but the agreed-upon expectation of *how* those quotas were to be fulfilled. Day after day, thousands and thousands of people of color were drawn into the system by the gravitational pull created by each individual police officer looking to get his numbers. And the racism was sewed in so tight most didn't even realize or question it.

I refused to artificially reach my quotas, but that didn't mean I never met them. It was just inconsistent because I wasn't purposely seeking it out: hunting, ice picking, or playing in the rooms like my colleagues. Sometimes, because of the way things worked out, I'd even double the quota in a month. Though even then, there would be a problem.

Early on in Conditions I had a busy month, with eight arrests, and the special operations lieutenant (SOL) pulled me aside after roll call in the muster area. The SOL was a down-to-earth and muscular Black man who lived in the gym. Around us was the bustle of shift change, people grabbing their radios out of the box, checking their batteries and turning the units on, all the while busting one another's balls, talking about their days off, and complaining about the Knicks.

"Hey, Raymond," the SOL said.

"What's up, boss? How's everything?"

"All good, all good," he said. "Listen, good job with activity this month—"

"Uh, thanks," I said, wary about the praise.

"But you know, your two-fifties* were light," he said, looking at a printout. "Looks like you only had one last month, so see if you could step that up."

While I stood there flat-footed, the SOL got called into an office.

Step that up? According to the Constitution, I could no more "up" my stop, question, and frisks than I could control the weather. I needed reasonable suspicion, which made any SQF a matter of happenstance. It's as random as a bird dropping on your shoulder; there's no methodology to get more, unless you're going to profile. Spotting a Black teenager in Flatbush and assuming he's up to no good doesn't qualify as reasonable suspicion, though plenty of cops had once stopped me on exactly that pretense and continued to do so. In that year, 2009, Blacks and Latinos were ten times as likely to be stopped in New York City but no more likely to be arrested, proving that profiling was not only unconstitutional but ineffective.[1]

What I didn't realize at the time was that Mayor Bloomberg and Commissioner Kelly had specifically pressured precinct commanders to increase stop, question, and frisks, who then pushed it down the chain to us. That's what was pressing on my lieutenant, who then was pressing it

---

* Stop, question, and frisks.

on me. Word was that at CompStat, SQFs were the new flavor. The commanders were safe in front of the chiefs—even if crime went up—as long as their commands had a high number of stop, question, and frisks.*

For all their focus on numbers, the NYPD wasn't very good at using them. Statistics had shown that no matter the number of stop, question, and frisks month to month, year to year, roughly the same number of guns were pulled off the street. Not the same percentage, the same *number*. It got to the point that the ratio was embarrassing for the NYPD. Commissioner Kelly would never address it, even when directly asked about it, but Mayor Bloomberg eventually gave up the game. He admitted that the increase in stop, question, and frisks was not a matter of practical policing but rather a psychological deterrent, to make it "too hot to carry."[2] The thinking was that if you're getting stopped and frisked every other day, you would think twice before grabbing that gun from the shoebox under the bed.

But in practice that's just race-based harassment. Keep in mind that in New York City that year, 0.1 percent—that's one-tenth of 1 percent—of stop, question, and frisks led to a gun.[3] Eighty-four percent of those stopped and frisked were Black and Latino (despite being 51 percent of the city's population) and 88 percent of all SQFs led to nothing. Of the remaining 12 percent that led to an arrest or summons, a substantial chunk was for things like marijuana[4] or pocketknives[5] found during the search.

Despite these overt discrepancies in the numbers, Mayor Bloomberg actually claimed that *whites* in New York City were stopped and frisked *too much* and minorities *too little*. His proof? Looking at a data sheet that broke down the percentages of stop and frisks by ethnic group,

---

* In 2011, "87 percent of those stopped were African American or Latino" and "41.6 percent of all stops were of black and Latino men between the ages of fourteen and twenty-four, even though they make up only 4.7 percent of the population of New York. The same study found that no crime had been committed in 90 percent of the stops." In fact, the total number of Black men stopped that year "exceeded the city's entire population of black men" by nearly ten thousand. (Angela J. Davis, "Introduction," in *Policing the Black Man: Arrest, Prosecution, and Imprisonment* [New York: Pantheon, 2017], xv.)

Bloomberg saw that the ratio of whites stopped was a few percentage points higher than the percentage who were murder suspects. Not only was this faulty logic, but it proved that stopping New Yorkers based on their race was the foundation of what they were doing! Grouping everyone based on race leads to the blanket overpolicing of hundreds of thousands of innocent people of color. Ninety-nine percent* of young Black men aren't carrying illegal guns or doing anything wrong at all, yet they are still getting harassed by cops day in and day out as a so-called deterrent.

This is so important, so I will state it as plainly as possible: Just because a large portion of guns in a certain neighborhood may be carried by Black men does not mean a large portion of young Black men are carrying guns. One thing does not mean the other. The percentage of those who commit the violent crimes in a certain area—even in high-crime areas—is extremely small. It's a handful of people carrying the guns, doing the robberies, shooting at one another. The rest of us share nothing in common with them except skin color, yet that seems to be enough to put us in the police's crosshairs.[†]

Those at the top misperceive violent crime as being far more widespread than it is, especially in Black communities. It's a process that started long before they became cops. Throughout their lives, the mass media has been planting the image of the dangerous Black man into their minds. If someone has a predisposition to view Black men as dangerous, becoming a police officer will only exacerbate it. Now it's their job to pay attention to nothing but violence and crime, as is the job of

---

[*] A neighborhood like East Flatbush may have ten serious crimes (violent and property) per thousand residents. That's 99 percent of the residents doing nothing wrong, and even less if you consider that those who commit these crimes tend to be repeat offenders.

[†] In a similar vein, the NYPD was forced to admit in 2011, after vociferous denials, to the existence of a "Demographics Unit" that was secretly surveilling Muslim Americans based on nothing but their ethnicity and religion. After years of pressure, Bill Bratton disbanded the unit in 2014. (Matt Apuzzo and Joseph Goldstein, "New York Drops Unit That Spied on Muslims," *New York Times,* April 15, 2014.) I would later learn at John Jay that this kind of racial profiling is known as "rational discrimination" and is widespread in the department.

most of those with whom they talk and socialize. Confirmation bias runs rampant in police departments. Black officers, particularly ones who have grown up in Black neighborhoods, may have a more nuanced picture of these communities, but they are not immune to the stereotyping.

Think of it this way: In the first half of the twentieth century, when ethnic whites had a monopoly on violent crime, none of this race-based overpolicing was deployed because the negative activity of a few didn't reflect on the entire group. Yet for Black people it does. This is precisely what Mrs. Cross was teaching us in fifth grade when she said Blacks are treated as a group for negative things but as individuals for positive things. In general, the opposite is true for white Americans: there's nothing in white America that 1 percent does that the other 99 percent have to pay for.

To take one glaring example, the overwhelming majority of school or mass shooters are white men,[6] but you don't see any push to focus on them punitively as a group. *Never.* There's not a single voice saying white men's homes need to be searched or white kids need to go through metal detectors or white schools need to have a stronger police presence or white men should be screened for weapons at movie theaters. But the driving force behind how the NYPD responds to crime is an inability and refusal to see nuances in communities of color.

My sergeant in Conditions, an Ecuadorian named Ferruzola, was a bulky, light-skinned man in his thirties with gelled, spiked hair. He had a competitive streak regarding his squad's numbers and was a true believer in the gospel of broken windows. Ferruzola would regularly use something known as "team-lead enforcement," in which he followed us out on patrol specifically to increase the unit's overall numbers.

By 2010, all the remaining loopholes regarding quotas were closed and they were fully banned in New York City. But nothing changed. It was enraging, but I was careful about whom I complained to. In a paramilitary organization, you have to be. I wasn't yet ready to stick my head out for what would be read as disobedience. This wasn't the business world where there were brainstorming sessions or the media world where collective suggestions were sought. This was the police force, and there were orders and insubordination. Those were the two lanes. I knew I was veering, but I wasn't ready to occupy that place just yet.

I would mostly vent to my fellow rookies. One of them, Kushnir, would debate with me freely. He had emigrated from the former Soviet Union as a baby and still spoke Russian like a native. In American schools, he had run-ins with his Black peers, which framed how he saw everyone with darker skin. I'd met people like him before, formerly bullied kids who grew up to be cops in order to take psychic revenge. Tall with dark hair and glasses, Kushnir would regularly tell racist jokes in the locker room, seemingly indifferent to my presence. But he also was a team player who would always have his fellow cops' backs; I still felt like I could talk to him, even if it was just to debate his prejudices. I even convinced him to watch one of my favorites shows, an adult cartoon called *The Boondocks*. He became a big fan of Uncle Ruckus, the older character on the show who is always ranting about his own race. "If every Black person was like Uncle Ruckus," Kushnir told me, "the world would be a better place."

Over lunch we'd get into these back-and-forth arguments. "The same people the department claims it's protecting and keeping safe are the ones who are overenforced because of this broken-windows shit," I said.

"That's how we get the perps," he said, biting into his sandwich. "You never know who has guns."

"Yeah, but there's no reasonable suspicion for these stops."

"Sure there is."

"What's that? A Black kid with a hoodie? That's reasonable suspicion? C'mon, Kushnir—"

"Look at the numbers. The numbers don't lie, man. Look who's committing most of the violent crimes there."

"Yeah, we're just harassing people who share the same ethnicity as them. They're not the same people just because—"

"I'm just doing the job, Raymond. That's the job."

"But that's the problem! The job shouldn't be about perpetuating an inherently racist system that sees all Black people the same!"

He took a beat and stared at me. "Raymond, there's no way you're Black," he said, tossing his napkin on his plate. "You're way too smart to be Black."

How do you respond to something like that?

Kushnir was indeed racist, but he was also a product of what the department incentivized. He did what was expected of him to get his numbers. A Mafia-like system of "showing gratitude" infected the force: if an officer got his chosen day off or if he was picked for overtime, he knew to go out there blazing, summonsing and collaring well past the quota. He had to protect his favored status. There were a million little ways that your superior could make your life hell. The path of least resistance was to simply go along, but I just couldn't treat my fellow citizens like a meal ticket.

I remember at the academy, one of the instructors—the same one who told us about making money—would use this phrase I'd never heard before: "body up." "I'll tell you what," he said to the recruits. "On the job, I was never cold, never wet, never hot. *Never.* Because anytime I was in those conditions, I bodied up."

Bodied up. He would find a way to arrest someone in order to get indoors to process the paperwork. Somebody's freedom was climate control to him. This cop was no outlier; he was an instructor at the academy. Cops were indoctrinated to think of people's lives and freedom in terms of their own payday, their own promotions, their own comforts.

People's humanity could be discarded because of nothing but a cop's laziness. One night I was working plainclothes during overtime with Kushnir and Sergeant Ferruzola, and we were supposed to head out to New Lots Avenue in East New York, which had been experiencing high crime. Our job was to "address conditions as they occurred," which in reality just meant enforcing broken-windows offenses because of a string of robberies out there. As though those two things were connected. But that's broken-windows logic.

At two a.m., the three of us walked into the Franklin Avenue station planning on taking the train out to New Lots. We spread out because a Russian, Ecuadorian, and Haitian hanging out, especially at that hour in Crown Heights, made people look twice; they might notice the outlines of our vests, guess we were cops.

Down the platform, I saw Ferruzola talking to a guy on a bench who was getting increasingly heated. He was with a woman and a baby stroller, and I was too far away to hear what they were saying. Ferruzola made eye contact with me to summon me over. I started approaching, pulled out my shield, and said, "Listen, brother, get the ID—"

The guy seemed alarmed—shocked—that I was a cop. "Why?" he asked. "Why the fuck I gotta show my ID for?"

"Just get the ID and everything will be explained after," I said.

The woman next to him was trying to calm him down: "Babe, just show them your ID."

"Nah, fuck that. Why do they always gotta bother me? I'm sitting here with my baby, trying to eat my food!" The guy was now screaming, getting the attention of others in the station.

Kushnir then walked up. "Listen, if you don't want to show the ID, we're just going to get it anyway."

At the sight of Kushnir, a third officer, the guy's face twisted in rage. He blew up. "Y'all not telling me for what! Why? Why do I—"

At that moment Ferruzola hit him with the OC spray—pepper spray—to neutralize him; he bent down and covered his face, yelling,

"Ahhhh! What the fuck?!" Then Kushnir and I stepped in to keep him in place while Ferruzola worked to cuff him. My eyes were red and I was coughing from the chemicals, which had hit the woman and the baby, who was now screaming. After struggling with the guy for a minute, we finally got him in cuffs, the baby's wails bouncing off the tiled walls.

Breathing heavily after the struggle, I pulled up my radio. "Central, can we have transport?"

"Is everything okay?" she came back. "What's your location?"

"Everything . . . is okay," I said. "All good." But no one is going to hear a cop breathing heavy into a radio and think everything is okay. A few minutes later, thirty cops flooded in from various exits, all while the guy kept on screaming. It became a distress call, a full-on scene.

Once things settled down and the guy was being transported, Ferruzola and I walked back to the station house. The sergeant turned to me and hit me in the right shoulder. "That's good police work, kid," he said.

"Thanks. What'd we stop him for?" I didn't even know.

"Uh . . ." He hesitated. "For littering and—"

"Littering?"

"Yeah," Ferruzola said. "I didn't feel like going all the way out to New Lots and he looked like he might pop so I just wanted to run his name and check. But he wanted to be a dick, so fuck him."

While eating on the bench, the guy had put down a cup of soda on the floor, which the sergeant considered littering. The guy was rightly annoyed. Why did he have to deal with police for putting a soda on the ground? A soda he was still drinking? When people say, "Just comply and there won't be an issue," they're just regurgitating cop talk. Would you just comply if it happened to you? What if it had happened twice a week since the day you turned sixteen?

That's why this father and husband was spending the night in a cell, why his wife was in a panic, why his baby had been pepper-sprayed in the face. The sergeant, pressured to get a collar, didn't feel like going out to New Lots. To save himself the trip, he just hunted closer to the station and bodied up.

Twelve

Problem Cop

The late-night subway incident with the pepper spray lingered, hovering like a heavy cloud. It reminded me that cops were part of a historical continuum, the latest incarnation in a long line of systematic oppression. Some of the first police forces in America were slave patrols, and for all the progress Black people have made in America, there was still connective tissue there. In fact, as scholar Angela J. Davis writes, "The number of black men in prison or jail, on probation, or on parole by the end of 2009 roughly equaled the number enslaved in 1850."[1] These are the things that kept me up at night and in a boiling rage all day.

After venting about the soda incident to other cops in the locker room, word got back to Sergeant Ferruzola, most likely through Kushnir. After that, I felt this shift in energy in the unit and the cold shoulder from the sergeant. He became flippant with me about little things, stopped backing me up when I asked for specific days off, and kept me out of group meals. We all used to meet up to eat during our shifts at a predetermined spot shared at roll call. At some point, he stopped mentioning it at the start of our shift, so I figured we'd stopped doing it. But everyone else was still meeting up; Ferruzola was just texting them all directly.

In the NYPD's own evaluation system, there were twenty-eight different categories for grading a police officer, characteristics like ethics/integrity, reasoning ability, and community interaction. Summonses and arrests were nowhere to be found anywhere on that scale, to preserve deniability about the quotas. But they mattered more than all the other factors put together.

The idea that meeting your quota shows that you're a proactive cop is not just dangerous, it's also patently untrue. I saw plenty of cops who'd reach their quota early and then spend the rest of the month hanging in those subway rooms, killing time on their phones, not even looking up. They'd say they were "good for the month" and wouldn't show themselves in the subway station to deter or spot crime. Yet on paper these were the "good cops," while someone like me was getting reprimanded.

To play the game was not just to go against my education, my identity, and my nature; it was to admit that the system was just. And I simply couldn't do it. My stubbornness had gotten me this far, and I wasn't about to let it go for something I knew in my heart to be wrong.

TRANSIT IS ACTUALLY one of the worst offenders of this institutionalized oppression because collars are easier there. Technically the subway stations are private property—owned by the MTA—so there's an additional set of rules that makes people more arrestable. Among the rules specific to the underground world is a status called "transit recidivist," which essentially means repeat offender. If you've had five summonses in a twenty-four-month period, or if you have *ever* been convicted of a felony in the state of New York, you do not qualify for a summons in

Transit; you have to be arrested for *any* infraction.* If you are a "transit re-cid" and you drop your MetroCard receipt on the floor, you'll be arrested for that. I've seen bored young men waiting for the train, picking flecks of paint off a column in the station, and then arrested for "defacing property." I saw a young man bite into a jelly donut where the filling squeezed out onto the floor and the sergeant stopped him for littering, ran his name, and he came up a transit recid. So he was arrested. For biting into a jelly donut.

In Conditions, Sergeant Ferruzola had actually been making it even easier for his officers to arrest people. At the time, the MTA was closing down token booths, so we used this special paper to cover up the booth from the inside but cut slits to monitor the turnstiles. Then we would radio a description of whoever jumped the turnstile to officers waiting downstairs, who would catch them on the platform and run the names. Fish in a barrel.

One day we were hiding in the covered-up booth at the Utica Avenue station when we saw a short, dark-skinned young woman with dread-locks, doubling up with a young man through the turnstile. We radioed to the officers on the platform and gave a description of the two: the officers stopped them and Kushnir and I came down to confirm it was the right couple. The young man was issued a summons; the young woman didn't have ID on her, though we gave her the benefit of the doubt that she was who she said she was. But when Kushnir ran her name, she came back 10-18, and I transported her to the precinct to process the arrest.

I felt awful for her. Only twenty years old, she had just come here from Barbados to meet up with her high school sweetheart and had been in the country for a little over a month. She was crying in the cell, dis-traught: "I'm never coming back this country!" she kept saying.

I didn't understand how she could already be a transit recid in such a short time. In processing her arrest, I had to print out her history, but I

---

* There are obviously serious and dangerous felonies, but a felony also includes things like selling at least one hundred bootleg CDs.

didn't know how to run names on that particular system, so I had a veteran officer help me. "Wait a second, Raymond," she said, "why'd you collar her? How she's a transit recid?"

"I don't know," I said. "Ask the sergeant. He said she was."

She turned the computer screen to show me. "Look, she's not a recid. She just has an arrest. And it wasn't even a felony. It was a domestic misdemeanor."

I went over to the cell and asked the young woman about her previous arrest, which had happened a few weeks earlier. She told me when she came to the United States, she found out that her boyfriend had been meeting up with other women. Devastated, she got very angry at him and it led to a domestic incident—she scratched his face—where she got arrested for assault.

The veteran cop was annoyed and went over to Ferruzola to ask about the arrest. As he started explaining it, she made eyes with another officer like, *Another one of Ferruzola's bullshit collars.* Ferruzola then came at me, visibly red.

"Raymond, what are you doing!" he yelled. "Why you bringing in other people? We handle things in-house here."

"I was just asking for help logging into the system. I—"

"Listen," he said, lowering his voice slightly. "I'm trying to look out for that bitch. She doesn't even have ID but I put her in for a DAT anyway. She still gets to go home soon."

Ferruzola wanted credit for giving the young woman a DAT (a desk appearance ticket, meaning a court date) instead of putting her through as a regular arrest, which would've sent her to Central Booking. Once there she would have had to wait for fourteen hours before she got to see a judge. The sergeant had the gall to make it like he was doing right by her. His reasoning made no sense. Obviously he had already identified her—that's *why* she was arrested—so her not having ID was irrelevant.

"Raymond, if you don't want to take the collar, you don't have to,"

Ferruzola said, annoyed. "Kushnir can take it. He was there and witnessed it too."

"Okay," I said. "Kushnir can take it. That's fine."

"Okay. Kushnir'll take it. But then she doesn't get the DAT."

"Wait, what?" I said. "Just because—"

"Put her through!" the sergeant yelled to Kushnir, meaning, *Send her to Central Booking.* He was punishing her to punish me. Then he walked off, fuming.

Transit recidivism never sat well with me—it felt like double jeopardy—but as far as I understood, it was a felony *conviction* that put you in that database. However, Sergeant Ferruzola was pissed because I had exposed what he was doing. After learning that other units were getting higher numbers by enlarging the pool of transit recids, he started to do the same. The extra step was this: cops would run names, and if that person simply came up as *arrested* in the past—not convicted, just arrested—officers were bringing them in as a transit recid. Having been arrested before, even for a misdemeanor, was a reason to arrest them again.* I've yet to see a more crystal-clear example of the feedback loop that gets people locked into an unjust system. Arresting someone because they've *previously been arrested*? What kind of self-fulfilling nonsense is that? What country are we living in?

The transit recid racket was just one part of a series of regular and egregious practices. There was also citywide initiative in Transit known as Operation Toolbox, which essentially meant zero tolerance or discretion—any little infraction required you to run someone's name. Toolbox would be triggered when an enforcement unit's numbers were low compared to the year or month before. It wasn't in reaction to any conditions on the ground, just what the spreadsheets said. All the lieutenant had to say was "Toolbox," and there was this Pavlovian response

---

* I later found out that prosecutors didn't know anything about this and certainly hadn't approved it.

in the command: they'd just go crazy on the community to get those numbers up.

During Toolbox, four hours of post-tour overtime were distributed to incentivize arrests and summonses. I watched all common sense and empathy go out the door as my colleagues looked for any reason to run someone's name. Every five to ten minutes another officer would run a name over the radio. "Ten-nineteen" here, "ten-eighteen" there, grabbing people for spitting on the tracks, for littering, for lighting a cigarette on the steps before they were completely out of the station. It was madness.

One time, backing up an officer, I heard her running a name and met up with her from three stations away. When I got there, I found out it was for blocking a turnstile.

"Jesus," I said, losing my patience. "You're stopping her for that?"

"It's Toolbox, man," she said. "It's Toolbox."

"So all someone has to say is a bullshit word at roll call and your humanity goes out the window?"

I didn't even bother hiding my disgust. Toolbox was supposed to come from the very top, but the captains noticed that cops worked "harder" when it was on, so they started lying and claiming it was "Toolbox" just to raise their numbers. I'd be talking to cops in other units, and when I mentioned it was Toolbox, they had no idea what I was talking about.

There was also a junior version of this called Operation Pencil Point, which was designed specifically to nab juveniles, those under sixteen. Pencil Point would go into effect simply if the number of juvenile reports, which recorded less serious incidents, were low compared to the year before. Again, a pure numbers chase.

After one roll call during Pencil Point, a Black female sergeant told us, "I know we usually don't bother to even stop kids if they look like they're under sixteen, or we let them go, but you gotta take them in now. You never know if they're out here committing robberies." She was trying to rationalize callous, backward policing. The fact that this was a Black female officer, who knew which kids would be disproportionately arrested, made it hard to process. Didn't she see what all this led to? And all because of some data sheet that was sent downtown? Decisions made by—or in order to please—One Police Plaza (NYPD headquarters) reverberated across Black neighborhoods and ruined lives on the street.

Watching the mass of young Black men coming through the system like water through an open drain, I kept thinking about Jacob. It had been almost a year since I'd met the shy fifteen-year-old in the juvenile room after he was caught snatching iPhones. Once, visiting Transit District 34 in Coney Island, I was standing in the muster room next to the wanted posters when I spotted a list on a corkboard: names of juveniles to be on the lookout for due to past behavior. Jacob was on it. Every few months when we'd visit Coney Island, I'd search the list and see that Jacob's photo was still stubbornly there. I didn't know if it was left over from his last arrest or if he had committed a new infraction, but I kept checking that list. It became this routine for me, thinking of this single boy and whether or not I—or anything, really—had gotten through to him. It was just one name, but the connection I'd made with him, my belief that those kinds of interactions mattered, made it weigh heavily.

About a year later, while we were assigned to the Mermaid Parade, I checked the list and couldn't find Jacob's picture. I double-checked to be sure. It was gone. I exhaled a breath that I hadn't realized I'd been holding in. He hadn't reoffended.

It was a small moment, but it gave me hope. One pebble in a large lake, but still, those stones cause ripples.

"RAYMOND," Sergeant Ferruzola said to me, "it's not like we're making this stuff up. You're not the one who made these people pop. You just ran their name; if they have a reason they need to be arrested, that isn't your problem." This mentality pervaded the unit. I didn't agree with the sergeant entirely, but I had a conception of where he was coming from. I assumed warrants, with a judge's signature, meant that they had previously done something serious.

Then I learned how deep the bullshit actually went.

One afternoon I was processing an arrest in the cell area. When I glanced up, I noticed a young girl alone in one cell, separated from the males, staring down at the floor. I looked around to find out her story, but the arresting officer wasn't there. This was typical. Though I preferred to process paperwork near the cells after making an arrest, in case the prisoner needed to make a phone call or something, many cops did not. They put the prisoner in lockup and then processed their arrest over at a desk on the other side of the building, gun belt off, kicking back and doing paperwork.

The girl in the cell needed to be at least sixteen to be in there, but she looked far younger, slim and fragile, with hair freshly braided in cornrows. A kid.

"What are you doing here?" I asked.

"Huh?" She looked up, surprised at being addressed.

"What are you doing in here?"

"My friend and I went through the turnstile together."

That gets you a summons, not an arrest. I stood up and approached the bars. "Yeah, but why'd you get arrested?"

"I don't know. They said I had a warrant," she said.

"A warrant? What was the warrant for?"

She shrugged.

"How old are you?" I asked.

"Sixteen."

I got her name and pulled up her paperwork. "What happened on your birthday?" I asked.

"Oh yeah," she said. "Oh yeah. In Queens. We go out of the movie theater and a cop walks up to us and yells, 'Didn't I tell you guys to move?' But we were in the movie the whole time. Then he asks for our IDs, and I was the only one who was sixteen, so he wrote me a ticket." The charge: blocking pedestrian traffic.

Up to that point, I knew people were getting stopped for low-level offenses, but I assumed the warrants that led to their subsequent arrest were for something serious. But this girl had a warrant because she (supposedly) blocked a sidewalk and then missed a court date, a not uncommon occurrence for a teenager. And because of that, she was being transferred to Central Booking, something no child should be exposed to. It was an experience bound to traumatize her something fierce. *This is how it starts,* I thought. *She's about to be flushed through.*

This incident sent me digging deeper into the system's pipes. Whenever I was assigned prisoner transports, I'd make a point of talking to people in the cells. If they were arrested because of an outstanding warrant, I would look into their history and kept finding that the warrants themselves—the things cops were stopping people for, running names for, putting people behind bars for, the *prime focus* of all of their work— were usually also entirely inconsequential. Two minor infractions do not equal a serious crime just because a court date got missed or a fine didn't get paid. But that's how the system ran.

The feedback loop made it so that the Blacks who were already disproportionately targeted and overpoliced were getting pulled in on these warrants, leading to fines, court dates, and jail time. The math was overwhelming: cops in Black communities were pressured to write twenty-five summonses per month, which led to thousands and thousands of warrants a year. In this way, the police department was operating as a preserver of the social order, a natural extension of American enforcement methods like the Black Codes, keeping minorities down, always playing catch-up, forever in their place. But in the twenty-first century, it was all under the guise of public safety. It's called "firehose policing": to put out what may be a contained fire, you're drenching the block.

To go deeper into the system, I had to look beyond Transit, because that's where a lot of these original warrants were coming from. I knew topside had quotas, too, but until I learned about that young girl who went to the bookings for blocking a sidewalk, I hadn't put much thought into how their enforcement fed much of ours. The court date that got missed for a minor infraction topside became the warrant that led to our arrests.*

My topside colleagues told me weed was the easiest arrest because it's in the air, easy to smell, and even the hint of marijuana can be used as a pretext to search an entire vehicle. Other common summonses were for open containers—sometimes for people drinking right outside on their own stoops—and the baffling "bicycle on the sidewalk." That's the only summons you can write to someone under the age of sixteen (as young as thirteen), and it's just another moneymaking scheme for the city. Even if someone hops on the bike at the door and quickly rides perpendicular from the door to the street—a distance of twelve feet—that's an infraction. However, in white areas, where there are five times as many bicyclists and plenty on the sidewalk, no one gets stopped for it.

All of this was hard to digest and even harder to answer for. I had to go back to the community and hear even more of these stories. Neighbors would call me to explain a recent stop and frisk they experienced, complain about a car stop where they felt violated, recount incidents where cops were rude or overstepped bounds, and ask me whether or not the officers' actions were legal. Almost all of them were frustrated with the innocuous nature of their offenses. In a city where violent crime

---

* Missing a court date is more complicated than it sounds. Bob Gangi's organization, Police Reform Organizing Project (PROP), is a court-monitoring initiative that captures the reality of this process: from the lopsided racial breakdown to the insane line that people have to wait on for hours before seeing a judge. Some people leave without even realizing that this gets them a warrant; they have to go to work or pick up a child and don't have the luxury to spend the day on that line. And that is what gets them arrested.

occurred regularly, they figured cops should be focused on that instead. They'd ask what recourse they had, if any.

I had a lot to answer for, but I really couldn't: I was questioning it all myself.

The NYPD calls itself a paramilitary organization, instills in you a rank structure, and then cajoles and threatens you to stay in line. You are not free to think for yourself. You're following orders. If you question it, you're a problem. I wasn't me out there—I was a pawn on the front lines of a systemic attack on my own people.

I'd always assumed, especially as a teenager, that the problems with cops had to do with problematic cops. But I found out that many were just operating and surviving inside a problematic system. It started so much farther up the chain than the single cop. Because I was pressing against these expectations, as far as the department was concerned, *I* was the problematic cop.

I remember complaining once to a female sergeant who had something of a smirk on her face while I was talking. I stopped. "Sarge?"

"You know, Raymond, I just figured out what the problem is with you."

"What's that?"

She shook her head. "You think this job is real."

Thirteen

Pushing Through

Once it became clear that I wouldn't get on board, Ferruzola couldn't wait to send me out of Conditions. Not too long after our exchange of words over the young Bajan woman he sent to the bookings, he offloaded me to the Coney Island summer detail, a retaliatory post. It would be my first of many.

In the summer, cops from all over the city were temporarily reassigned to the Sixtieth Precinct and Transit District 34 in Coney Island due to the millions of residents and tourists who headed out to the beaches, boardwalk, and amusement parks on Brooklyn's south shore. Commands tried to get cops to volunteer, but few ever did. You were stationed away from your home command, your routines were interrupted, and you didn't get a summer. The shift was Wednesday to Sunday, six p.m. to two a.m., and it was almost impossible to get a weekend night off. People hated it, so it was reserved for rookies who still had to pay their dues and those whom supervisors were looking to punish. I later heard someone in my command actually volunteered for it but was told no: they *wanted* to give it to me.

One night on the detail, at the Kings Highway subway station, a short white woman with dirty-blond hair ran up to me and literally jumped into my arms. She was crying into my uniform and talking rapidly in a thick eastern European accent.

"Miss, slow down," I said. "Please."

"No, you don't understand!" she said, clawing at me. "He's coming. He's coming right now!" As I tried to calm her down and get her story, I could make out that her boyfriend had been cheating on her, and when she said she was leaving him, he beat her up.

As I was trying to get more details from her, a tall, slim guy with dark hair came up the stairs right behind her. He began speaking softly to her in what sounded like Russian, all the while smiling at me, presenting an innocuous tone and expression. But she was translating to me in a panic: "He's saying he's going to kill me! He's saying I'm a stupid bitch for coming to you! He knows how to hit me so I won't bruise and so you won't believe me. Please, please, help me," she said. She kept squeezing my arm and shoulder, refusing to let go.

Then she held out her laptop. "Look! Look! Look at the computer. He hit me with!" The screen was cracked and the metal was bent, something that would have required repeated blunt force. That was enough proof for me. My partner and I cuffed the guy, arresting him for felonious assault in the second degree, because he used the laptop as a weapon.

Back at the station, as I was filling out the Domestic Incident Report (DIR), the sergeant said, "Raymond, make sure not to mention the laptop on there."

"*Not* mention it?" I asked, making sure I heard him correctly.

"Yeah," he said.

I left it out, but I hoped that the victim would mention it in her own statement on the second page. That way, the assistant district attorney would clearly see it was a felony case.

"Ah shit," the sergeant later said when looking over the completed DIR, "why the fuck did she write about the laptop?" Without much thought, he ripped up that second page—the victim's statement—and threw it out. Then he attached a blank second page and wrote *refused* across the narrative section, which is what we did when a complainant refused to fill it out. But she *had* filled it out—he just didn't like what she had written. I was new there and doing my best not to rock the boat, so I just stood there, stunned.

The sergeant disappeared her statement and, consequentially, the real charge. The reason: the laptop made the crime a higher degree of assault, which raised the overall crime numbers. According to the powers that be, *those* numbers had to go down. Whether they actually did or not was beside the point. We simply had to make them look like they were going down.

That's not just fudging paperwork or taking a bureaucratic shortcut. It has real-world consequences. When I went into work the next day the Russian man was already released and picking up his property, charged with misdemeanor assault. Beating a woman over the head with a laptop so badly that it bends is obviously not a misdemeanor. If it got filed properly, he would've been remanded to Rikers or at least out on bail. Now he was free to go home and finish his business. It haunted me. We set him free to potentially go kill her because we didn't do what we were there to do. And the reason? Numbers. Always with the numbers. They infected everything like a virus.

The two-headed monster—broken windows and CompStat—led to a two-pronged manipulation. The number of broken-windows arrests and summonses—"activity"—fulfilled on the backs of Black and Brown people had to go up. But index crimes—the seven majors— needed to go down. That was the equation: *activity up, crime down.* Make it look like the police were everywhere, clamping down on serious crime. And everyone knew it. In Black and Brown neighborhoods, we had to provide the evidence that broken windows was working, create the illusion that we were cracking down on crime. It was a massive tail-wagging-the-dog situation, orchestrated at the highest levels and regularly executed by numerous commands across the city.

The only word to describe it: conspiracy.

What the sergeant had done, erasing any reference to the laptop, was relatively common. It's known as downgrading or "cooking the books": classifying a crime as something lower than it was or not reporting it altogether ("shitcanning"). Downgrading threatens public safety, the thing cops are supposedly focused on, often what they claim is their top priority.

I had been seething about all the harassment done in the name of public safety, but meanwhile an actual public safety issue was getting intentionally ignored. And why? Politics and job protection. The commissioner and the mayor needed the crime numbers to go down so they could promote the fact that crime was down—it helped their careers, protected tourism dollars, and justified increased development revenue. Every cop in the chain pushed the person below them to make sure crime appeared low. Forget about what was actually going on. The demands from the top turned to harassment and manipulation at the bottom.

Not only were we locking people up for nonsense to get one set of numbers up, we were letting people go who had actually committed violence to get another set of numbers down. Everything was backward; it was *Alice in Wonderland* shit. If you create a system like CompStat that evaluates and promotes based on numbers, then people are going to work to manipulate those numbers. That creates a rot that will seep into every corner of the institution.

Downgrading was so prevalent that officers would literally contradict what victims were saying in order to disappear the crime. I was backing up an officer at Flatbush Avenue when a thirteen-year-old girl had her cell phone snatched. The officer called the sergeant over and told him the situation. The sergeant then turned to the girl. "That's not what happened," he said to her. "I think you put it down and someone grabbed it."

"Nah, no, it didn't happen like that," she protested.

"Well, you go home and think about it," the sergeant said. "I think you put it down."

If you put the property down and someone grabs it, it's petit larceny. But if it's snatched from your body, that's grand larceny—a seven major. That summer a guy was arrested for cutting the pockets of sleeping passengers on the train and stealing their wallets and phones. Rather than charge him accordingly, for grand larceny, the sergeant made the charge "unsafe riding," since he used the end doors of the train car looking for victims. It'd be like charging a murderer with nothing but breaking and entering because of how he got into the victim's house.

According to police reporter Graham Rayman, back in 1998, "Then Commissioner [Howard] Safir was forced to disclose that subway crime had been under-reported for 20 percent for years."[1] Even with that admission from the highest-ranking police official, in fifteen years not much changed. There was too much incentive to keep crime numbers low. An anonymous survey of New York City police officers around this time found so much downgrading going on that they deduced that there were "conservatively . . . at least 100,000 manipulations" *just* from those who answered the survey.[2] Downgrading was its own cancer.

Leonard Levitt, a longtime New York City police reporter, got a number of cops to admit to him that downgrading was the "unwritten policy [of the department] to lower the official crime rate."[3] There were even institutional bulwarks that existed solely for this purpose. For instance, anytime officers had to take a report for one of the seven majors, you had to first call a supervisor to the scene. There's no reason for this except that the supervisor had an opportunity there in the moment to quash or reclassify the crime. One commander I knew was called "the Slasher" because of his willingness and creativity in making sure a crime didn't go on the books as a seven major. Those at the top, despite cooking books themselves during their ascension, actually punished any commander they discovered doing this, so it all had to be done very quietly and stealthily. The crime rate was just another fiction maintained by the powers that be to protect careers, keep the money flowing in, and make sure no one on the outside knew what was going on.

I HAD NO PROBLEM being isolated, marching to my own drum. My experience in the NYPD mirrored my youth in a very palpable way: again, I was forced to go it alone. Despite the push and pull of the crowd, I worked to keep my feet firmly planted and refused to be part of the problem. When I was younger, I distanced myself from my friends when they were breaking the law because I cared about who I was and what happened to my community. Later, as a cop, I distanced myself from colleagues who were harassing people because I still cared about these things. I didn't make the right choices in those days to make the wrong ones now.

Around the time that I was clashing with Sergeant Ferruzola in Conditions, there was something else that was drilling its way into my core. Drinking had taken over too much of my life. A once innocuous thing, an afterthought, had become a focus of my entire week. At first, I wasn't even aware of the problem. Alcohol is a pillar of Caribbean culture, and I grew up around it. My dad let my brother and me try beer when I was six, and all parties—even children's birthday parties—would eventually morph into adult drinking parties. With our older friends, Billy and I would sneak coquito and crémas around the corner, downing them like milkshakes and then finding we couldn't walk straight. As a teenager, I'd show up with my Hennessy to basement parties or the skating rink, and when I started hanging out with DJs, I'd get into clubs underage as part of their crew and drink freely. Drinking was an escape hatch, a way to celebrate during a youth that offered few chances to do so. It never seemed dangerous or unhealthy; it just was.

Then as a cop, alcohol became a bonding agent; it just flowed naturally from the work environment, especially when my shift ended at eight p.m., just as the night came alive. Most cops feel entitled to a drink or two after work. It's a tough job, you're on your feet most of the day, facing the elements, navigating the chaos of the city, dealing with some of the worst moments in people's lives. It makes you want to kick back, numb your mind to it.

Though I would drink right there alongside my colleagues, I could tell we were there for different reasons. While they drank to let off steam and socialize, I was drinking because I couldn't stand seeing what the system was doing to my people. We came to it from opposite ends of frustration. The cops working alongside me, wearing the same uniform as I was, were perpetuating a system that maintained the racial and social order. They drank because of the headache and the hassle, and I drank to stave off the pain of seeing it up close. It haunted me: the systemic and deliberate caging of kids, the harassment of my community, the destruction of my neighborhood, the apathy and disregard for my people. I got to see the ways that the hood became the hood, how and why it remained the hood, how and why the powers that be *needed* it to remain the hood.

I didn't get to hop on the Long Island Expressway and leave it all behind after work. I went home, spent time with neighbors on my block and school friends who were getting harassed, thrown in those cells, caught in a system that didn't see them as people, that benefited from *not* seeing them as people. I'd see my dad at the nursing home, watch him slowly deteriorating, and the stress of work would be on my mind. I'd visit with my young niece and be thinking about what she'd face when she got older, remembering the kid that day in the cell whom a cop tossed off his bicycle and arrested for riding on the sidewalk. Being part of this machinery of oppression was too much. I had front-row seats to the madness and it was tearing me up inside.

For everyone I saw in a cell who didn't belong there, I'd extrapolate what was going to happen to them, their schooling or job, their families—none of which was ever discussed on the police side. If anything, the job was romanticized on the cops' end; they thought they were doing God's work, "saving these people from themselves." Everyone in those cells was branded a perp—violent offenders and turnstile jumpers all mixed together with little distinction. The dehumanizing was a necessary part of it, a way for officers to go home with a clean conscience. But I needed to drink.

I didn't know how to cope or process it, so I self-medicated in the way I knew how, in the way I'd learned how. At the time I had Sundays and Mondays off, so Saturday night after work was the start of my weekend, and we'd all go directly to the bar from the station. Closing out the workweek with a few Hennessy on the rocks, maybe a Heineken or Guinness to top it off, took some of the sting out. (The Long Island cops even got me drinking Bud Light.) Then I'd be back at work on Tuesdays, counting down the hours to Saturdays. Alcohol had never called to me like that before, and it struck me as a festering problem. It gnawed at me and gnawed at me, until I could no longer ignore it. I had to do something about it.

At the time I was seeing someone. She'd always call after work to make sure I was good. Saturday nights I'd miss the calls when I was at the bar. Next morning when we'd speak, she'd be concerned. She could see what was happening and didn't like it. She pushed the issue and touched on things that I was finally ready to see for myself. In October 2009, she and I made a pact to quit drinking together.

"Not even a glass a wine?" people ask. "A toast?" *Nothing.*

When I tell them I quit after a period of drinking too much, they'll say, "Oh, it's the stress from the job? Being a cop? Chasing bad guys?"

No. Not at all, I tell them. *The opposite, in fact.* It was seeing what the "good guys" were up to.

Removing alcohol from my life kept me off the path of self-destruction. It also gave me the space to do something about the pain. Once I chose to stop numbing it, the only other choice was to take action. That was how I came out the other end. It would be years before I put anything into motion, but back then I took that first step, deciding to open up to the world instead of closing myself off.

And I made the decision at a time when the person most responsible for who I was was falling apart.

DAD'S STROKE BACK in 2003 had left him mostly incapacitated. Through the end of high school, then my time in the academy, my years in Impact, Conditions, Coney Island, he had been lying there in that nursing home. Life went on and the world spun, but Dad just lay there, a feeding tube now attached because he couldn't swallow food.

There was a small TV set in his room permanently set to ABC to ensure he never missed *Jeopardy!* and a radio for him to tune in to his beloved Haitian programs. On the dresser and windowsill were get-well-soon gifts, birthday and Father's Day cards that had accumulated throughout the years, along with a framed photo of my brother Winer in his U.S. Marines uniform.

A few years earlier Dad had been diagnosed with mild dementia. He spoke with difficulty, and his body was almost fully contracted, his limbs stiff and brought inward. According to the staff he was completely nonverbal, but I never accepted that diagnosis. I'd do whatever I could to get him to speak, even if it was just one word.

On my visits, I would play his music, Tropicana and Celia Cruz, and see how his face got lighter, knowing the sounds penetrated into him, the real him, the one trapped inside this body that had betrayed him. I wouldn't let what I could see be the final word on what was going on in there, and I learned to read his faces: his agitated face, his thinking face, his reminiscing face.

The day Obama was elected in 2008 I couldn't wait to get over there and tell him. Since I was a kid, he had been insisting this day would never come. "America's the land of opportunity," he'd always said, "but a Black man can *never* be president."

"Look, Papi, you see that?" I pulled out my phone and showed him news articles about President-Elect Obama. He lifted his head to see. "This man, this Black man right here, won the election. He is going to be president." Just saying the words aloud brought tears to my eyes. And knowing the moment had come, that Dad was able to see it in his lifetime, was a gift.

I liked to visit him in my uniform, so he could be proud of what his son had become, this honorable position that he had first suggested to me. I would pull out my badge and show it to him, squeeze the plated metal into his hands.

Sometimes, I'd point to my firearm and show it, asking him in Creole, "Papa, kisa sa ye?" *("Pops, what's this?")*

"Re-re-vòlvè," he'd stammer. *("Revolver")*

I saw how much he struggled when he tried to speak, how the words were like blocks in his throat he couldn't push out. I came up with another way to communicate with him.

Years ago, I'd watched an episode of a TV show in which one of the characters, a teenager, volunteers at a nursing home. He becomes close with an Alzheimer's patient who used to love driving his car. When the old man starts to fade, the young man shakes him out of it by jiggling his car keys in front of him. And it works. The keys return him to the world.

I remembered those patients at YAI who'd act out—break things or bite—because they were frustrated that they couldn't communicate. I wanted my dad to feel seen and heard. Not just for him, but also for me.

I came up with this exercise where I'd walk to the far corner of the room. Then I'd say, "Papi, can you lock your eyes with me?" Even though he was contracted, he could still move his head and neck. He'd turn his head slowly until he met my eyes and would stare at me.

Then I'd go to the other side of the room and say, "Dad, can you lock your eyes with me?" No matter how sick he was, he always did this. Those eyes across the room, the eyes I knew so well because they were my own. That moment held a lot. It was his way of saying, from deep within himself, *I see you, son. I see you. Do you see me?*

Because of him, I knew where I came from, had Haiti running through my bloodstream. I read so many books, watched so many documentaries, and had endless conversations with peers and older folks who had migrated, but I'd still never been there. In the winter of 2010, I was watching TV in the command lounge at work when I saw footage of the devastating earthquake that hit Port-au-Prince. After my shift I was glued to CNN and couldn't believe the images—the misery, the rubble, the grieving faces that looked just like mine. My mother had two children who lived there whom I'd never met, along with various uncles, aunts, and cousins. I realized that I could've lost my entire family before even getting to know them; immediately, I applied for an expedited passport.

The next summer, I finally made the voyage. After all those years, meeting my sister and brother, seeing my mother's face in their faces, was an emotional experience. I met so many other relatives, from the Dominican Republic and even Suriname, that I felt the expanse of my history stretching out before me. The experience helped me understand my culture, my ancestry, and even my father so much better.

I watched little kids fetching water from the village and walking two miles with the bucket on their heads to flush the toilet or wash their clothes. It made me think of the plumbing issues in our East Flatbush apartment and why they were nothing to my dad. I went to the quarters of the founding fathers and the ruins of the National Palace, saw the statue *Le Negre Marron* that has famously survived every Haitian disaster, the anchor of the *Santa María* from Columbus's maiden voyage to the "New World," and artifacts that belonged to Haitian heroes such as Charlemagne Péralte. Seeing those things up close, to have them taken out of books, lit me from the inside.

Because I wouldn't be able to tell Dad about the trip in a way that he'd understand, I borrowed a camera from a photographer friend to take high-resolution photos. When I came home, I put them all on my laptop, set the computer on my supine father's stomach, and just started scrolling. He could barely move by that point, but he could not contain himself: the tears just *flowed*. I could see it in his eyes: seeing his homeland and knowing I'd been there touched him in his very core.

In late October of that year, 2011, I went to visit Dad, and when I did our routine of walking to the corner of the room, he wouldn't lock eyes with me. After that, I just knew.

Heading home that day, I steeled myself. I was finally at peace with the idea of him dying, because it really wasn't a life anymore. It was no longer him in there. On a cold morning two weeks later, I got the call. I rushed over, pushing through medical staff and officers to see a sheet over his face. I pulled the sheet back and quickly put my head on his chest. As a kid I used to lay there listening to his heart; with my left hand like a metronome I would tap his right shoulder matching the rhythm of his heartbeat. But now nothing. It was deafening, the loudest silence.

I'd been preparing for my father's death for many years. But no matter what your brain knows will happen, you still can't be ready for something like that. He loomed so large in my identity, in my history, in my childhood, that it was like I had been disconnected from something elemental. It was like I was floating, just myself, out there—uprooted from the very concept of home.

In more ways than one, I was an orphan in the world.

Fourteen

Officer Lil Wayne

2012

The sergeant who said my problem was that I thought the job was real? She was right; the issue was that I seemed to be the only one. Despite the interactions I'd had with cops as a teenager, the horror stories that penetrated my community, the biases that taught me how police viewed my Black body, I still became a cop. Because I believed in what it could be. I believed in the noble oath we swore on our first day.

But what I found was an entire institution rotting from within, structured around oppressing minorities, motivated by self-interest and empty statistics. I desperately wanted to hold the job accountable for what it professed to be. What it had the potential to be. That was my conflict: whether or not I had the power, the will, the stamina to wrestle it into submission and *make* it be.

As part of the retaliation against me, I had been thrown the previous fall on the midnight shift, which eats up any semblance of a life you might try to have. You're working when everyone's asleep, asleep when everyone's hanging out, and out patrolling the city during the ghostly hours. I was starting to see that this was going to be part of the price to pay for not getting with the program.

Because of low ridership on the midnight shift, the Transit police's focus moves from fare evasion to "outstretched," taking up more than one seat on the train. Like Ferruzola, our lieutenant would come out with us on patrol to make sure we hit our numbers. The Grand Army Plaza station underneath Flatbush Avenue is made up of a single platform with trains going in opposite directions. This made it the ideal station to look for outstretched collars; you could stand in one place and scan the windows of two different trains as they slowed into the station. A Manhattan-bound train would pull in and our lieutenant would walk the platform, often looking for homeless people sleeping with their bags—literally all of their possessions—next to them on the seat. It's not like anyone else was using those seats, but he'd have his officers write them up anyway. He'd then wait for the train to come to a stop and signal to the officers which car held the outstretched passenger, while also scanning the other track to do the same thing on the Brooklyn side. It was embarrassing to me that this is what the police were up to in a city of eight million, but the numbers had to be served.

Enforcing so-called quality-of-life issues so heavily was not just a nuisance and harassment; it perpetuated the racial and class differences that plague every city. Broken windows wasn't enforced everywhere, certainly not in white areas. It's *selectively* enforced, which makes it that much more damaging.

A colleague of mine once stopped two white college girls and pulled them off the train. They were outraged. One of them, who had a nose piercing and painted black nails, kept asking, "For what? For what?" The officer didn't reply. Cops go robotic when they can't rationalize what they're doing to civilians. When people ask questions, they get technical ("It's illegal," "It's the Transit rules"), but I was willing to dialogue with anyone.

"What for? What'd you stop us for?" she kept asking.

"Outstretched," I explained. "Taking up two seats. It's against Transit rules."

"What!" the other one said.

"What do you mean?" the first girl said. "This is my Chanel bag! I'm not putting it on the dirty floor."

"According to the New York City Transit rules and regulations," I said, "you're in violation."

"Wait, wait. Since when is this a thing?" she asked. "I've never heard of this. You have people getting killed, raped out there."

I shrugged. "It's called the broken-windows theory," I said.

"What?"

"Broken. Windows. Theory," I repeated more slowly.

She wrote it down on the cover of a notebook. "I'm going to look this up," she said. "This is insane." I didn't disagree with her, but what stood out to me the most was that she'd never heard of it or experienced it. Very few Black people made it to her age without being exposed to broken windows.

The job could be repetitive and frustrating, though never uneventful. Once in a while there'd be a moment of sheer terror. Heading back to base one early morning after a midnight shift, a guy came flying out of the corner store. "Officer, we're being robbed! Someone's robbing us!"

"Does he have a gun?" I asked.

"Yeah, yeah."

"What is he wearing? How many?"

"He's the only one in there."

I put the distress call out over the radio. "Central, can I have a ten-eighty-five, robbery in progress, possibly armed." It was intense, more real than real. Dispatch started asking for these vivid details while my adrenaline was pumping and my fine motor skills were fading.

I pulled out my gun and I waited. The guy finally came out, a black plastic bag in his left hand.

"Get on the ground!" I yelled.

"For what?"

"Get on the fucking ground!"

"What the fuck do I have to get on the ground for?" he asked, like I was being unreasonable. "What's wrong with y'all ni**as? You ni**as always fucking with me!"

"Drop the bag!" I screamed. He did. "Get on your knee! Get on your other knee!" He did as he was told. "Now, get on your stomach."

I was proning him out, getting him flat on his stomach with his limbs extended to give me the greatest tactical advantage. As sirens drew closer, I approached him, gun to my side. He started bringing his arms in toward his stomach, trying to push himself up. If he did have a gun, it would've been right in that spot, the pelvic area. I couldn't know for sure if he was reaching for it and I had to decide in an instant.

I came so close to shooting him.

Instead, I ran behind the car, my gun still on him. "What the fuck is wrong with you? Get on the fucking ground! You don't see I have a motherfucking gun on you?" I was speaking in ways I didn't know I could speak. Finally, when he saw the waves of cops coming, he proned himself out again. With backup covering me, I stepped out from behind the car, reached in, and pulled out his gun. It was an orange water gun spray-painted black to look like a TEC-9.

Back at the base, as my heartbeat steadied, I watched in disbelief as my superiors tried to undo it all. An armed robbery was a seven major, which the department didn't want. The lieutenant ran back over to the bodega and got to work manipulating the report, making sure it didn't get recorded as an armed robbery. The bodega owner had to travel the next day and was unavailable to immediately speak to the district attorney; therefore, the robber ended up walking. It would be laughable if it weren't so enraging. I risked my life in that moment, but the precinct didn't want to get stuck with the number.

"Yo, Ray, why didn't you pull the trigger?" an officer asked me.

"I didn't see the gun," I said. "He didn't necessarily reach for it."

"I would've done him. You're playing with your life, man."

Growing up in East Flatbush, guns were just around, so I had a higher tolerance for seeing one. I didn't just panic at the sight of a gun. I knew I still had the upper hand and I would've taken action if I didn't. Some cops just see the gun and react. If I had shot him, it might have been justified, but it would've sat on my conscience forever. Even a justified shooting will haunt you.

"You're lucky it was Raymond," they told the guy in his cell. "Because if it was anyone else, you'd be dead right now."

Midnight shift was also when lush workers were out in full force, preying on the passed-out drunks and the sleeping, stealing wallets and sometimes assaulting them. I've certainly arrested my share of those who deserved to be locked up for assaulting passengers, sometimes sexually.

On those shifts, I also did a lot of prisoner transports. I'd come into work and automatically go check the cells because I'd have to take prisoners to Central Booking and wanted to have some rapport with them in advance. If there was time, I'd look into their file, find out what the original warrant or charge was. One night there was a kid in there who was sitting quietly on the bench. I asked him what he was doing there.

"My MetroCard wasn't working," he said quietly.

"What?"

"Well, I slipped under the turnstile when I heard the train coming. And the undercovers arrested me."

This kid was going into Central Booking? It still didn't make sense, so I got the whole story.

At around ten p.m., this young man, whom I'll call David, had been playing video games at a friend's when his mother called for him to come home. His school MetroCard, which cut out at nine p.m., wouldn't work and he had no money, so when he heard the train coming, he crawled underneath the turnstile. Two plainclothes cops grabbed him. It's exactly the kind of case that should be discretionary, but if an officer needs his number, discretion goes out the window.

When they asked for his ID to run his name, David said he didn't have any. Though this isn't illegal, if the cops can't ID you after you commit an infraction, they can arrest you. But since David was under nineteen, they were required to make a notification to a parent or guardian. The cop was stuck: if he made contact with the parent, the kid would then be identified, which meant there was no reason to arrest him.

This cop's solution? He purposely didn't call David's mom and filled out a missing person's report on the kid just so the arrest would stick.

When I heard this, I almost lost it. Both for the mother who must've been in a blind panic not knowing what happened to her kid and for David himself. David was sixteen, had never been arrested once in his life, and now I was going to take him to the bookings, a place that held some violent criminals. Brooklyn Central Booking was a massive underground dungeon that warehoused hundreds of people, mostly Black and Hispanic, crammed in filthy cages. Prisoners would have to wait nearly two days to see a judge and pray they weren't remanded to Rikers Island, which is hell on earth.

In her book *Crook County,* Brown University professor Nicole Gonzalez Van Cleve notes not just how cruel it is to arrest these kids for minor infractions, but how counterproductive. As she writes, "Racially disproportionate incarceration contributes to a cycle of poverty, growing structural inequality, and *higher (rather than lower) crime rates*."[1]* Before they go into Rikers, they could be anything. But when they come out, they're the kind of people who can survive Rikers. We should be sure that those we're sending to jail belong there. The consequences are far too high.

---

* Italics mine.

One of the plainclothes officers who arrested David was Officer Adé, a military veteran whom I was friendly with. He was a good guy, and he and I had spoken before about the damage of these kinds of arrests, especially to young people. As I expected, Adé told me he and his partner were out on plainclothes overtime looking for a collar because the partner *needed* one for the month.

"Ray, what can we do?" he asked me. "You think you're not part of this because you don't get down with the numbers game? You're part of this."

"Nah, I'll never be a part of this," I said. "This shit doesn't make any sense."

"It's the job, my man. When I was in Iraq, I had to do all kinds of things that made no sense. What am I—a Black man—doing out in the desert shooting Iraqis? They ain't got no problem with me. But once you join the job, and you know what it entails, you do what you gotta do. Not everyone is willing to suffer like you. I got kids, I got a wife, I can't do what you do, Ray. I need my overtime, bro."

"But we have benefited from the sacrifices of those before us who took steps to change things," I said. "Now that we're in these pivotal positions, shouldn't we be trying to do the same? It's for those same kids you just mentioned."

It was hard to blame a single cop when this was the soil that he had to thrive in. But after countless interactions like this with fellow cops, I saw how ingrained the behavior was. I started looking for a different place in the NYPD to plant my flag, one where I could value what I would be doing and one that valued what I could do.

And I knew exactly the place that would be.

In Conditions, we sometimes would be called by the Truancy Unit to help out with the after-school crowds, especially at the Franklin

Avenue–Eastern Parkway stop in Crown Heights where five different schools (four high schools and one middle) all converged. That spot was like a teenage Grand Central Station and dismissal time was a nightmare.

I was easy to recognize because of the dreads, and they started to call me "Lil Wayne," after the rapper. Flooding in from upstairs and spotting me in the train station, the students would sing the hook to Lil Wayne's "Mrs. Officer," imitating a siren: *Wee ooh wee ooh wee.*

One time when I was called in as backup, I came up the subway stairs to the intersection of Franklin and Eastern Parkway to find nearly a hundred teenagers circled up and yelling, instigating a fight.

"Get that bitch!"

"She pussy!"

"Yo, fuck her up!"

It was chaos, the heat and anticipation of the crowd all pushing to the center, where two groups of girls were about to square off. Officers tried to get kids to clear the intersection, but they had no control of the situation. As I pushed my way inside the circle, I immediately recognized the two main girls in the middle, tying up their hair and removing their earrings while cursing each other out. I'd talked to them before about how loud they were and how people heading home after a long day didn't need to hear all that. We'd crack jokes at one another and I tried to drop little gems on them about thinking with their futures in mind.

When I got between the girls that day, I looked closely into their eyes. What I saw: pure fear. These girls didn't want to fight. They just needed a reason to get out of it without bruising their egos or reputations. I'd been inside those scrums before, and the energy and pressure pushed you until you felt like you had no choice. But you always did.

I pulled each girl aside to talk separately and listened as each vented about the other. "I hear you," I said. "I understand you're angry right now." Then I calmly reminded them about the advice I had given them to think beyond the moment. As they encountered crossroads in life, they should ask themselves what choice puts them closer to who they want to be.

"We're standing right now at one of those crossroads," I said, the sound of the adolescent crowd rumbling behind us. "We're right there. Now, what are you going to do? Which way do you want to turn?"

It seemed to deflate the girls' tempers. After they cooled off, they both seemed relieved. They parted ways and the crowd dispersed, a disappointed mumbling emanating from the groups.

Afterward, Sergeant Ruane, short with dirty-blond hair and blue eyes, who was in charge of the Truancy Unit, came up to me. "Good job, kiddo," she said. "You should put in an application to join us."

That's exactly what I wanted to hear. I felt like someone had seen my value, in action, and wanted to reward me for it.

"Will do, Sarge."

A few weeks after I broke up that fight, I ran into a friend of mine from Truancy. We got talking about how I'd put in for the unit. "Raymond," she said, "you know Sergeant Ruane don't want you in there, right?"

"What? Why?"

"Remember that day you stopped that big fight on Franklin? With the two girls?"

"Yeah. Ruane came over to me and told me 'Good job.' She was the one who told me to put in for the unit."

"Yeah," she said, "that's all bullshit."

"What do you mean?"

"You know what she said right after you walked away?"

"What?"

"'I'll never take Raymond. If we get him, we'll never be able to collar these kids.'"

"Bullshit," I said.

"Swear on my life. I heard her. Word for word."

We'll never be able to collar these kids.

I'd heard cops complain about Ruane before, about how she pre-ferred the white cops for plum positions, but she really was just a creature of the system. A few months later, when Sergeant Ruane left Truancy, I was hopeful about my chances of getting in. Then a new captain, Cap-tain Griffith, came in to the command. Griffith was from Flatbush, with Guyanese roots, walked with a noticeable bop, and possessed a street-like edge. He brought with him a newly promoted Black lieuten-ant, Lieutenant Reid, whom he made the special operations lieutenant (SOL). The SOL was in charge of all units that weren't regular Patrol, which included Truancy.

Lieutenant Reid seemed like the coolest cat I'd yet seen inside the department. He opened my mind to what a Black cop rising up the ranks could be. A well-dressed and young-looking guy from Brooklyn who drove a fancy Mercedes, Reid carried himself relaxed and easy, like noth-ing fazed him. But there was also another, deeper thing drawing me to him: cultural recognition.

As a Black man from the hood navigating his way inside a white in-stitution, I hadn't found anyone like me to look up to. *We cannot be what we cannot see,* my friend Michael K. Williams used to say. But now here was a Black man from my neck of the woods in a position of power. In three years in uniform, I'd seen maybe six or seven Black lieutenants to-tal, and none carried themselves like Reid. I pushed the new captain to transfer me to Truancy. He agreed, putting me in there under SOL Reid.

Wearing the uniform while interacting with teenagers, especially ones of color, came with all kinds of potential: of second chances, of community building, of righting wrongs, of changing habits. When I was their age, I never saw the cops as anything but a nuisance, but they were unavoidable, sewn into the fabric of the streets. Now I would be playing the other side of those interactions. Maybe I could change what those conversations looked like and what they led to. I had come from these kids' world, could relate to the lives they were leading, and I'd be talking to them from the inside of an institution they'd only known as a threat.

While those like Sergeant Ruane were incentivized to "collar kids," the collateral damage was playing out on the other side. Statistics show that interaction with the juvenile justice system has a monumental effect on kids' futures—from their potential criminality* to their education to their mental health. Cops are hunting these kids on the street, and nowadays, with the help of faculty and administrators, they're arresting them in schools as well. Despite representing only 15 percent of the U.S. school population, nearly a third of those arrested in schools are African Americans.[2]

This tendency to single out Black kids for adult-type discipline, especially Black boys, has led to the "school to prison pipeline," whose very existence should make us all ashamed. In her essay "Boys to Men," law professor Kristin Henning points to evidence that "black boys are more likely to be treated as adults much earlier than other youth and less likely than white boys to receive the benefits and special considerations of youth."[3] For the same behaviors, the white kid is getting a detention and a call home while the Black kid is getting cuffed and booked. As author Claudia Rankine has poignantly asked, "Whose boys get to be boys?"[4]

There's also evidence that these negative interactions affect their learning, development, and growth. "Stress can disrupt learning by preventing the brain from retrieving and retaining long-term memories and from updating old memories in light of new information," Henning notes.[5] We are going beyond harassment into something even more damaging and nefarious.

Truancy was not just another assignment or post. I went in with a

---

* Having any kind of juvenile record drastically increases the likelihood of returning to the system before the age of twenty-five. (Rosa Brooks, *Tangled Up in Blue* [New York: Penguin Press, 2021], 26.)

clear awareness of the high stakes. I showed up on my first day charged with the possibility of what could be done there.

"MORNING, GUYS," the sergeant said from the front of the muster room. "Happy Monday. Okay, according to the database our number last year for this week was forty-two. So that's this week's number: forty-two yellows. Let's hit that number, maybe go over a bit. Have a good one out there. See you guys after meal."

Besides managing the after-school chaos, Truancy's job was to find those kids who were cutting school, so-called truants. When we encountered a kid who was supposed to be in school, we had to fill out the youth referral forms, known as yellows, after the paper's color. The metric of activity in Truancy was how many yellows we filled out as a unit. At the start of every week, the sergeant would look up our quota—based on the same week in the previous year—and that's what we had to hit at a minimum. If we were rounding up kids, calling parents, and incentivizing them to go to school, the unit might have had a positive effect on school attendance. But that wasn't the actual objective of Truancy; it was just getting the number. The number *itself.* Because the yellows didn't lead to anything.

At one time the unit would round up kids cutting school and take them to truancy centers throughout Brooklyn. Then officers would notify the parents or guardians, who would come pick them up. It wasn't perfect, but it at least kept the adults in the household aware of the child's cutting while also acting as a deterrent, since the adult had to show up in person to collect the child.

But a couple of years before I got to Truancy, due to budget cuts, most of the truancy centers closed. There was one in Bushwick, but it became burdensome to keep taking students from Crown Heights and Flatbush all the way out there, so the Truancy cops stopped doing it altogether. They simply found kids cutting school in parks, alleyways, and train stations, filled out a yellow on them, and let them go on their way. No one else even knew about it. It was just about the piece of paper. What does a kid care about a yellow piece of paper filed somewhere? What does anyone care?

I would make calls to homes and parents, as would one other officer, but this was considered unnecessary. Most officers just dropped their yellows into a box so the record was kept, so it would appear on a spreadsheet somewhere. The next year, the sergeant would count those up to see what their number was supposed to be. And on and on. It was just a cog, a widget.

Once we had gone slightly past the week's number, the other Truancy officers would walk by a whole group of kids cutting school and do nothing.

"Shouldn't we be writing yellows?" I asked the first time I saw this.

"Nah," an officer said. "We don't want to go too high."

"Why not?"

"Because then we'd have to reach that number next year."

I just shook my head, filing it away as another part of the charade of being a cop. These truant cops would even give yellows to exceptional students who had unique schedules that let them start school later in the day. So they were essentially punishing kids for doing well. Within the requirements, I was still finding ways to make the job my own and positively interact with kids. During our downtime, I would go visit the schools just to be a presence in their day.

"What's up, Lil Wayne?" they said when they saw me, giving me a dap or asking me questions about what kind of action I had seen that day. "You shoot that gun today?" they'd ask. "You stop any bank robbers?" They had an impression that being a cop was more like the movies.

"Not yet," I'd say, laughing.

I'd visit the school safety staff, walk the hallways, go to the dean's office to see if I could talk to any kids there facing discipline. Most of all, I was just present, part of the school community, not patrolling or contributing to the pipeline. The students appreciated it as much as I did. That actually *was* the work, because when things got real and I had to take police action, so much of the foundation was already laid.

There was this Jamaican teenager, Kash, wrapped up in gangs, who was nosediving in school. After we arrested him for something minor, I stayed on him and stayed with him. One day I spotted him waiting for the bus while I was driving off duty. I pulled over and picked him up, gave him a ride to his job at McDonald's. I shared with him that I had started working at only twelve years old, how it kept me in line, and told him to stay focused on the future version of himself.

"With all due respect," he asked, "why you doing all this?"

"Doing what?"

"This," he said.

I smiled. "Don't think because you got arrested that I don't see my little brother. You still my little brother."

He gave me this look, like he didn't want to drop his guard. But I could tell he was surprised. "Thanks," he said.

Next time I saw Kash, I gave him my talk about understanding the opportunities that he had being in this country. He eventually respected me enough that when I saw him hanging out in large groups, he'd step away just to give me a pound. His friends often looked confused. They would jokingly ask him if he was a snitch or an informer, as they say in Jamaica.

"Nah, nah," he'd say, "this one's different, yo. I don't care what none of you ni**as say, he's real."

If that's all the job was, pointless yellows, chaotic afternoons, and I could do my thing, I would've been fine with it.

But it wasn't. Not by a long shot.

THERE WAS A second thing expected of the officers in Truancy, one I wasn't totally aware of until a few weeks in. Between the hours of ten a.m. and two p.m. when I was hitting the schools, sometimes calling parents, the Truancy officers were still expected to get summonses, stop and frisks, and arrests like any other unit. Because we were a specialized unit, I just assumed we didn't have the same quotas and expectations. But I would eventually learn that plenty of specialized units—from Anti-Terrorism to Crime Analysis to Task Force—all had to bring in broken-windows-type activity.* It wasn't related to their mission or objective; it's just that the unit, and the unit's supervisors, looked good if their arrest numbers were high. Again, there was a reluctance to collar people for any of the seven majors, because those would raise the crime numbers. So during school hours, it was time for the Truant officers to get petty.

Late one morning I was back at the command making parent calls when two Truancy officers brought in a young Black man who had been arrested at the Utica Avenue subway station. He had been standing on the Brooklyn-bound platform, in one of those sweet spots where cell service works, when his phone rang. His ringtone was Rick Ross's boisterous anthem "B.M.F.": *Rozay, that's my nickname / Cocaine runnin' in my big vein.*

It is unlawful to play music in the subway, but that's not what he was doing. Despite explaining and demonstrating to the officers that it was his ringtone, he was charged for using a "sound reproduction device," as if he had been blasting a boom box. Although it does happen, a cop doesn't have to invent anything to harass someone. There are just so

---

* In the years after 9/11, federal dollars flowed to New York City for counterterrorism efforts. The NYPD created the ATU (Anti-Terrorism Unit), which fell under the Transit Bureau. It was composed of young officers out of Impact. Now they got to be in this highly specialized unit with nearly unlimited federal funds and additional training (which paid them overtime). Aside from the dollars being spent on the training and bag searches, which required that officers come in early pretour, the rest of the money was used to fund overtime completely *unrelated to counterterrorism*. The money paid for guys to stand around turnstiles in plainclothes and arrest people for theft of service all day.

On the day observers came from Washington, DC, the commanding officer divided the platoon into groups for bag search, groups to inspect every train car, and groups that carried long guns and radiation detection devices to check for things like dirty bombs. The DC observers were highly impressed, and the department convinced them to keep the funds coming. The next day the commander at roll call talked about how yesterday they had to put on a show to make sure they paid the bills and the officers should now go back to the work they'd been doing.

many rules on the books that can be squeezed and manipulated in order to get an arrest if you want or need one.

At the end of the first month, I had one arrest and a couple of summonses. This was partly because I was spending my time in the schools and calling parents.

My sergeant was a blond, blue-eyed sneakerhead who wasn't familiar with our area of Brooklyn and often relied on me to get around. He pulled me aside one morning after roll call.

"Raymond."

"Yes, sir."

"Find out what everyone else is doing and get on board."

I knew what he meant, though of course his language was coded, coated in deniability.

Special Operations Lieutenant Reid, who had been one of the big draws for me going into Truancy, was also a creature of the numbers racket. Reid was constantly asking about my summons and arrest numbers, though he tried to be casual about it. It was his frequency that gave up the game. "How's it going, kid? How's it looking, you get anything today?" he'd ask me, usually sometime in the early afternoon.

"No, nothing yet, sir."

Reid himself was evaluated based on the enforcement of every cop under him, no matter the unit. He wanted all his teams to chase numbers because it reflected on him and his commanding officer, made them look like "superstars." Reid was using his informal talks with me to get an impression of my overall numbers. He could've checked the database, but he had been making an assumption about my "activity" based on these brief interactions. A few times I'd actually gotten an arrest later in the day after speaking to him.

A month and a half into Truancy, on a Friday afternoon, I was on patrol by myself when Reid popped up at the Church Avenue train station in plainclothes.

"Hey, Lou," I said, giving him a handshake.

"What's good? You get anything today?" he asked.

"Nah, nothing."

"All right, let's see if we can get something real quick."

It was thirty minutes until the end of my tour, and I was ten minutes away from jumping on the train back to the command. "Go downstairs and wait," he told me at the turnstile. "It's easier for me to get something in plainclothes."

Downstairs I watched trains careen toward Prospect Park, the bustle of a Friday in spring. Waiting and watching, ten minutes became twenty minutes. When I came back up the stairs, Reid got excited. "You got something?" he asked. "You got something?"

"Nah, boss, I'm approaching the end of my tour."

He shot me this look. "All right, let's take the train back and if you see anything on the way, you take it."

We took the train back to Prospect Park, where he was eagle-eyeing for an outstretched, an unsafe riding, anything. Then I parted ways with him on the way back to the command on Carroll Street.

When I got there, the sergeant said, "Lieutenant Reid says give him a call."

"From a while ago? I was just with Lieutenant Reid."

He pointed at the phone. "Two minutes before you walked in that door he called."

"Okay, but I don't have his number."

"All right, get changed," he said, "and when you come back, I'll have his number for you."

I got changed, got Reid's cell number, and rang him. "What's up, Lou?" I said. "You call?"

"Yeah, yeah," he said, panting. "I got a collar for you, kid. I'm coming into the station for you to process."

He hung up before I could even explain that I was out of uniform. It was now well beyond the end of my shift. A few minutes later, Reid walked in with this frail-looking Black girl, skinny and scared. He didn't notice me in my street clothes and walked past me.

"What's up, boss?"

He stopped short when he saw me. "You're already changed? What the fuck?"

"Yeah, my shift's—"

"What the fuck would you do that for!" he snapped. Everyone stopped and turned. "Do I look like I need a fucking collar? I'm a lieutenant and I'm standing out there like a fucking monkey. You're not holding your weight in this unit, Raymond! Now that you have weekends off you have to bring in a lot more bodies!" Gone was the cool cat I had first met. He was livid.

Reid started putting on rubber gloves to search the girl before he threw the gloves at me. "Do your fucking job and search your perp!"

"Lou . . . ," I said.

"What?"

"She's a female," I said. Inside the command, the rules were that a same-gender officer had to conduct the search.

Reid's shoulders dropped. "Jesus," he said, walking off to find a female officer.

The young woman had no business being there. Reid hadn't even run her name. Here's what happened: As she stepped onto the train, a bird feather flew in her mouth and she spat it out. Desperate to grab anyone for anything, Reid ran up on her and stopped her. Then he found an officer standing nearby and had him cuff her. For spitting out a bird feather.

When we ran her name at the command, she was clean as a whistle. Reid had essentially kidnapped her.

We had to let her go, but not before writing her a summons for spitting, which Reid wanted me to do so I'd get the number. But for violations, the issuing officer had to witness it. I couldn't sign the summons without committing perjury.

"I can't sign it," I said.

"What? Why?" Reid asked.

"It's a violation, boss. I didn't see it."

"Oh, you really want to play like that? We were out there together."

"But by the time you stopped her, I already was walking to the command."

"I get it. I get it. No problem," he said. But everything in his tone and body language said he was done with me. And he was.

I lasted all of six weeks in Truancy. In the one place I felt like I could finally be an effective police officer without losing my integrity, where I occupied this special role in the community. *Six weeks.* I was born for Truancy and it couldn't digest me.

The most painful part was that I was kicked out by a Black special operations lieutenant with the approval of a Black captain. I once thought that having Black faces higher up in the command structure would be a cure for what ailed the department. But in Truancy I got a heavy dose of reality.

Like a lot of mainstream institutions, the NYPD may claim diversity, but it doesn't tap into what diversity can bring. The police force had Black chiefs, Black people in important positions, but it never penetrated past the symbolism. If an institution doesn't utilize minorities as assets, listen to their unique perspectives, then it means nothing. In the twenty-first century, American institutions want the credit for having Black faces at the top without it being accompanied by Black experience and Black intellect. That's the problem. It's not about all Black cops being "sellouts," which I still hear all the time, blaming powerful Black people for not doing more. It's about the institution rejecting who they are.

Cosmetic diversity ("the illusion of inclusion") allows people to feel good about themselves, puts forth the idea that the problem is being addressed, even solved, and lets everyone off the hook. It allows white supremacy to fester in a stealthy way. You could change the skin color of the entire command, but as long as they're incentivized to operate within a certain framework, the systemic racism remains.

I once had a conversation with a white sergeant who was shocked that I felt racism was still an issue in the NYPD. The first thing he went to: his bosses' skin color.

"What are you talking about, Ray?" he said. "The chief who oversees Brooklyn North is Black. My lieutenant is Black. I *only* answer to Black men. How can you say that?" His argument was exactly why cosmetic diversity is so dangerous. It's like painting over a building's structural problem—hiding it doesn't mean you solved the problem. It just allows you to move on to something else. But inevitably, one day, it will all come crashing down.

Putting Black faces in charge doesn't automatically dismantle and uproot how a system operates. The criminal justice system has been crafted by white males who know nothing but the white male experience. Much of the existing protocol in the police department grew out of a racist era when Black voices weren't even allowed in the room where things were decided. Now we have Black people in the room, but they're incentivized to keep their mouths shut. Most end up toeing the line because the culture demands it. In fact, they likely only got to the top by toeing that line.

I wasn't received with open arms in the police department because what I had to offer—everything that made me unique as a Black cop from an immigrant family in the hood—wasn't embraced by the culture and the leadership. They didn't even understand how to value it.

Fifteen

Hardheaded

2012

After getting kicked out of Truancy, I was sent to the 4 × 12s, the four p.m. to midnight shift. I continued to push to find instances where I could be a different kind of cop, one positively impacting his community. While standing on the subway mezzanines, people asked me for assistance for things like buying MetroCards from the vending machines. One time, while I was trying to teach a middle-aged African American man how to use the machine, he said something I couldn't make out among the clatter and whoosh of the station. I leaned in closer.

"Sorry, what was that?" I asked.

"Young brother," he said into my ear. "I can't read."

This was far more common than I imagined. After walking him through how to use the machine, I decided to make it my duty to start introducing local kids to books as early as possible, keeping children's books with me on patrol or, later, in the trunk of my car. I'd include books written for adults by Black authors to give out to the community as well.

Meanwhile, my "activity" wasn't keeping pace with my peers. A sergeant who hated me back in Conditions was part of my platoon in the 4 × 12s. Alfredo Ruiz was a Puerto Rican with slicked-back hair who seemed to want to shed his identity and be white, even pronouncing his name *Roo-ez,* rhyming with "Suez." And he didn't go by Alfredo; it was Al.

Back in Conditions, Ruiz perpetuated a "don't talk to me, rookie" culture. He came from an era in the NYPD when hazing the new guys was routine. You'd be standing in front of his desk and not be able to interrupt him, forced to wait until he put his head up and asked, "What do you want?" Just for spite, he'd have you stand there for fifteen minutes to get his signature, then rip it up and make you start from scratch for a small error. The hate coming off this guy not just for me but for what I believed in was fierce. It was the extra motivation I needed to move up in the ranks. I wanted to get out from under every small-minded cop like him.

One time after roll call, Ruiz started talking about his early days on the force. "I don't think any cop should start their career in Transit," he said. "I'm the senior sergeant on this tour, started out in the seven-oh before I got promoted. When I was there, I got into a shooting and killed a kid," he said, practically bragging about it. He was talking like he was in the Mafia or prison, flashing it as a badge of honor. It made me sick. This guy's in charge of serving and protecting our community? And because he got the numbers, he was treated like a star by the higher-ups.

Ruiz and I clashed on a fundamental level. Other officers told me Ruiz would ask, "Why the fuck did the department hire Raymond?" or "How did he get this job?" His thinking—like a lot of cops'—was if you don't like what the job is, don't be a cop. He'd complain about my dreads and ask why they didn't make me cut them at the academy. He'd perpetuate talk that I got into the force because they lowered standards.*

Ruiz would show his dislike for me in petty ways, like giving me a hard time about taking an hour for lunch. Technically the hour doesn't include travel time, but everyone took the full hour. One time, when I was heading back out to patrol, he called across the room. "Hey, Raymond, what time is it?"

"Twenty-one hundred," I said.

"And what time did your meal start?"

"Twenty."

"So, what—oh, you're the commissioner, you get travel time now?"

Everyone stopped what they were doing and watched. The whole room went quiet and tense. I didn't even know how to respond. It was such a humiliating moment that, from then on, I would no longer eat inside any police facility. I would be the lone cop in the back of the restaurant or would take my food to an MTA break room.

On his assigned days off, Ruiz came in for overtime with handpicked people from his squad to join him. It was a racket, a money-printing machine. They went out in plainclothes, grabbed Black and Brown folks for minor subway infractions, and made sure the paperwork took them further into overtime. Then Ruiz signed some arrest-processing documents and they'd all cash in. As long as he could make income on top of his salary, Ruiz never questioned a thing.

Jean, a Haitian officer from Ruiz's squad, used to call me Tet-di, Creole for "hardheaded."

"Tet-di," he'd say, "just make your money. You cannot fight the system." Jean was not a bad guy; he was just incentivized out of his ethics. He was aware of his moral center; he just wasn't listening to it. It didn't get him paid or make his life any easier.

---

* This is pretty ironic considering the entire police department is run on nepotism. White conservatives tend not to see their own affirmative-action programs, but they're everywhere. They just use nicer words for it, like "legacy."

He told me his kids lived in the city and he was glad someone like me was around. This baffled me: he appreciated what I did but couldn't see his own agency in the matter.

"HOW HARD IS it to get a collar?" Nickson asked. I was standing in his nicely furnished living room, hardwood floors gleaming. "If you're struggling to get activity, I can show you. I started out in Transit and we used to—"

"No, no, no, Nickson," I said. "That's not it. I *know* about playing in the rooms. Looking through the vents. I'm objecting to the *way* things are done."

He took a beat, his face a mix of resignation and pity. "Just play the game, Edwin," he said.

I'd meet up with Nickson for counsel, or just for the company of someone who knew the job. But we were talking past each other. I shook my head at the same advice I'd heard far too often, from far too many people I respected. *Play the game.*

"Why are you bringing all this unnecessary stress on yourself?" he asked. "This is what the job is. There's nothing you can do about it. Just do what you got to do. You want to change things? Fine, but make it to chief—*then* you can change things."

Nickson wasn't even being cynical; he was just looking out for me. He knew my mom, my story, and he wanted the path of least resistance for me. His argument was that life was already stressful and here was one stress I could choose not to bring on myself. But I could no more ignore the big picture than I could walk around with my eyes closed.

Nickson and Jean, like plenty of cops (of all colors) might've been initially put off by what the job actually was, but they suppressed that feeling because it did them no good. They got on board because what was the alternative? It's a battle everyone goes through: How much do I care about myself and how much do I care about others? And is it a zero-sum equation? Can I do the right thing without somehow taking away from myself and mine? It's a tension in the heart of every citizen.

But I was educated—by my father and my teachers and Black role models—that getting in, making good for ourselves, was just phase 1. Phase 2 was what we did once we were in. I thought of my hero Marcus Garvey, who sparked a revolution regarding Black strength and independence and exceptionalism. A century ago, when he first tried to spread the word to others, they couldn't hear him. In colonies like his home in Jamaica, they couldn't grasp what he was saying. He had to go to Harlem to get himself heard. And it was from there that his ideas spread across the Black diaspora and around the world.

Most people don't join a group to change it. It's inherently illogical to do so. When you enter an organization, you enter from the bottom and can only rise—and get enough power to change anything—by playing the very game you're trying to undo. But if you do that, then you become part of the problem. It's a paradox.

Many of my colleagues and superiors came into the department to have a steady job with a pension and benefits. Even when they witnessed racially motivated policing—behavior that threatened everything they were, everything their family and friends were—they still went with the flow. It's called "normative social influence." No matter the absurdity of what was going on, everyone just went along, like the famous Stanley Milgram experiment from the 1960s where volunteers kept increasing (what they thought were) powerful electric shocks on strangers just because a guy in a white coat told them that was the requirement. Our desire to belong—and our fear about pushing back—is so overpowering that it can overtake our values, our identity, and our common sense.

To effect change I had to rise to the point where I had the autonomy and influence to shake things up. I turned my focus to becoming a captain, a role where I could do things differently in my own command. I wanted to prove you could achieve public safety without playing the numbers game. My success would reveal the lie that undergirded the police and expose the unnecessary collateral damage destroying my community. The goal was to ascend and then become too loud to ignore.

On my off hours and days, I buckled down and studied for the sergeant's test, which is given every few years and is notoriously difficult. There were study courses where the instructor essentially read from a weekly packet and told you what to highlight. After a couple of weeks of going to class, I realized that I was just being read to. My reading comprehension was fine, so I skipped class and instead went to the twenty-four-hour study center at Brooklyn College after work, staying from midnight to around three a.m. before going home to bed and crashing hard. Then I'd get up, study for a few hours prior to work, and do it all over again.

It was a rigorous year, and I minimized distractions: no recreation, no leisure, just work and studying. I rarely went out and barely saw anyone but my girlfriend and her six-year-old son. I'd review at her place and she'd quiz me. She was supportive of what I was trying to do, partly because she was concerned about what kind of policing her son would face in a few years. She appreciated the fact that I wasn't just going along to get along, that I was trying to make things different for him.

No matter how much my seniority increased, on the days that Ruiz worked, my assignments were the punitive ones that mostly rookies caught. The upside was that those posts—things like watching a hospitalized prisoner or prisoner transport—had tons of downtime. I took advantage of those pockets of time and brought index cards or a packet with me to review for the sergeant's test. It was like jujitsu, flipping Ruiz's retaliation to my benefit.

I even leaned into it sometimes. On the weekends there was a post known as CRV (critical response vehicle). Fifty or so police cars drove in formation with lights on through the heart of the city as a show of force, a counterterrorism initiative. They pulled two cops from every command who would then go guard specific high-profile sites. I actually loved CRV because it was a break from the tunnels and brake dust of Transit, from Ruiz and the headaches. It was also a post that had downtime where I could review for the test.

"Sarge," I'd say to Ruiz, "I had CRV for the last two weeks. Am I going to have it again next week?"

"What are you, Lieutenant Raymond now? Since you're the lieutenant now, you let me know who you'd like to send to CRV. You wanna send me?" It was reverse psychology, because I knew asking him about it would guarantee CRV for a while. I knew how petty he was. Ironically, even though he was unknowingly giving me all this study time, Ruiz, a big gambler, told everyone he had bet heavy against me passing.

The moment the test was over, I knew I'd done well. Even with a punitive assignment from Ruiz on the night of the test—when all the test takers were wiped out—I wouldn't keep my eyes off the prize. Now I just had to put my head down and wait months for "the list," the ranking of everyone's score. Before it was posted, Ruiz sent his minions fishing around for my score, looking to collect on his sure bet.

Doing well on the test didn't automatically make you a sergeant. When the list was posted, you found out whether you passed and where your score put you on the list. Once that list was activated (the existing logjam of sergeants had to be placed first) and promotions began, you waited for your number to come up. Several things could hold or kill your promotion, from discipline issues to low evaluations to pending investigations. Before the list even came out, people were already warning me that the powers that be were going to block it. *Just play the game, Ray. Don't let them fuck with your promotion.*

A cop lives and dies by his superiors' evaluations—it's the difference between a smooth career and a bumpy one: where you're placed, what promotion you land, what raise you get, when you work, whether you get time off, what posts you get, how you're treated by superiors, even little things like if you get a meal break—everything.

Sergeant Stapleton, a caramel-skinned Black man with a bald pate, was my direct superior. On my quarterly evaluations he had been giving me 3.0, a barely passing grade. The scores were not great, but they weren't low enough to damage my career. Not yet. One morning after roll call, everyone started heading to post and Stapleton asked me to stand by in the muster room.

"What's up, Sarge?"

"Ray, listen." He waited a beat for the last stragglers to leave the room. Then he took in a breath. "Listen, they want me to give you a two point five on your evals. Put you on performance monitoring."

"What? That's—"

"I know. Listen, I know," he said, shaking his head. He seemed genuinely pained about it. "I'm not going to do it, you're a good cop."

"Thanks. Yeah, I mean, what do they—"

"I understand you, what you're about. And I'm going to protect you as much as I can, but remember, I'm just a sergeant. There's only so much I can do. I understand your position, I respect it, just know you're taking on a big challenge right now."

"I know it."

Once they gave you an evaluation below 3.0, they could put you on performance monitoring, a type of probation. It was the beginning of a path that made cops—who were union protected—easier to fire. Performance monitoring wasn't supposed to be about your activity and numbers, but that's what it was used for. It was supposed to be for disciplinary issues and excessive civilian complaints, but it was linked mostly with officers whose numbers weren't on par with what the leadership wanted.

"I gotta be honest," Stapleton told me that day. "This usually doesn't end well for those who go against this thing."

After five years as a cop, I knew how much power the department's leadership had, how comfortable they were in lying to protect their image, how easily they could railroad someone who threatened that image. Just look at what happened to Adrian Schoolcraft.

Schoolcraft was a white NYPD officer originally from Texas who became a police officer in the wake of 9/11. Over the years, he objected to similar things I had: the way that the quotas were expected to be filled through harassing minorities, the systemic downgrading of crime to keep the index-crime numbers low. He just wanted to be a cop and do good police work, but the system itself—and the culture that supported that system—made it hard. He was retaliated against and penalized for his complaints. Around the time I was joining the force, in 2008–2009, Schoolcraft had taped conversations with his superiors proving that this behavior was rampant.

One day in October 2009, a frustrated and isolated Schoolcraft left work about an hour early and went home. When he didn't answer his phone, his superior officers declared it a "psychiatric emergency." A squad was sent to his house and forcibly cuffed and then confined him to a psychiatric hospital for six days. His father had to search the city even to locate him.

Fortunately, Schoolcraft had taped that interaction as well, which showed the cops—his colleagues and superiors—inventing a reason to make him look crazy to absolve their own behavior. Schoolcraft eventually brought all of his tapes to *The Village Voice*, which did a four-part series on the NYPD, leading to investigations and lawsuits. Schoolcraft eventually won a settlement against the city, the department, and the hospital, though he was shaken up good and ultimately left the police force. The department treated him as an unstable and lazy cop, then as a greedy liar, but he was holding the proof. Without those tapes, who knows what they would've been able to do to him?*

---

* To this day, Adrian Schoolcraft is still called an EDP (emotionally disturbed person) by the New York City Police Department.

Reading about Schoolcraft left a heavy impact on me. While I was studying for the sergeant's test in 2013, another ground-shifting case in the news caught my attention. The case, known as *Floyd v. City of New York*, was a class-action suit filed by Black and Latino residents that directly took aim at stop, question, and frisk.* The plaintiffs claimed they were racially profiled when they were stopped and frisked in violation of their Fourth (illegal search and seizure) and Fourteenth (equal protection) Amendment rights. At the time, 86 percent of stop and frisks in New York City were of Blacks and Latinos.[1]

What made the case an even bigger deal was that active NYPD officers Adhyl Polanco and Pedro Serrano, as well as retired police captain and state senator Eric Adams (New York City's current mayor), all testified for the plaintiffs. It was a huge step for an institution where cops simply did not testify against other cops—ever. It just wasn't done.

Polanco had already been in the news a few years earlier, around the same time as Schoolcraft, having complained to Internal Affairs about the rampant quotas and racial profiling that flowed through the NYPD. He had been suspended and retaliated against before eventually going to the press in 2010.

In the *Floyd* case, State Senator Adams testified to being present at a meeting with then governor David Paterson and Police Commissioner Ray Kelly, who admitted that his officers stopped minorities with such frequency because "he wanted to instill fear in them, every time they leave their home, they could be stopped by the police. How else would we get rid of the guns?"[2] Adams said he was "amazed . . . [Kelly was] comfortable enough to say that in the setting."[3] It was about sending a message, not about reasonable suspicion, which the Constitution requires.

Officers Polanco and Serrano both testified that they were required

* Also known as Terry stops, named after the 1968 Supreme Court case *Terry v. Ohio*.

to hit quotas for stop and frisks, by focusing on "male, blacks fourteen to twenty-one." Most importantly, they had evidence to back up their testimony, recordings of roll calls where quotas were mentioned and retaliations threatened. I followed the case closely, excited about what was finally coming out into the open and disgusted with what the NYPD tried to do to protect itself.

For instance, in filling out the stop-and-frisk form, an officer has to check a box that explains what provided reasonable suspicion.* In 45.5 percent of the stop and frisks on Black suspects, the "furtive movements" box was checked. But on the stand, the NYPD cops gave such a generalized description of "furtive" that it "encapsulated virtually any type of behavior, such as sitting on benches, looking over a shoulder or going into a building with a broken front door."[4] Stop and frisk is a useful tool if it's coupled with reasonable suspicion. But cops were under pressure via quotas to treat being Black alone as reasonable enough.

The Schoolcraft and Polanco cases, along with the *Floyd* lawsuit, showed me how easy it was for the department's leadership to lie. The amount of lies coming from Paul Browne, deputy commissioner of public information (DCPI), was overwhelming. I'd read quotes in the paper from Browne about how there were no quotas or racial profiling in the NYPD and then at roll call be told to reach my quota and stop more of "the right people" for minor offenses.

The judge in *Floyd v. City of New York* ultimately ruled in favor of the plaintiffs that stop and frisk as employed by the NYPD was unconstitutional, highlighting the fact that it was based on profiling and quotas, not reasonable suspicion. A federal monitor was appointed to ensure that court injunctions were followed. In order to execute a stop and frisk, cops now had to go through a more convoluted procedure with ample documentation and the endorsement of a supervisor. If the stop lacked

---

* We were told to check if people were "casing." Leadership told us that standing at the turnstile meant they were looking to rob someone.

the minimum standard, then the cop was retrained or possibly reprimanded. I had mixed feelings about this result. The problem was never
the cops at the bottom. It was the supervisors putting pressure on the
rank and file to hit quotas. These supervisors were the same people who
were now in charge of making sure stop and frisks were done along legal
parameters.

In her summation, the judge made clear she understood that the
quota demand was coming from superiors, yet she made those same people responsible for ensuring that cops were meeting reasonable-suspicion
standards. The amount of stop and frisks was drastically reduced, but
the arrest and summons pressure remained. It didn't make sense that
stop and frisks were singled out when the profiling and quotas system
infected everything. Stop and frisks in New York City dramatically
dropped from over 685,000 in 2011 to under 46,000 in 2014.[5] The
Floyd ruling helped to reduce overall incidents, but the system itself remained undefeated.

I KNEW THAT when the shit hit the fan with my career, as it was looking
more and more likely to do, the only thing that could save me was the
truth. And the only way to get the truth was to have it in my hands.

I met with my union delegate for the Patrolmen's Benevolent Association* (PBA), Gentry Smith, a dark-skinned bald man with a round
head. Most union delegates were dinosaurs who operated as the institutional memory of every command. Commanding officers changed every
few years, sometimes every year, and the first thing they did when they
arrived at the command was to find the union delegate to help them get
their bearings. Unfortunately, this process invariably bonded the commanding officer to the delegate, who's actually supposed to be there for

---

* In 2019 this was changed to the Police Benevolent Association.

the rank and file. Plus, many delegates are old-timers who no longer really go on patrol or do whatever they can to avoid it. They tend to have cushy indoor positions they don't want to lose so they're reluctant to go against the brass as they sometimes need to. Gentry patrolled like the rest of us and went to bat for us whenever he could. He had been inspired to join the police when he was wrongfully arrested as a teenager and was pissed off at how he was treated. We talked about my issues all the time and he'd agree with me, but that's where it ended; he didn't know what could be done about it.

When he realized after the sergeant's exam what they were going to do to me, he didn't mince words. "Raymond, you have to protect yourself. They're gonna fuck with you, gonna fuck with your promotion. Document *everything*."

I knew what he meant, but I was still on the fence about recording my superiors. I knew I needed to do it, but it still felt like crossing the Rubicon, an action that could never be undone.

On his last day assigned to our command, a sergeant in my platoon, O'Brien,* asked me to be his driver for the day. O'Brien was a redheaded Irish guy with pale skin and light freckles. We weren't close, but he was a gentleman, approachable and optimistic, not uptight like Ruiz. We'd have a conversation now and again, and he stood out as a Democratic voter among a very conservative crowd. At the time, so many cops viscerally hated President Obama, beyond any logical reason.

I didn't know why O'Brien had chosen me to be his driver that day, but once we were alone in the car, he came clean. He was talking about his time at the command, how it was his last day, and then he got quiet for a moment.

"Raymond, listen," he said, "I wanted to talk to you. I'm not going to name names, but I want to warn you. When I first got to the command,

* Not his real name.

there was a separate orientation just for you, warning incoming supervisors about you."

"What, seriously?"

"Yeah," O'Brien said. "I was there. But the picture they painted of you . . . it doesn't add up. After getting to know you, I understand what you're about. I realized they're just not ready for you. The way you see things, they don't see it. Just . . . be careful."

It was the final straw. I had always known they were gunning for me, but this was a level of targeting that even I couldn't have predicted.

I knew I wasn't going to budge, and if they were coming after me, I'd better get prepared.

Sixteen

On the Record

January 9, 2014

Raymond, see me after roll call," my new platoon commander, Lieutenant Long, told me one frigid January day after giving us our assignments. There was no doubt in my mind what the conversation was going to be about. I'd sat through too many of them already. Before I went in, I pulled out my iPhone, hit record on the voice messaging app, and tucked it inside my jacket pocket.

Lieutenant Wei Long had jet-black hair, an athletic build, and spoke in Chinese-accented English. Most of the time his face fell into a serious expression, as though he were concentrating deeply on something. His uniform was always squared away and he carried a more stoic, professional air than the high-school-with-guns-type cops. He was new to the command, not yet there a month, so this was my first real one-on-one conversation with him. In the empty juvenile room he stood up against a desk.

"What's up?" I asked.

"The CO talked to me. He asked me about you. When you look at the activity for the past two months compared to your own peers, you're a little bit low."

"Is it something—"

"I don't want you to be on monitoring. When you get promoted, you go see the board, the whole nine yards," he said, then he caught himself. "You might not even get promoted."

"Okay."

"I don't want to do that. I don't want to give anybody low ratings. I want to give everybody at least three point five, but I told these guys you have to help me out. I can tell them, 'You know, he's a good guy, he did this, he did that.' But, you know—the department is all about the numbers."

I saw my opening. "In all honesty, I go out there and I do my job," I said. "You see me, I'm always on post, always visible; I always do what I have to do. The only difference between me and my peers is I don't hide. That's the reality, that's the difference. They hide so the infraction can be committed in the first place by the absence of their presence. I don't do that; I do the job the way it's supposed to be done. I'm there, I'm visible to the public, and if something occurs, as my activity proves, you know I do something."

Cops are measured in twenty-eight-day cycles, so those who operate based on numbers will always look good in each cycle. But crime doesn't operate on that cycle. Some months are higher than others, I tried to explain, because that's reality. The fluctuations are reality. Show me someone who always has exactly the same numbers and I'll show you someone manipulating that system.

"You gotta understand," Long said, "they don't know you," referring to the commanding officers at Transit District 32 and the higher Transit chiefs.

"I'm out there," I said. "I'm always there."

"I know you're always there. I see you. But when it comes to activity, you know the deal."

"It's people's lives we're dealing with," I tried to explain to Long. "The whole numbers thing, you know—"

"But that's how they rate."

"If you want me to go hide in a room just for the sake of a number, that's a shame. I would tell the cap, I'll tell the inspector himself, I'll tell [Transit] Chief Fox—if anyone asks me, I'll tell them the same thing. The difference is, I'm not hiding just for the sake of the infraction. You're gaining pennies by getting the infraction but you're losing dollars because that's less presence."

"All you have to do is you have to look harder then . . . ," he said, a little exasperated.

We went in a circle like this for thirty minutes. He kept telling me to "look harder," and I'd explain that looking hard had nothing to do with it. It's a question of how you're working, or even what's considered working. What are cops even for? Are we there to prevent crime and stop it when we see it? Or are we there to rack up numbers so that the people above us can look at a spreadsheet and see that we're "working"?

Long was new to Transit, so he didn't seem to understand that my numbers were low compared to my peers because *they* were solely focused on producing those numbers. Does anyone think cops would be hiding in storage rooms to catch turnstile jumpers if they weren't forced to meet a quota? It's absurd.

You're not supposed to disagree or debate with a superior; it's considered "boss fighting." I was presenting it logically, not emotionally or discourteously. Additionally, as a Black man I have to be careful never to show my anger. That's always on my mind.

I felt sorry for Long. He didn't even know his own argument. This was the job, so this is what he did and instructed others to do. Forget about actual public safety. Forget about collateral damage to the community and relations with the neighborhood. Give the bosses their numbers.

Long kept referring to a faceless "they"—a term most supervisors used. It was a way to make the department seem like this large, amorphous thing, not made up of people. Commanding officers could take responsibility off themselves, which contributed to the problem. No one was willing to rationalize or defend the system on its merits.

WHEN IT WAS OVER, I took out my iPhone, pressed stop, and went out on patrol. I didn't know what the recording was for, if they'd come for me like Gentry warned; I just knew that I had to protect myself. I didn't want to be in a Schoolcraft situation without anything backing me up.

Around that time, in early 2014, Sergeant Stapleton, who had warned me that he wouldn't always be able to protect me, moved on. After repeatedly refusing to lower my evaluations, he was eventually sent to midnights in retaliation. Soon after, he got out of the command entirely, but not before giving a warning to his successor, Sergeant Campbell: "Leave the Raymond thing alone."

Sergeant Campbell was a dark-skinned man from Trinidad and Tobago with a subtle Caribbean accent. Heavyset with a round face and puffy cheeks, he came from the Sixty-Ninth in Canarsie, Brooklyn, a middle-class West Indian community. He had just been promoted to sergeant, which meant he was on one year of probation, closely watched. But I was excited when we first met; he seemed cool, down-to-earth, and easygoing. We had people in common and had a few positive interactions.

Campbell embodied a change in the culture. When I started out, my bosses were mostly like Ruiz, "don't talk to me, rookie" types. The rumor was that leadership-training courses—BMOC*—used to beat any kindnesses out of the supervisors, but things were changing.

The new batch of bosses getting promoted were different. Campbell was a Black Caribbean man who understood the larger plight of his brothers and sisters, treated us with respect, and took time to greet us with a handshake or pound.

In March, about a month after Campbell arrived, he pulled me aside for a private meeting. I again secretly pressed the record button.

"I guess they already got their stuff about you from before in the past," he said. "I don't know what that issue is, all right? This dude"—Lieutenant Long—"is telling me that based on your activity, the CO† may have something out for you, I don't know. I haven't spoken to him about it. This is from what I'm hearing from other people. I don't usually listen to what people say, but my lieutenant says, 'Listen, if Raymond doesn't X, Y, Z based on his activity, she is gonna put him on performance-monitoring evaluation.'"

"Okay."

"Now here's the problem with that: usually if you get performance monitoring, nobody gives a shit because, you know, you're not losing your job. But when it comes to getting promoted it's a different story. And if you have to ever go before the board‡ for anything, performance monitoring is not one of the things you want to go for. 'Cause if you go for that, they treat that worse than like if you get collared. There's people who got collared on this job who get promoted." It's true, there were officers who got promoted after getting arrested, whom the chiefs didn't treat as harshly as those not hitting quotas.

Campbell sprinkled "I don't knows" throughout the conversation, a

---

* Basic Management Operations Course.
† Commanding officer.
‡ CARB: Career Advancement Review Board. Officers who pass their promotions test but are red-flagged for various reasons have to meet with a panel of three-star chiefs who determine their fate.

way to distance himself from the message. I got the impression he might be an ally who wasn't going to lie down just because superiors were out to get me.

"You don't want to go before chiefs," he said. Campbell proceeded to tell me a story about an officer going before the board whose numbers were down. When he was pushed on why, the cop said his wife was dying of cancer.

Chief Fox had told him, "You have to be able to put aside those things and when you come to work, you gotta be able to separate them."

Apparently, the guy lost it, telling them, "Let me see your fucking wife almost die from cancer and then you come back and tell me what fucking performance . . ." He was passed over *twenty-eight times* before he got his promotion.

I listened to the story, unsurprised, and repositioned the focus back to me. "I don't bother anyone; I do my job. I respect my community; I do what I gotta do."

THAT SUMMER, we got a new platoon commander, Lieutenant Hayden. She was a young and attractive Black woman who had risen through the ranks quickly. Hayden made a real effort to try to raise morale among us, which is no small thing: celebrating birthdays, buying meals for everyone at the end of the month. Like Campbell, she represented something of a new breed, especially compared to my early supervisors. Inevitably, she made a beeline for me. Clearly every supervising officer sent to the 32 was told to deal with me, in one way or another.

One day after meal, she caught me inside the command near the main desk, walking down the corridor that led to the back offices.

"Hey, let's take a walk," she said. "How's everything? Is everything okay lately?"

"Nah, everything's fine," I said. "I miss my dad now and then." My father had been gone two and a half years by that point, but his absence was still a giant hole.

"Listen," she said, lowering her voice. "I didn't like cops growing up. I mean, cops used to lock up my dad."

"Yeah?" I didn't want to correct her; she was trying to connect with me, but she was oversimplifying everything: I wasn't against cops at all. She was trying to show empathy, but she had me wrong. I never hated cops as a whole. It's just I saw firsthand that so much of what they did was trash.

"I'm good out there," I said. "It's just Transit—the numbers game is much more egregious than topside."

"Listen, when I came out of the academy I was put in Transit and I purposely got out of it for that same exact reason. Honestly, I thought about leaving this job because of it but then I passed the sergeant test and figured, hey, I guess I'll stick around for a bit."

"As minority members of the service, shouldn't we push to do things differently?"

"Of course," she said. "When you're out there, you treat the community with respect."

"What's respectful about locking a whole bunch of people up for two dollars while people a few miles away are left alone for the same thing?"

She just stared right at me. "You know what, then you should be an activist or politician. The department isn't the place to have this fight."

Hayden was pushing numbers not because of any ingrained belief in broken windows, but because it was her job as lieutenant to do so. No one was questioning the larger purpose. What are we doing out there? What should we be doing? What effects are our actions having on the community? On crime? On one another? On the city?

The system was running on autopilot because of outdated practices, paramilitary obedience, and racially based policing. And even though so many cops seemed to feel there was something wrong, no one would do anything about it.

AT THE SAME TIME my promotion was being threatened for low activity, the department itself was acting like it had turned a corner. Twenty years after his first term in 1994, Bill Bratton was back as police commissioner and sounding very different. He was saying publicly that the NYPD's new focus would be on the quality (not quantity) of arrests and developing positive community relationships, in addition to public safety.

The new mayor, Bill de Blasio, a self-proclaimed progressive, had a lot to do with the change. At first, de Blasio's selection of Bratton, the father of broken windows, seemed strange. I was skeptical but hopeful, immediately buying and reading Bratton's two books to get a deeper understanding of who he was. It was clear he had changed over time, but I still wasn't convinced that he had the will to do what was needed.

As part of this new direction, Commissioner Bratton started a program called Reengineering 2014* in order to make changes from within. It was a series of presentations, discussions, workshops, think tanks, and research over the course of a year. The program included mandatory training that select officers helped design. The idea was to diagnose issues in the department by reaching down to the lower ranks, to solicit and listen to any ideas of how things could be improved. (It was very different from the previous commissioner, Ray Kelly, who believed only in the top-down approach.)

From his time in corporate America, Bratton saw that changes that include input from all ranks could be more effective. It was a revolutionary idea to bring to a paramilitary organization, and I commend him for

---

* This was a follow-up on a program he did twenty years earlier, called Reengineering.

even trying it. Bratton seemed to understand a universal truth: the people closest to the issue are the ones at the bottom. They are on the front lines so they are going to observe and process things differently than the bosses.

A captain whom I'd taken as a mentor, Oliver Pu-Folkes, selected me to be part of his team. I was one of the only rank-and-file officers invited to contribute to developing the program. It begged the question: If I was such a bad seed, why were they asking my opinion on how to change things?

In recent years, I'd vent to people on the job whom I trusted. Captain Oliver Pu-Folkes was a Black captain, something of a unicorn at the time, whom I was introduced to through a friend. On my day off, decked in business attire, I took the train to meet him in Manhattan. Caramel-skinned and youthful looking with a shaved head, Oliver was from East New York but reminded me a little of Barack Obama, not so much in appearance but in manner. He was also a lawyer and an impressive speaker, with a wide vocabulary and Harvard-level elocution.

Sitting down with Oliver was a revelation. I hadn't yet found anyone that high up who really understood what I was talking about. I just assumed the executives were all compromised because they needed to hit their numbers for their promotions. (After captain, there's no test for promotions. It's all up to the chiefs' discretion.) The last thing I thought I'd see was someone who benefited from those numbers agreeing that the numbers were a problem. Oliver and I had a candid conversation about the high barriers to change, the implicit bias not just in the officers but in the policy itself. He talked about how by using the term "high-crime area" to justify blanket policing, you end up with racially disparate results despite the overwhelming majority of innocent people.

"Look, Edwin," he said, leaning forward from behind his desk. We were in his office at the Nineteenth Precinct, the walls decorated with his many accolades. "This is all they know. It's going to take a lot of effort to get them to see things differently."

"Believe me, I see it every day."

"But I think you're the one to do it," he said. "And I hope you'll rise in the ranks."

Oliver was a forward thinker, a visionary, someone willing to challenge what *is* in anticipation of what *can be*. Every time we spoke from that point forward, I always grabbed a pen and pad to write down his gems. I didn't have any role models on the force, people I truly recognized myself in. He was the first. It wasn't just that he existed and provided that solidarity, but it was the fact that I could see myself in that role. *We can't be what we can't see.*

I had been told so many times, *Maybe this job isn't for you.* But I always thought, *No. It's exactly for me.* Who better to police East Flatbush? Oliver represented a better future of what police executives could be.

With Oliver's encouragement, I sent him a detailed letter to be passed along to the chief of Transit that outlined my concerns about racially motivated quotas and how the messaging from Bratton was not matching what we were seeing at the ground level. I essentially wrote the letter to test the contradiction. If the new direction was sincere, then the letter would be embraced. If nothing happened, then I'd know for sure it was all public relations.

For Reengineering 2014, the entire platoon went back to the academy for three days of training together. One of the other platoons went first, and a friend of mine came back from it in shock. "Raymond, you won't believe what they're saying in there."

"What?"

"Man, it's literally as if this training is saying 'Be like Raymond.'"

What? I'd been in philosophical conflict with the department from day one, so I was curious. I was still hearing from my superiors that my numbers were low and being told that my promotion might be in jeopardy. It was like whiplash.

The training took place in a huge room in the new academy building in Queens, which was like a modern college building, sleek metal and tall windows filled with light. Throughout the presentation, everyone was craning their head looking for me. All the slides were things I'd been saying for years:

Officers should use the **least coercive** means to correct the condition, whenever possible

The goal is **Correcting** the condition

Arrests and summonses are **NOT** the goal—they are more coercive methods

Quality over quantity of arrests

Everyone was shocked. There was no press there, no public. They were telling *us* these things.

Supervisors were cringing because they couldn't believe it was real. Their view, which they shared openly, was, *They're telling us not to do our jobs.* They'd been brainwashed into thinking the numbers were the job itself.

AT THE SAME TIME we were being introduced to this new kind of policing, I was also seeing evidence of the old way everywhere I turned. On patrol one Saturday afternoon at the Atlantic Avenue–Barclays Center stop in downtown Brooklyn, I saw some young shirtless Black teens sprinting past me, followed three seconds later by three plainclothes officers chasing them. I joined the pursuit, as a cop does, not knowing what was happening.

The kids made it up the steps and blended into the street crowd, out of sight. I caught up to the plainclothes cops, who were huffing and puffing, hands on knees.

"What's going on?" I asked.

"We were . . . trying to collar . . . and they ran on us," one of them said.

"Robbery?

"Nah."

"What?" I asked.

"They were dancing," he said.

I did a double take. "Wait, what?"

Kids. Dancing on the subway.

One of the new initiatives making its way through Transit from the top was for us to come down hard on the street performers dancing on the subway, often known as "showtime" kids because that's what they yell at the start of their performances. These kids could've made a lot of destructive choices, but they chose the arts. It's not Juilliard, but those kinds of places are rarely accessible to these kids. They have their bodies, their music, and public spaces. Not to mention the showtime kids were catnip to the tourists, which was one of the major forces behind the drive to lower crime. It was more broken-windows nonsense. These kids could be selling drugs, doing robberies, but we're supposed to arrest them for dancing?

I don't know a better example of counterproductive policing than criminalizing the arts, hurting the communities in the name of keeping them safe. You couldn't come up with one if you tried. Meanwhile, at press conferences and in the papers, you'd think policing in New York City was going through an overhaul. But at roll call, it was the same as always. In fact, there was a marked increase in arrests for panhandling, open container, and other "quality-of-life" offenses.*

---

* Halfway through 2014, arrests of subway and street performers more than quadrupled. (Matt Flegenheimer and J. David Goodman, "On Subway, Flying Feet Can Lead to Handcuffs," *New York Times,* July 28, 2014.)

Broken windows was ingrained in the system so deep it didn't even have to adhere to logic. At roll call, a captain once explained that broken-windows arrests lower violent subway crime because they all warn one another. His logic was, "Perps at Central Booking talk to each other and when they ask, 'What you get locked up for?' and they hear for walking through the train, outstretched, littering . . . they say to themselves, 'Damn, they don't play in District Thirty-Two. Let me not try to rob anybody there.'"

They came up with these stories to justify zero tolerance for minor offenses. It was delusional.

AT THE TIME—mid-2014—I was still getting 3.0 evaluations, which were right on the line. It couldn't hurt my career but it definitely wouldn't help, especially with promotions coming down the pike. Then the sergeant's list came out, the rankings of who passed the test. I was number eight.

Eight out of 932 passes. Eight out of around six thousand test takers.

But a good test score alone wasn't enough. Soon after the list was posted, Sergeant Campbell called me in to meet with him. Before I went in, I pressed record on my iPhone app. Campbell opened the conversation by guessing that the first class of sergeants would be promoted that December.

"Okay," I said, "so they want to watch to see if I get more arrests and summonses? Or they already have their mind made up and they want you to put me on performance monitoring."

"Based on your monthly performance according to—you know, the guidelines, coming from the CO*—because there's no numbers, you

* At the time, the commanding officer was Captain Maldonado, a Puerto Rican woman who had bought fully into the numbers game. She didn't interact with me much and chose to deal with me through subordinate supervisors. She wanted my evaluations to be lowered from the moment she arrived in 2014, and Lieutenant Hayden and Sergeant Campbell initially had protected me.

know, there's no nothing, there's no quotas, supposedly, nothing like that." This was a dizzying sentence but typical of the coded ways superiors talked. "She's saying you go to work eight hours thirty-five minutes a day and you come back eight hours thirty-five minutes a day, what did you show for you being out there eight hours thirty-five minutes a day?"

"Okay."

"She said, 'It's not just standing out there in presence looking pretty.'"

"No, understood," I said. "But if something does occur in my presence, I take action. But the thing is, I'm not gonna take myself out of sight just so something can happen. And, in a nutshell, that's what the difference between me and pretty much everyone else is."

"That's already established, that's what was explained, you know—"

"It's already made up that they want me to be put on performance monitoring," I said, "due to not arresting and getting a certain amount of summonses that they want." I explicitly wanted this on the record, punching through all the "they" and "I don't knows" and circular talk. Performance monitoring was not supposed to be about low activity, though it often was.

"Right," he said, "due to whatever your enforcement is, that's what it is. She said based on your enforcement, your monthly performance." Campbell took a beat and switched to a friendly tone. He explained how he had tried to defend me, that my philosophy of law enforcement was different. The CO wouldn't hear it. "She said, 'This is a law-enforcement job. We enforce the law; you know . . .'"

"If I was such a problem officer, why in all the thirty-five thousand officers why would I be chosen for [Reengineering]? Obviously, someone sees that I have good insight. I don't want to get you in trouble and I'm not trying to make a point or anything, I just go out there and I police. I don't go out there and hide . . ."

"Here's the thing," he said. "When you're getting promoted, the number-one person that you should have on your side is your CO, because she holds the power . . . This job is a big beast, a very big beast. In order to do those things, you gotta get yourself in those positions, and sometimes you just gotta say, 'All right, whatever, I see what it is.'"

"Yeah, this is stressful," I said. "It's unfortunate. I know I'm doing nothing wrong, this is crazy, but I know this is just the way the job is, unfortunately."

"And just remember your commanding officer has the power to say based on the way you carry yourself, based on the way you do your job, you are not cut out to be supervisor material. She can do that. That's her opinion, but they will take her opinion . . . Just know, whatever you do has actions, and I'm not in agreement with some of those things, but I also have to follow instructions."

It was the same pass-the-buck stuff I got from Lieutenant Long and others. No one wanted to defend the way things were done, but no one had any interest in questioning it either. It was stagnation and narrow thinking taken to an absurd level. The recordings were not just about protecting myself. They were about exposing the whole broken system.

I never recorded conversations with another officer at my level, neither in the locker rooms nor at my post. Regardless of how my peers treated and ostracized me, they weren't at fault because they were operating within a system. They were victims of a paramilitary, top-down culture. I've watched people who need assistance or even medical attention get ignored because stopping for them is not going to help a cop reach his quota. Whose fault is that? Just the cop's? Or the system that made that cop and signs his check?

The numbers game was everywhere. That's why I call it a cancer. It's not just a metaphor. It spreads and kills in the same manner.

Seventeen

The Unheard

A riot is the language of the unheard.

—DR. MARTIN LUTHER KING JR.

July 2014

The word "quota" may have an innocuous, bureaucratic ring to it, but it's the catalyst. The individual cop's quota is the foundation of profiling, harassment, community mistrust, violence, and, ultimately, death. A New York City plainclothes officer's quota is high: four felonies a month. A cop, even out of uniform, will not just naturally witness a felony a week. I don't care what neighborhood they are patrolling; they will have to agitate to get those numbers consistently. It's why, on a hot day in Staten Island in the summer of 2014, Eric Garner was choked to death for selling loose cigarettes.

Selling untaxed cigarettes can actually be a felony; that's why the cops got so rough with him. It's why these types of nuisance crimes are policed so aggressively and why discretion is rarely used. Those cops can't afford to toss out that number; their jobs, salaries, and promotions depend on it. If a commanding officer tells them to get four felony arrests in a month, they're going to start behaving like cowboys.

I had friends from the academy who were in Housing and Patrol, and we compared our experiences across the three bureaus. One thing I learned was that plainclothes units topside (what I knew as "the Dees" growing up) were like a cult. They felt they were better than everyone else and saw themselves as the "real" cops doing the "real" work. In their eyes, regular patrol cops were simply enlightened social workers. There were regulations about uniformed officers having beards that don't apply to plainclothes, so they purposely grew them as a signal, a clear indication that they were part of this elite unit. One officer I knew who had left the precinct's Anti-Crime Unit told me that the sergeant instructed them, "Don't talk to anyone else." That separation from others feeds into the cowboy mentality, though it is also about self-protection, because there are likely things they've seen and done that they are going to take to their graves.

Those units look for felonies, but really they're pressured to find one thing: guns. And every piece of the "gray area" they can exist in, any way they can manipulate the rules, they'll do it. The upper echelon incentivizes this behavior with rewards and praise; that's the way into the Detective squad and other coveted units.* So they get what they need by any means necessary. Those of us paying attention have long known what it leads to. And starting in 2014, with the ubiquity of cell phone video cameras, the larger public began to see what the racial-based quotas had been creating, like a monster in a laboratory.

"The order to arrest Eric Garner came from the very top echelons of the department," writes Alex Vitale in *The End of Policing*. "Treating

---

* The Street-Crime Unit, which was the predecessor of Anti-Crime, was the group that killed Amadou Diallo by firing forty-one shots at him in the vestibule of his own building in 1999. As I write this, five plainclothes cops in Memphis, who were part of a similar unit, were charged with murder in the killing of Tyre Nichols during a traffic stop.

this as a crime requiring the deployment of a special plainclothes unit, two sergeants, and uniformed backup seems excessive and pointless . . . No amount of procedural training will solve this fundamental flaw in public policy."[1]

Eric Garner was far from the first, but the video of him being choked to death by Officer Daniel Pantaleo generated a response reminiscent of the Rodney King video twenty-three years earlier. Would there be justice at the end of it? No one who'd been following such things had reason to be hopeful.

A couple of weeks after Garner's death, Officer Darren Wilson shot and killed an unarmed eighteen-year-old Black teen named Michael Brown in Ferguson, Missouri, leaving his lifeless body there in the hot street for hours. Though the incident was grayer than the Garner one, the community responded in force to what they saw as another example of police oppression. Ferguson was a suburb of St. Louis where the Black population had been living as second-class citizens, at the mercy of a police force intentionally raising revenue off their bodies by way of aggressive enforcement and high court fines. It was a localized, highly concentrated version of what was happening in New York City.

Brown's death set off an explosive uprising in the streets of Ferguson, media flooded in from all over the country, and the BLM movement was born.* Eric Garner's final words—"I can't breathe"—became a battle cry. Footage of the last moments of Garner's life and the images of Ferguson on fire spread throughout the world, triggering statements from leaders up to and including President Obama. Although witness accounts from Mike Brown's killing varied, what was not in dispute was the overaggressive policing that residents of Ferguson had suffered for years. Overall, these incidents were seen as yet another example proving this nation didn't value Black lives.

---

* The hashtag #BlackLivesMatter began trending after George Zimmerman, who murdered Trayvon Martin in 2012, was acquitted. But it was the Brown and Garner killings and the ensuing protests that catalyzed the BLM movement.

I remember watching the protests on TV that summer—officers in helmets with batons hitting unarmed protesters and cars on fire and smoke rising like in a war zone, anger on Black faces and tears in Black eyes. The reaction was much bigger than the incident that sparked it. Years of frustration released in the streets. I understood where they were coming from—the language of the unheard. When you feel you have no other voice, no other outlet, you do what will get attention.

And it got people's attention.

DAYS AFTER Mike Brown's death, as the streets of Ferguson erupted, I was sitting in a brightly lit classroom on the West Side of Manhattan, a muggy summer day beyond the tall windows. At John Jay College of Criminal Justice, I was participating in the school's NYPD Leadership Program, which police officers were given the opportunity to attend for free. Each semester, hundreds of cops took at least one of four courses that the faculty believed would have a positive impact on law enforcement's ideology and perspective.

I was surprised to be introduced to something so progressive and open-minded with the encouragement of the department. The professors weren't afraid to go to places that the mainstream, especially cops, were not willing to talk about. Those courses went right past the illusion, ripped up the revisionist history, and dug into the hard reality. They taught about the origins of the police in America in the slave patrol. They lectured on the ubiquity of implicit bias, which doesn't look like outright bigotry and can be far more dangerous since it's built into the foundation, merged into mindsets, and regurgitated as policy. I was one of only four Black people in my class, so I was learning these things in a room of mostly white, mostly conservative, and very uncomfortable cops.

One time, during a class discussion on illegal stop and frisk, a white cop classmate had an outburst. "You know what? I have to say something.

I know a lot of people feel how I feel, but they're just trying to sit through the class. I can't take this anymore," he said. "You show me any neighborhood where a cop can stop and frisk and search anyone, and I'll move there tomorrow! Why would I be against cops wanting to keep me and my family safe? That's what's wrong with this country!"

"You know what?" I said, interrupting him. "It's easy for you to say that, when you're not the one who has to go through this. You might feel like you're making logical sense, but we have a recent example showing that when white folks start getting treated like this, they don't like it."

The professor jumped in, "Where's Raymond going with this?" Everyone just looked at me.

"TSA PreCheck," I said. "After September eleventh, for the first time since the turn of the century, white folks were treated with as much suspicion as anyone else, and they hated it! It is only when white people are forced to give up personal rights that people start calling it a 'police state.' So what did they do? They created TSA PreCheck to circumvent being treated like everyone else. You pay money to get you in a club of people that go through metal detectors without extra levels of security."

As we debated in class, I shared personal anecdotes from my time randomly checking bags in Transit, where no one gave us more pushback than white women. "Do I look like a fucking terrorist?" they'd complain to us. Or they'd turn away from me and say, "I'm not letting you search my bag." I'd calmly say they didn't have to let me, but then they couldn't enter. The idea that anyone would want to live in a place without the Fourth Amendment protection of rightful search and seizure was nonsense, and I called him out on it.

Professor Bornstein's anthropology class, Policing in a Multiracial and Multicultural City, was especially eye-opening in the sense that it gave me names and terminology to what I'd been witnessing, such as:

Reasonable Racism (a.k.a. Rational Discrimination): The notion that because a particular racial group is overrepresented in a particular crime category, it's common sense to treat the *entire group* as suspicious. This was the basis of many of the NYPD's policies. A prominent example of this was when former mayor Mike Bloomberg saw nothing wrong with 88 percent of the stop and frisks being of citizens of color[2] because shooters were 92 percent Black or Brown.[3]

Rudimentary parts of our minds can oversimplify things that are actually quite complex. There are times when snap judgments have to be made with limited information, and what we see has a larger bearing on our thoughts than what actual statistics show. The discussions in Bornstein's class revealed that many white perspectives on Blacks and Latinos were almost entirely secondhand. This ignorance is what's at the base of implicit bias and the so-called reasonable racism it produces.

Noble-Cause Corruption: Situations where, in order to enforce the law, unlawful "shortcuts" are taken and "gray areas" are exploited. It's a version of "the ends justify the means," even if the means are illegal. An example: in the name of getting guns off the street, cars are pulled over and illegally searched.

Procedural Justice: When members of the public are fine with their negative police interaction because they felt they were treated properly and fairly.

The implicit bias exercises blew my mind, exposing what I had sensed in my gut and witnessed from other cops. For instance, one day our professor gave the students a survey:

Of the entire Black and Brown population in New York City, what percentage are murderers?

A. 50 percent
B. 25 percent
C. 10–15 percent
D. Less than 1 percent

This seemed easy, and I confidently chose D. Afterward, on a projection screen, the professor showed a bar graph of our answers. Shockingly, 7 percent of the class picked A (50 percent), which meant two police officers in that classroom thought *half* of all citizens of color were murderers. I tried to just shake that off—it was too baffling even to process— but what was less dismissible was that most of the class picked B or C. As the professor knew, this was exactly part of the problem. Cops thought one out of every four Black and Brown people in the city was a violent criminal? A million New Yorkers? It's not hard to imagine the kind of policing produced from such a mind.

It felt like I was back at the academy, getting a look inside these white minds. I started to see the cycle, how these cops would one day be in charge. How the institution's policies and practices operated from this faulty foundation. That's how you get broken-windows overpolicing. That's how you end up implementing and protecting a system that harasses minorities for the kind of small things that white people do with impunity.

I've talked to colleagues who admit that Black communities are policed stronger than others. When I push them further on why, they'll blame Black people—as a group. "In my neighborhood," they'll say, "we can enjoy a beer outside on the stoop. Maybe if the people in their neighborhood could stop people from shooting one another, they could too."

"Wait a minute," I'll say, "you want the law-abiding community, ninety-nine percent working folks, to tell those who engage in violence to clean up their act? Does the Italian community tell the Mafia to cut it out? Are white people responsible for those who share their skin color?"

Usually, they don't have much to say to that. Their logic holds no water.

You don't need racist cops to run a racist system—officers will do what they're told—but it certainly makes it run more smoothly. There are plenty of bigoted, small-minded people who join the police force and the job just frees them, allows them to be who they are. If you are motivated by prejudice and assigned to Harlem or the South Bronx, and you're aggressively getting numbers, you're hailed as a hard worker. If you believe that Black people are the problem, then treating them this way seems natural and just. *Shake the tree and something will fall out because that's how Black people are.* If you already think a group of Black teenagers walking down the street are causing trouble, it's easy to rationalize putting them in a cage. Not only are cops not corrected for this thinking, they're *rewarded* for it.

At John Jay, we learned about critical race theory (CRT), the study of race as a social construct, and how history, institutions, and systems operated out of rooted, systemic bias. CRT—which has been unfairly demonized by much of the Right—is a forty-year-old academic discipline that tries to understand and explain the lasting effects of yesterday's legal, political, and cultural landscapes on today's racial inequalities. *How racism is baked in.* The objective of CRT is to explicate these issues so we can take proper corrective action to eliminate the lingering inequality.*

"C'mon," a white colleague said on meal break. "You've never been a slave. No one *alive* has even been a slave or slave owner."

"Sure, outright slavery was abolished," I said, "but it was followed almost immediately by decades of systemic discrimination. People of African descent weren't then accepted into the American family with open arms. All sorts of official and de facto things were put in place to keep the group as second-class citizens."

"Yeah," another said, "but at what point are you guys going to get over it? It's not like it's the nineteen-sixties."

"You think most white people in the nineteen-sixties understood

---

* As a parallel, any study of Christopher Columbus and the European slaughter of Native Americans *without* understanding that the whites saw them as "savages" and "less than human" would be incomplete. The story literally doesn't make sense otherwise. CRT just looks to give a fuller picture on how things actually unfolded.

that things needed to change? If they did, we wouldn't have needed a civil rights movement!"

Just about everyone reveres Dr. King in hindsight, but when he was alive, he was detested by a large segment of Americans.[4] People today have the audacity to reference Dr. King as an example of what's wrong with the BLM protests, but did their grandparents support Dr. King? If Dr. King had been openly embraced, we wouldn't have needed a Dr. King!

The present never sees itself on the continuum of history. Everyone thinks they're living the endgame. We need to have the foresight to see that we're living some future history and get people to understand how they're currently suppressing progress.

John Jay was like a second wave of my education, the next phase after encountering Malcolm and African history in my early twenties, digging into all those books Bishme recommended on our lunch break at YAI. It was what was missing from the academy. I wanted to understand the causes of the system in order to develop a way to change it.

Even though the John Jay classes were free, as were plenty of other educational opportunities, very few people in the department valued them. There is little respect for academia in the police department. Higher learning is viewed as a bastion of liberal ideology spewed by people who don't even have the guts to put on the uniform but are comfortable criticizing from the safety that the police provide.

One time in the locker room, I was sitting next to a Mexican American officer known to aggressively meet the quota; he had recently been caught in a viral video arresting someone in a train station. I was reading my school notes and he asked, "Are you in school?"

"Yeah, I'm at John Jay, working to get an international criminal justice degree."

"Oh, that's the degree I got." He had recently graduated. I didn't say anything then but was perplexed. Stunned, even.

After I got to know him, I approached him and asked, "Can I ask you a personal question, no disrespect?"

"Sure. What's up, Ray?"

"If you already have this degree, thus this education, why do you police the way you do?"

He shrugged. "Because I'm trying to get into the Detective squad."

Even those officers who did take classes viewed them as a formality to meet requirements for certain promotions. They didn't bring what they learned back to the department.*

I did, and over time, I would get slammed for it.

EVER SINCE SERGEANT Stapleton was reassigned for not giving me low evaluations, my career felt at risk. And every conversation with every superior felt like a tightening of the screws. On Thanksgiving, right after roll call, Sergeant Campbell pulled me aside again to talk. The holidays were always rough for me—I missed my dad—so I was already irritated.

"What's it now, man?"

"The CO," Campbell said. "It's always something. The CO told Lieutenant Hayden that it's only one post you're getting now: David Twenty-Two. That's where she wants you."

David Twenty-Two was code for the Barclays Center, the new basketball arena in downtown Brooklyn. "David" stood for "dual"— meaning there always had to be two officers there. Twenty-Two was the location: Atlantic Avenue–Barclays Center. It was the most demanding station in the command—probably in all of Brooklyn: ten subway lines plus the Long Island Rail Road covering several city blocks. Because of this, David Twenty-Two was often used as a retaliatory post.

---

* There were, of course, exceptions. At the end of the semester, a white officer spoke movingly about how he'd grown up in a house of racist views and how his eyes had been opened to the way historical oppression still affected communities of color.

While I recorded him in my jacket pocket, Campbell—in his round-about way—was telling me the CO, Captain Maldonado, wanted him to do an interim evaluation on me. Evaluations were given quarterly and yearly, but supervisors had discretion to add an interim evaluation. Technically it could be mitigating (positive) or aggravating (negative), but it was only ever used for COs to get a paper trail on you, a way to build a case to get you on performance monitoring and, ultimately, out of the department. The CO told Campbell to make sure the total score of my eval was below 3.0. His issue was that he wouldn't rate me below 3.0 for the individual categories, so the final score wouldn't make sense. She didn't care.

"It's weird!" he said. "I was like, 'So what's the proof and the facts? Because if you use the point system for this—'"

"But what's the purpose of this evaluation?" I asked, even though I knew.

"According to the CO, you're underperforming. According to her." As he told it, the CO kept pushing him to put down negative reasons for my evaluation, but he refused. "And then even with those three things that she picked that was negative," he said, "I wrote a positive. She sat in there and she changed the whole shit, kid, she changed the three whatever it was . . . You know, for the most part she said, 'He has great ideas, he has great communication skills . . .'"

"But why are they trying to do something to me, that's the thing. I do my job quite well. It's just—"

"Unfortunately, we're still puppets, we're still puppets right now. No one is individual: we still push buttons with strings on us."

"You know what it is?" I asked. "It's old habits die hard, and despite the direction the department is moving, I'm always gonna stick out like the problem . . . But I understand for twelve years that's how this department has operated under the previous administration: numbers, numbers, numbers. But if I have to be the poster boy for it to change, I'm more than willing to be that poster boy."

It was beyond frustrating; I'd explained this multiple times to Campbell that year, and he understood. But he wasn't the one calling the shots.

"David Twenty-Two is very busy, it's the limelight . . . ," Campbell said.

"I have no problem with that," I said. And I didn't. It tells you a lot about the culture of the job that the busy posts are considered punishment. I had no issue with actually *going to work*. And David Twenty-Two was about to become one of the hot spots in the country, ground zero for the burgeoning conflict in the police-citizen divide.

A WEEK BEFORE this conversation with Campbell, a young unarmed Black man named Akai Gurley was shot and killed by a cop in a stairwell in East New York, Brooklyn. Mayor de Blasio simply called it a "tragedy," refusing to single out the cop who killed Gurley for no reason whatsoever.

On the heels of the Gurley shooting, and the police killing two days later of twelve-year-old Tamir Rice, who was playing alone with a toy gun in a Cleveland park, came the decision out of Ferguson not to indict Mike Brown's killer. Between those three events, New York City was simmering to a boil. I could feel it back home in the neighborhood—there was tension in the air akin to the days of Abner Louima and Amadou Diallo, with an extra seventeen years of pain and anger piled on top. At work, the cops were tighter, edgier, feeling like maybe something was going to combust.

Then, a week later, the match.

A Staten Island grand jury—assisted by a DA who had aspirations for higher office in a very conservative, pro-police borough where many cops resided—decided not to indict Officer Daniel Pantaleo in Eric Garner's death. New York City exploded. People marched down the West Side Highway and up Sixth Avenue, laid down at Grand Central

Station, got arrested in Times Square, and flooded outside the Barclays Center—David Twenty-Two—in downtown Brooklyn.

It was a strange time to be a conscious Black cop refusing to go along with the system. I understood these people's pain, written on their faces and in the strain in their voices. It was less a cry about an individual cop—there were few protests right after Garner's death—than a broken justice system. It was less about the choking than the impunity. That's what gets the people out in those numbers: a systematic breakdown, not the behavior of a single bad actor.

People forget that the 1992 LA riots were not in response to the video of Rodney King's beating. The city erupted over a year later when a court of law acquitted the four men caught on camera beating King within inches of his life. The outrage was big picture, a collective scream of anger about what cops get away with in the name of law and order and public safety.

The day the news broke about Pantaleo, I heard a call for additional units at one of the Barclays entrances due to the growing crowd. On one side officers stood in formation with hats and bats (helmets and batons) and across the way, a loud and angry crowd of all colors held signs and screamed their frustrations at us.

"Murderers!"

"Pigs!"

"How could you wear that uniform?"

"No justice, no peace!"

I was on the side of the people, but they wouldn't know that just by looking at me. The uniform has a way of hiding and subsuming one's identity. Not only did I support the protesters, I had been fighting from the inside, knowing where these preventable deaths came from. I had seen the pipes, the wiring, the faulty system that left unarmed Black men dead in the streets. I understood why it would continue to happen until crucial steps were taken to ensure otherwise.

Previously, under Mayor Bloomberg, officers were more aggressive to protesters and made arrests almost immediately once the technicalities allowed them to do so. The message under Mayor de Blasio, though, had been to let people vent. Protesters came just inches away from the faces of officers as they offered a piece of their minds. Some officers stood there stoically, while others wore the discomfort on their faces.

The only previous experience I'd had with a spontaneous crowd of this size was the Occupy Wall Street movement in 2011, but this was another level. Occupy had a communal vibe, collective indignation at a faceless finance system, whereas this felt more emotional, more electric. Additionally, this was geared toward *me*, my uniform, my identity. That in itself made it charged; the two sides of the conflict were physically facing each other in the street. Protests against police always retain that extra level of urgency because of this fact.

The BLM protesters took it out on the cops they could see. They were asking for punishment of the cop they knew, Daniel Pantaleo, understandably angry that he was free. But they didn't know the commissioners, the chiefs, the commanders who threatened and incentivized him to *get that number* that left Eric Garner dead. Of course, there should be justice at the bottom of the chain, but there should be consequences high up that chain as well. Any movement overly focused on arresting individual officers is missing the forest for the trees.

As a conscious Black cop, I was straddling both sides. It weighed on me, stressed me out, kept me up at night. I was wearing the uniform, believing in the ideals, but was treated like the enemy. It got to me, hit me where I lived. I don't care who you are: facing that kind of anger and hate from your own people will do a number on you.

FIVE DAYS BEFORE CHRISTMAS, tragedy and horror hit the department. In Bedford-Stuyvesant, two officers, Wenjian Liu and Rafael

Ramos, were gunned down at point-blank range by a mentally disturbed person who claimed it was revenge for Eric Garner and Michael Brown. He had posted on social media: *They Take 1 of Ours . . . Lets Take 2 of Theirs.*

This was unfolding at the start of roll call and I saw real fear in my platoon's eyes as we all followed the aftermath through our radios. It sounded like an ambush; I had visions of the Black Liberation Army in the 1970s calling for cops' heads. Everything came to a halt as we followed the radio calls, with officers chasing the shooter into the Myrtle-Willoughby Avenues subway station, where he took his own life.

The Liu and Ramos murders put cops on a war footing, afraid that people would begin to take matters into their own hands. The collective fear around the precinct was that we were now on the front lines of something that we couldn't control or influence. Cops were being killed because of decisions made far above our pay grade, orders coming from up the chain from men and women in climate-controlled offices inside well-protected buildings. The brass at headquarters would never be the ones in the squad car getting shot. Never.

It was a terrifying moment, both as a cop who was indistinguishable on the street from any other cop, but also as someone who supported the Black Lives Matter movement. I didn't want the movement co-opted by those who thought violence against random cops was the answer. On social media, people were getting whipped into a frenzy, not seeing fathers and husbands eating their lunch in the car, just trying to get through their workday. They viewed it as taking out two enemies in the larger war.

The Liu and Ramos shooting shook me in another way. I couldn't just keep my head down and do things my way; I had to say something, get involved, lay the groundwork to change this thing before more people were killed. I had joined the police to act as a counterbalance or protective force for the oppressed, but in the midst of BLM I saw the other side of the coin: I could also be a messenger for cops themselves. I wasn't just a representative, a voice for the communities. I could be the voice of justice-minded officers who believed cops can do better, must do better. And I could say so while wearing the uniform.

The powers that be had run the police department into the ground, to the point that some people thought it had no legitimacy, that armed insurrection was the answer. There was a growing number of people who wanted to use the universal language: violence. They thought courts, marching, legislation was all a waste of time because people only understand violence. That's just how things operated. It begged a much larger question: Was I willing to die for this thing?

Eighteen

Front Lines

G rowing up, I saw my friend Buffett and his brother from Crown Heights, younger Haitian kids from the neighborhood, as kindred spirits. They were among the very few who regularly showed up to work at Food County, and that job was about survival, not name-brand sneakers. Buffett had come to the States when he was eleven without any money or English, but he carried this unmistakable air of confidence. He smiled and laughed at everyone's jokes, even ones I could tell he didn't follow. But if you looked closely, you could catch a serious demeanor behind his eyes. I saw it, because I had one of those too.

What stood out to me about Buffett was his complete lack of fear; no matter that he was the youngest there, he never shied away from anything. After he stopped working at the supermarket, I'd see him hanging out on the stoops of Crown Street and could tell he had switched to a more lucrative job. Around the time our mutual friend Jigga was killed in gang violence, I heard word that Buffett had been arrested for dealing crack cocaine—a felony—and then deported back to Haiti around 2004. That sometimes happened to guys from the neighborhood: one day you stopped seeing them and then you got word they'd been sent away and you never heard from them again.

Fast-forward to 2009. Five months out of the academy, I was standing on the platform at Grand Army Plaza with my partner when I saw a young man coming into the mezzanine. *Buffett.*

I was surprised, but it was unmistakably him. He was muscular and filled out with a slight mustache, more mature looking than the skinny teenager I remembered. But he had the same energy, same bright eyes. We caught sight of each other from across the station, and I saw his face change. "Dread!" he exclaimed. "Dread! Oh shit!"

I instinctively cringed, tried to hide inside myself. At the time I was still struggling with my new identity as a cop, not exactly advertising it around the old neighborhood. I knew I would eventually develop a way to carry it, but at the time I held it awkwardly, like an extra limb. I was just figuring out myself how someone like me could be police; I wasn't ready to explain it to others yet. Also, the Buffett I knew had been involved in the streets, and I didn't want him to say the wrong thing. I froze like I'd been caught.

As Buffett approached us, I panicked. Taking a step toward him, I gave him a dap while quickly muttering, "Pale Kreyòl. Pale Kreyòl" ("Speak Creole"), hoping to protect myself inside our shared language.

But then Buffett blew my mind. "Dread, that's what's up!" he said, raising his chin. "I respect what you're doing, man. I was considering doing the same thing."

My jaw hit the floor; the last thing I expected from him was admiration for my uniform. Before I could make sense of it, he got on the train and disappeared into the city.

We ran into each other a few more times and I learned his real name, Jim St. Germain, and his story: he had been arrested for dealing drugs off his bicycle when he was fifteen, but he wasn't deported back to Haiti as I'd heard. A few months shy of sixteen (when he could be charged as an adult), he had advocates who secured him a bed in Boys Town, a residential facility that operated as an alternative to juvenile detention. The experience drastically changed his trajectory. He had a family-type support system in there, peers with whom he could learn from and with, and parental figures who got him interested in his education and his future. After discovering *The Autobiography of Malcolm X* in a drawer in that house, he developed a strong sense of purpose. Other books lifted his consciousness and, by the time he was released, Jim was enrolled in college and a new man.

When we reconnected, he was coming into his own, but a side effect of that is you clash with your former self, in the form of the old neighborhood and old friends. He talked about being a loner now because the people he grew up with wouldn't go with him to museums or poetry readings. Just as I had in that supermarket all those years ago, I sensed a kindred spirit.

Jim came by my new condo, in a modern building with a gym, roof decks, carpeted corridors, and floor-to-ceiling glass. "Damn, Dread," he said, looking around. He knew how poor I'd been growing up because he was the same. "You doing all right. I need something like this." I let him borrow my car sometimes when I was working and we started meeting up at the gym to work out together.

Jim had recently gotten a job working at Boys Town, the same place where he had once been incarcerated. This was a beautiful thing to me, a perfect distillation of phase 1 and phase 2: taking care of himself and then rerouting that energy back into the community. He was now working with kids who mirrored his younger self and, over our workout sessions at the gym, we'd share stories about the kids we encountered in our respective jobs.

"I had this one kid who lost his temper," Jim said, "and it reminded me so much of myself. I told him about how I once punched through a glass door. Then he wrote me a note to apologize. I teared up, Dread, for real."

"Jacob, this kid from Guyana," I shared, "was snatching iPhones and I sat down with him, talked about the opportunities of this country, the mission we're on, and how he shouldn't let that go to waste." I told Buffett that a few months prior I had actually run into Jacob in the Franklin Avenue train station. We started talking—he remembered me—and it turned out he was in college. "I'm so proud of you, man," I told him. "Thank you for letting me know I'm not wasting my time." It was a huge moment for me, seeing the results of my efforts, but still, it felt inadequate, too piecemeal. These kids were growing up even faster than we had; by the time they were in our orbit, so many bad habits had hardened into place.

"Damn, I wish we could get to them before, you know," Jim said. "Before they're sentenced."

"Before they even get to a cell," I added.

We wanted to get involved further upstream. Jim was intercepted and changed his trajectory, which inspired him to do the same for others. As for me, that kind of work would let me contribute outside of uniform in a way that wasn't embraced by the blue.

The question became, How do we do that? We needed something larger, official. An organization. Two days later, I had the name: PLOT, Preparing Leaders of Tomorrow.

PLOT would be a mentorship program to give young teenagers in the community (eventually anyone ages nine through twenty-one) a support system and resource hub to embark on a different path. If these young folks got the bigger picture earlier, chances were better that they'd make smarter choices, more forward-thinking decisions. Too many were living in their own condensed reality, where they could barely see into next week. Jim and I would spend two years building the team, organizing, and in 2014, launching PLOT. I was going to make a positive impact in my community, even if it had to be through another outlet. It is an indictment of the entire police department that I couldn't do it through my job.*

Jim and I would meet up in the mornings to work out at New York Sports Club in downtown Brooklyn, a modern facility with multiple levels and large windows that let in swaths of natural light. There was a political edge to our discussions. Jim was getting involved in the Raise the Age campaign in New York, a political effort to get New York to increase the age of criminal responsibility from sixteen to eighteen.† Sometimes we'd get an entire section of the gym fired up about some issue to the point that folks complained we were ruining their workout routines. We'd trade stories from the news, and I'd give Jim the inside scoop on what was actually occurring in the police department, how what the leaders and spokespeople said in public was diametrically opposed to what we were told at roll call.

"I don't know how you do it, Dread," Jim said one day as we loaded free weights onto the bench press.

"What do you mean?" I asked.

"That fucking job, man. All the bullshit you got to deal with. My first day in there I would've exposed all of it: the quotas, the racism, the harassment. I couldn't do it. I couldn't keep my mouth shut. I would've said something."

"I can't just say something. This is my career."

"Yeah, but still . . ."

"C'mon, I can't just blow it all up. You see the life I can live because of this job. I grew up starving too, remember? Why would I want to jeopardize that? I want to rise through the ranks and be an example." I was still

---

* I invited everyone from Commissioner Bratton to Transit Bureau Chief Fox to Captain Maldonado to the launch fundraiser gala and didn't get a single response. That told me a lot about the brass's priorities. I thought back to that Truancy sergeant who told me she'd never bring me on because then "we'll never be able to collar these kids." Instead of seeing me and PLOT as working in tandem with the police, they saw me as wasting time or, worse, going against their mission.
† At the time, New York and North Carolina were the only states where it was that low.

operating from a place of self-preservation. I figured Jim, of all people, would understand that.

"Sure, I get you," Jim said. "Yeah." But I could tell he disagreed.

Caution had always served me well, but those talks with Jim introduced some doubt to my thinking.

By the time the Barclays protests happened in December 2014, Jim's position no longer seemed so out there. More people were going to die needlessly, get jailed needlessly, and have their lives upended and destroyed by people sworn to protect them. The radical way no longer seemed so radical. Then an opportunity to make an impact landed in our laps.

THAT WINTER, while I was finishing up my first semester at John Jay and working the BLM protests at Barclays Center, Jim got an invitation from the White House. The nonindictments of Officers Wilson and Pantaleo, the killing of Akai Gurley, the unprecedented nationwide protests, and the senseless killing of NYPD officers Liu and Ramos all coalesced into a flash point. President Obama formed the Task Force on 21st Century Policing, an effort to address the dangerous divide that had cleaved the police and the communities they were serving. Jim was asked to give testimony, and he forwarded the invitation to me with a short note at the top: "Need your help with this, bro."

Jim would prepare remarks for the panel as well as submit suggestions to the United States Justice Department, ideas that would be passed on to the president himself. He was overwhelmed, though I knew that his experience made him the perfect person for this role. "Don't worry about it, man," I told him. "You also got me. We're going to go above and beyond with this thing."

Jim loved setting up at a particular Starbucks in Park Slope, and we'd meet there to talk about issues to put into his testimony. He had a unique vantage point as someone who had gone through the system in his youth and was now working inside it. He commented on the necessity of police and youth relationships, and how that kind of thing can't simply be mandated. The cop has to actually care in order for that to work.

I worked with him on notes regarding the *systemic* dysfunction of police, how everything is connected back to the pressure and the policy. Far too much attention was given to the individual officer's conduct. We couldn't simply keep coming down hard on the single cop, expecting that would deter the behavior of others. Their behavior is policy dictated *from the top*. No matter how many individual cops got indicted (or not indicted, as the case may be), the institution itself was rotten to th core. When you toss out bad apples, you're not changing a damn thing about how they're grown and nurtured. As long as the process remains, new ones are going to turn out the same way.

"That's perfect, Dread," Jim said, taking down notes.

I then received an official invite to give testimony as well from the audience, the perfect opportunity to join the front lines and take a public stand.

I just had to get the day off work.

I knew they'd deny me the day off out of retaliation and spite. Lieutenant Hayden was on vacation at the time, but the administrative office, led by Lieutenant Reid, actually handled requests for leave. I put in the request slip with my sergeant and he ran it through that office. They're supposed to approve or deny requests based on manpower, and on a Tuesday in mid-January, when few officers would be on vacation, that should not have been an issue. I also asked Lieutenant Reid if he could find someone willing to switch days off with me if needed, and he made it sound like it was no problem.

When Hayden came back from vacation, I excitedly showed her the invite. "Check this out," I said. "An amazing opportunity, right?" Hayden and I had spoken about me getting into politics, and I figured she'd be excited for me.

Instead, her face clouded over. "Well," she said, "you're already on thin ice."

"What do you mean?"

She squinted like she was trying to figure me out. "Raymond, why would I authorize you taking that day off with the way your activity has been?"

"Well, the day off is supposed to be based on manpower."

"Oh," she scoffed. "Well, we're never at proper manpower. We just look out for y'all when y'all request days off. If it was about manpower then no one would get a day off because we're never at proper coverage." She then headed toward the office to speak with Lieutenant Reid.

The admin office sent me back the slip with "denied" written over it in red. I asked Lieutenant Reid if he was able to find anyone willing to switch, and he claimed no one was interested. Thankfully, I already had people lined up, since I was offering a free Saturday. The next day, when I told him someone would switch days with me, he had no choice but to approve it. I figured that was that.

TRAVELING TO DC on a late-night train out of Penn Station, I zoned out to the screech of metal on the rails, watched the lights shimmy off the landscape. I thought back to that long trip I took all those years ago, when my father brought us to live in Florida, the way it felt like a portal to another world. I thought about how long ago that seemed, how far I'd come, but I couldn't shake the feeling that that young boy was still right there, tucked closely underneath. My stomach started to flit at the thought of going to the nation's capital, wondering if maybe Obama himself would be there to hear me. I drifted off to sleep and woke as we pulled in to the sun rising above the Capitol building, the city majestic in the morning light.

At the Newseum, I watched Jim on a panel alongside the co-chair of the task force, Police Commissioner Charles Ramsey of Philadelphia, author and legal activist Bryan Stevenson, activists Carmen Perez and Brittany Packnett, law professor Tracey Meares, along with religious leaders, police officers, and public safety experts. It was the big leagues, for sure. Just seeing Jim—*Buffett!*—up there told me that change is possible if you push hard enough.

When it was my turn to speak, I took the microphone and stood up. Dreads pulled back and pinned up, sweater and sport jacket over a tie, I clutched my notebook in hand, nervous but focused. Other than Ramsey himself, I had the distinct sense that I was one of the only people in that room who actually knew how bad things were from the inside. I was standing up from within the bowels of the institution and yelling "Fire!"

I first addressed the weak panacea of "diversity" and how it alone doesn't solve a broken system. I called out the police department for hiding behind the myth of Black pathology to justify stop and frisk. I gave the lie to broken windows, which had been exposed in recent weeks as ineffective and counterproductive.

The weeks leading up to my DC trip had been something of a real-time experiment for crime in New York City. Soon after the decision not to indict Officer Pantaleo, Mayor de Blasio publicly expressed concern regarding the dangers the police presented to his Black son:

> I have had to talk to Dante for years about the dangers that he may face . . . because of a history that still hangs over us, the dangers he may face, we've had to literally train him—as families have all over this city for decades—in how to take special care in any encounter he has with the police officers who are there to protect him.[1]

A relatively innocuous and factually accurate comment from the mayor was twisted by Patrolmen's Benevolent Association (PBA) president Pat

Lynch into something anti-cop.* When Officers Liu and Ramos were killed a few weeks later, Lynch claimed that de Blasio had blood on his hands, a comment that led officers to physically turn their backs on the mayor. Lynch then signaled for a work slowdown: serious crime would be addressed, but everything else—essentially broken-windows infractions—would be ignored.†

As I testified to the panel, not only had this slowdown *not* led to criminal mayhem, but felony arrests actually *fell* 17 percent.[2] But what also fell was city revenue. With the slowdown, New York City was losing tens of millions of dollars a week,[3] not to mention crippling the industries that depend on broken-windows policing. The economic impact of overpolicing was driven home loud and clear.

The criminal-industrial complex was a gargantuan creature with tentacles reaching in all directions; judges, prosecutors, defense attorneys, court officers, police officers, correction officers, probation officers, parole officers, bail bondsmen, and clerical, custodial, and maintenance staff at those buildings were all paid from this beast. There are dollar signs on the other end of broken windows; the abuse of Black bodies is a lucrative business.

When I sat down, I felt a buzz running through me like an electrical current. It was the first time I had spoken publicly on these issues that were so close to my heart. It was like after being buried underground I was finally coming up for air.

There was a time when I thought that I would just lead by the example, be the best kind of cop I could be. But years in the trenches, day after day on the front lines, taught me that separating myself just wasn't going to be enough.

As Malcolm had said, it was time to start making noise.

---

* At John Jay College, a white officer with a mixed-race child admitted to the skeptical class that he too had this conversation with his son.
† Of course, Lynch didn't say this explicitly, but cops understood how to read between the lines.

Nineteen

Takedown

When I returned to work from DC, the buzz saw was waiting for me. Captain Maldonado had been pushing down the chain to get my evaluations lowered below 3.0 so I could be put on performance monitoring and, ultimately, pushed out of the job. Lieutenant Hayden and Sergeant Campbell had been protecting me, but after the DC trip, Hayden relented. She forced Campbell, my direct superior, to give me an interim evaluation of 2.5. The reasoning was a list of false or misleading sentences, copied and pasted throughout the document:

> PO Raymond does not take appropriate action when he encounters crimes and violations.
> He refuses to use enforcement to correct or address crime.
> PO Raymond is unwilling to adapt or adjust to new department policies and programs, such as addressing crime conditions.
> PO Raymond does not show any drive or initiative in addressing his monthly conditions.

When I went to Campbell, who ostensibly had written it, he indicated it was not what he had submitted.

"I still think it's a shame that they are putting your name on something," I said, my recorder running. "Did you read it? Did you read this stuff?"

"Yeah, I read it again just now."

"Do you agree with it?"

"No, I didn't write that," Campbell said. "You know what I wrote? I think I have the original copy what I wrote, before it was omitted." He tapped his pocket with a folded set of papers in it. "And she added a bunch of stuff. You read through the whole thing, right?"

"Absolutely, which is why I'm appealing it. It's misleading. So, appeal process goes to whom, her?"

"Whenever you appeal it, it always goes to the CO, but she was the reviewer."

"So, purpose defeated," I said. An appeal to the same channel that created it was pointless, a bureaucratic cul-de-sac. "But if anything gives me an opportunity to speak to her—because perception without challenge becomes reality. She's never spoken to me. This is coming from you," I said, trying to get him to clarify.

"It's from command, right," he said. "I don't agree with the interim. I'm being told what to give certain people. I didn't put all negatives on here. It only has the ones that are graded bad."

"Overall, you, as my immediate supervisor, you evaluate me," I said. "You are there with me, you work with me, and you have no issue with my performance. And for them to hijack your duty to evaluate me, simply because they have a complete other agenda . . ."

"She told me before that 'I am going to take away all your powers as far as a supervisor when it comes to dealing with Raymond. I'm going to have the ICO* help and the platoon commander do it. And if they can't do it, the XO† and myself are going to take care of it from there. I am telling you right now: I need an interim order *today*.' Those were the exact words. And I was like, 'Okay.' And when I did the interim—"

"What is the issue with me, just activity, the quota . . . ?"

"Do you really want me to tell you?"

"Of course, because I need to understand this."

"You are a young Black man with dreads, very smart, very intelligent, have a loud—a loud, say, meaning your words is loud."

"Okay."

"You understand what I'm saying by that?"

"Yeah."

"*Fuck this dude*," he said, implying what the bosses meant. "I never seen nothing like this, bro."

I **WALKED OUT** of there in a daze. Concerned for months about getting my rightful promotion, now I had to worry about my job. The confusion and anger started bubbling up from a deep place inside me. I had kept it buried but now it felt like it was going to burst.

I didn't put the onus on Campbell. My whole argument was that the individual cop's choices were subsumed to the larger pressure, so it would've been hypocritical to single him out. He was a military guy, on probation as a first-year sergeant, and he could hold out only for so long. It was not within his power to keep a lid on the coming surge.

Campbell understood my position about policing, even agreed with much of it, but the idea of trying to do something about it? That was

* Integrity control officer.
† Executive officer, the second in command.

a step too far. He had too much to lose. And he was far from alone. There are cops so afraid of the power of the department that even in retirement they won't speak out because they're afraid their pension will get taken away, an illogical fear, as even a cop convicted of murder would get his pension. It just speaks to the hold the department has over its officers.

My principles were solid, my rock. For six years, I felt that if I did everything by the book, avoided disciplinary issues, and made my arguments with logic and tact, I'd be insulated from negative consequences. I believed they couldn't derail my career.

Obviously, I was wrong.

I refused to sign the evaluation, checked off the box to register my appeal, and walked out of the meeting.

I felt my stomach clench like a fist, my intestines wrapped up tight. My instincts were to just get out of there, cede to the gravitational pull trying to drag me home. But I had a shift to work. I went out on patrol at the Atlantic Avenue station barely able to concentrate. All the activity felt muted, the bustle of the street unfolding like a dream. I compulsively replayed the sequence of events in my head, as if I turned it a certain way, it would make sense. It was such a shift from where I'd been two days earlier—returning from DC on a high and feeling empowered—like running full speed into a concrete wall.

I thought about the unreachable distance between what we could be and what we were, the gap between the task force members in DC believing a better police force was possible and the petty reality on the ground of what it meant to be a cop.

I thought of Officers Polanco and Serrano, whistleblowers who went public and testified for the stop-and-frisk suit. They were isolated and punished and scapegoated for standing up for what was right. I thought of Schoolcraft, committed to a mental hospital for saying the sky was blue. He just wanted to do his job and they *destroyed* him. I thought of

Serpico, who risked himself and single-handedly upended the entire New York City Police Department for the better. And how he almost paid with his life.

And now I was in the crosshairs.

WHEN I FINALLY GOT HOME, I continued to reread the printout of the evaluation. In cop world, what you put on paper is real. Everything else is treated as vapor. Those scathing comments were about a police officer I did not recognize. A stranger. An invention. A straw man created by the powers that be whom they could strike down.

I took a long, hot shower, my forehead pressing against the wall, the water like needles on my skin, the bathroom filling up in a fog. I tried to clean myself of the day, of my thoughts, of the backwardness of my life. Then I lay back on the sofa and stared at the ceiling.

For my entire life, no matter the struggle, the poverty, the hardship, I never had to doubt which way was up. The right thing to do and the smart thing to do were always synonymous, interchangeable. It was a fact as trustworthy as the sun rising each day. It had been like that when I was a young boy, a teenager, a young man, a recruit, a rookie, and now, as a cop. But the ground on which I stood was no longer steady. It forced me to question things that I took for granted: Was I being smart?

I'd worked so hard to get here, and because I tried to do what felt right, I was going to lose it all.

I thought back to a scene from the film *Serpico*, where Serpico, at the end of his rope, meets a captain in a secret location and tells him he can't take it anymore. When he mentions he's going to have to go to outside agencies to address the rampant corruption in the department, the captain tells him that's not how it's done, that "we wash our own laundry" inside the department.

"I always thought so," Serpico says, "but the reality is, sir, that we do not wash our own laundry! It just gets dirtier." Everything in his world is so upside down that he starts to question his own sanity. I understood that intimately.

As night fell over the city, and the streets of Brooklyn settled into a low hum, sleep eluded me. My body and brain were exhausted, but sleep never came. Before I knew it, light was peeking through my blinds. I got up, read the paper, worked out, tried to will some normalcy back into my body.

At work, a few colleagues asked me about the evaluation, wondered what it meant for my upcoming promotion. I told them the truth: I had no idea. I pushed through to the end of the shift, to finally make it home to sleep, but again, it never happened. The only thing that I could think about was that 2.5. By day three, the lack of sleep showed on my face, and it was difficult to concentrate. Toward the end of a shift, I finally felt my eyes getting heavy and my body shutting down just as I was transporting a prisoner. The last thing I needed was for him to escape, which would've been an automatic suspension, even more ammunition against me.

On the third night I finally fell asleep but woke up drenched in a cold sweat, with a phantom sense of my door being kicked in. I thought again of Schoolcraft, who could have been gunned down if things at his house had gone a little bit differently. An Emergency Service Unit, the NYPD equivalent of a SWAT team, forced its way into his home, pinned him to the ground, cuffed him, and imprisoned him in a psych ward against his will. All for asking basic questions like what are we even do-ing here?

I could either let them ruin me or take this fight all the way. I knew I'd be following in a long historical line, fighting something bigger than quotas, promotions, and police.

As with many people of color from tough neighborhoods, self-preservation was practically my religion. But to take on a machine of this size, I'd have to toss self-preservation out the door. There was no chance I'd come out unscathed.

I was ready.

What came with that decision was an eerie kind of calm. I was free: I didn't care what they did to me because I was not backing down. I whispered the words to myself in the morning dawn, just to hear them aloud: *I'm ready to die for this shit.*

For a long time, I'd always been frustrated by Malcolm's refusal to do everything in his power to protect himself once he knew he was a target. It baffled me that someone so brave and so wise could have had such a blind spot. But now I understood. He was ready to offer what needed to be taken, ready to go all the way. Even his life took a back seat to this larger thing. He knew those willing to lose everything are the scariest fighters of all.

PART III

It doesn't feel right if I watch other people suffer
and I do nothing about it.

—Vic Mensa

Twenty

Raymond v. The City
of New York

January 2015

The plan, at first, was to go it alone. That's what I was willing to do and what I thought I needed to do. No matter how many officers agreed with me in private, they weren't willing to engage in a public fight against the powerful entity that signed their checks. But I also knew—from Polanco and Serrano, from Schoolcraft; from Serpico—that going up the traditional chain of command would get me nowhere. The problem wouldn't be addressed by its own source. The leadership would never be a check on themselves.

I knew the Department of Investigation (DOI) had recently been made independent of the NYPD, so I reached out to the inspector general and began conversing with someone in his office, telling my story and sharing some evidence. A somber man in a buttoned-up shirt took notes, recorded our conversation, and said he'd look into it. My concern became that the DOI was still under the purview of the recently elected mayor, who was unlikely to support anything that made him look bad.*

At the same time, I talked with a civil rights attorney about getting a lawsuit off the ground. I was hopeful, though he was blunt about how long something like this would take. But while I was early in the process of going it alone, something came along that made sure I wouldn't have to.

One day in late March, as I was changing into street clothes after my shift, my cell phone rang. "How's it going, brother?" It was Oliver Pu-Folkes, cool and relaxed as always.

"Pushing through," I said, slamming my locker and heading out the door. "Not sleeping that great."

"I understand. Keep pushing, man."

"Thanks."

"So, uh . . ." Oliver paused like he was shifting gears. "You know everything we've been talking about . . ." Even Oliver was careful with what he said. "They're having a press conference."

"Who?"

"I'm not sure. A group of cops who have hired lawyers. Something about filing a suit against the department for quotas and retaliation."

"Really?"

"Yeah, and they're going big with it. Not sure what your schedule is, but if you can you should go out to One Police Plaza tomorrow."

The next day I took the subway downtown and as I was coming up the steps to city hall, I ran into retired detective Graham Weatherspoon. An older Black gentleman with a mustache and long salt-and-pepper dreads, Weatherspoon was one of the founding members of 100 Blacks in Law Enforcement Who Care, a groundbreaking group of cops who

---

* A few months later I received a letter from DOI stating that my complaint would not be investigated.

took initiative in supporting the community and speaking out against harmful policing. I'd been following him for many years, in articles and on TV, and he struck me as someone who had thrived without compromising his principles. When I finally met him, he had the air of the wise man who knew better but didn't always need to show it.

When I'd see him while I was on patrol, he'd take me aside and give me a pep talk, reminding me to remember who I was and saying in his deep bass voice, "Don't let this job suck you in." That day we walked to the press conference together, which was in a brick walkway alongside One Police Plaza, NYPD headquarters. Tripod cameras, microphones, and reporters gathered in front of a collection of police officers—I spotted Officers Polanco and Serrano, whom I recognized from television—lawyers, and supporters. Three cops stood military style in front of the group, holding blow-up copies of documented proof of illegal quotas on large posters.

As they were setting up, Weatherspoon quickly introduced me to Polanco and retired sergeant Anthony Miranda, the executive director of NLOA,* who was operating as the group's spokesperson. A large and imposing man, Miranda was once among the most outspoken cops on the force. Weatherspoon also introduced me to the two lawyers taking on the case: Emeka Nwokoro, a tall and distinguished Nigerian gentleman, and John Scola, a white guy with a square jaw and tough Italian demeanor. I had come to be a spectator, but right as the conference began, Weatherspoon motioned for me to stand alongside everyone, so on camera, it appeared that I was part of the group.

"Illegal quota systems are something that should be eliminated in New York," Miranda said in his booming voice to the arrayed cameras and microphones. "This mayor came in and this police commissioner came in with a promise to eliminate the quota system and protect our

* National Latino Officers Association.

community, but instead the system that they have operated is worse than ever before."

"Ever since CompStat, it's all about numbers," said Emeka in his African-accented English. "We're talking about enforcement activity and the kind of impact it has both on the police officers and the community."

Polanco and Serrano saw the impact they had as witnesses in the stop-and-frisk case. They realized they could make an even bigger dent as plaintiffs, so they had found a few more cops and filed the suit. Stop and frisks were irritating, but people weren't getting records, losing jobs and school time because of the practice. Stop and frisks didn't send you down the rabbit hole into the system the way aggressive summonses and petty arrests did. Those were the source of the problem, and their new lawsuit was going right for its throat.

Two days later, I met up with Emeka in his office on Wall Street. It was an old-fashioned building, from another era of New York, updated with cream-colored walls and carpeted floors. Emeka sat at his expensive oak desk in front of a wall decorated with accolades and degrees.

I brought my notes, recordings, and evaluations, telling him, "I got some ammunition that might help you guys out." Then I started telling my story. Emeka, sharply dressed and wearing a concerned expression, jotted down notes on a yellow legal pad, occasionally shaking his head in disbelief. I played excerpts of some recordings and watched his reaction. He was blown away.

"Right now, we have eight officers and we're looking to grow the group," he said. "We've had dozens of requests to join, but we're being very careful about whom we select."

"I understand," I said, thinking maybe he was going to explain why they couldn't use me. But instead, he said the opposite.

"But, this—this," he said, smacking his pen down on his notepad. "I'm going to talk to my partner, but I'm telling you: we're gonna need you to be the lead plaintiff. The face of the whole case," he said, spreading his hands wide.

"The face of the case? No, no. I'm sorry," I said, feeling there'd been a misunderstanding. "I'm just here to help. I just thought you could use the ammo for—"

"Edwin"—he said it *Edween*, like my mother had—"you have the most compelling story and you're the one who's up for promotion. Eighth on the sergeant's list?" he said, his voice raising an octave. "Can you imagine if they don't promote you? How much it helps the case? How it shows the lengths they're willing to go to keep the system going?"

I saw his argument, but I was still dizzy from how fast things were moving. I had jumped onto a moving train and, almost immediately, I was being asked to drive it.

I spoke to a few mentors and friends I trusted (including Oliver and Jim St. Germain) about whether or not this was the right thing to do. Emeka made it clear this was going to be a very public battle and I should be prepared for whatever they'd throw at me. I was ready in the abstract, but hesitant on doing it this way. I had already decided to take this thing to the courts, but I was still in first gear. The lawsuit was like immediately switching to fifth.

Jim put the finest point on it. "Dread," he said. "Seriously? You have to do it. You were born for this, bro."

As he always did, Jim put things in stark terms. He was right. What had all my struggles been for if not something like this? I called the lawyers and told them I was in.

The suit was now called *Raymond v. The City of New York*.

THE GROUP, eventually known as the NYPD 12 (after the number of plaintiffs) was filing a suit against the city and the police department for violating three things:

1. The illegal quota statute
2. The First Amendment (retaliation against cops for speaking out)
3. The Fourteenth Amendment (disproportionate retaliation against officers of color)

The goal was to lay the groundwork for change by stirring up the status quo. A suit, a trial, and the public pressure and media attention that come with those things are exactly how you take down an unchallenged and malignant system.

The NYPD actually gets sued pretty regularly, and it's not necessarily frowned upon. Most of the police unions have filed suits against the department. What stood out about the NYPD 12 (and what would make us targets) was two things: One, we were suing on behalf of the public because our disparate treatment was due to our refusal to harm them. Two, we were suing regarding the civil rights of a protected class. Policing is dominated by white males, and all civil rights suits are viewed as direct attacks to their hegemony. Many white males, especially in a conservative institution like the police, see themselves as the only *un*protected class, even though American society has been built around keeping them protected. In reality, they are the only automatically protected class; these white men are blind to those protections because they've always been there.

I had come to understand how ignorant my colleagues were about these issues. When NYPD officers had to go through implicit-bias training, the experience drove home how the average white officer really thinks. Round tables were set up where instructors handed out index cards and asked us to write down what implicit bias and systemic racism meant. The cards were shuffled and handed back out, and we took turns reading out peers' answers. Eighty percent of the answers were things like:

bigfoot

liberal bullshit

CNN nonsense

made up

doesn't exist

How can a system be racist? they argued. *A system doesn't have feelings!*

As frustrating as it was, I would try to calmly engage in conversations with them. Listen, I'd say, we all have biases. If you are in a leadership position making policy, don't you see how it's problematic not to acknowledge and address those biases? Even if you're not intentionally trying to cause harm? Can't you see how even a well-meaning system can have faulty outcomes?

Once in a while, I'd break through, but too often I'd smash headfirst into their defenses. It was hard for them to see the ways they benefited from the positive bias within that same system. The word "privilege" scared them off because they thought it meant "silver spoon," when really it just meant benefit of the doubt, obstacles that they didn't have to worry about. As a male I have privileges, like walking home alone at night and not having to worry about certain things—that's a privilege.

After years and years of being a police officer, it still baffled me how ignorant my white counterparts were about how race shaped society. They had taken for granted how embedded their privileges were, so they didn't even recognize them. It was oxygen, everywhere but invisible. They were so blind to it that they saw efforts to shape a more egalitarian society as "reverse racism." They felt like efforts to correct the past (and the present) were a "war on white people." They complained about not being allowed to have "historically white colleges" or to advertise "white-owned businesses," not realizing that *they already had those things. They were everywhere.* That was just mainstream society.

The implicit bias was not just in how citizens were treated on the outside but also how officers of color were treated on the inside. I encountered it all the time. Once I was in plainclothes visiting the Seventy-Second Precinct with two younger white guys and our sergeant, a Black Haitian in his midthirties. When we walked in, the cops at the Seventy-Second went right up to the twenty-five-year-old white guy as though he were in charge. That's implicit bias. The guy from the Seventy-Second was not thinking, *Fuck Black people.* He was thinking, *The white guy must be the supervisor.*

That kind of bias is reflected in positive assumptions as well as negative ones. The racial component of the NYPD 12 suit, how officers of color were singled out for punishment, was key. White officers with similar numbers didn't get railroaded in the same way. They got spoken to sometimes but rarely faced serious retaliation. In order to avoid disciplining a white cop, all the stops were pulled out. But when the officer was Black or Brown, the decision to reprimand was often swift and easy.* It wasn't just anecdotal. Studies across the nation have found a distinct discrepancy between the punishments white cops and cops of color receive for the same infractions.[1] This doesn't even get into the incidents that never make it on paper in the first place. And if cops haven't prevented discrimination from spreading inside the so-called blue brotherhood, what chance does the average Black person on the street have?

---

* After Eric Garner's murder, the only person immediately reprimanded wasn't Pantaleo, who actually used the unauthorized chokehold on Garner; it was the Black female sergeant who pulled onto the scene after it all went down. She was the only one suspended right away among all the cops who were there that day. An action like that doesn't make sense without understanding how racism is embedded into policy decisions.

Summer 2015

Captain Constantin Tsachas had a wide boxer's nose, permanent smirk, and a thin, reedy voice with a Brooklyn accent. He arrived as the new CO of Transit District 32 with a notorious reputation. In his previous command, a number of Black and Latino cops essentially chose retirement rather than be forced to deal with him. He had targeted their careers (and thus their pensions) if they stayed. He'd tell his officers things like, "You are stopping too many Russian and Chinese" and "You should write more Black and Hispanic people." He'd specifically instruct his officers to avoid what he deemed "soft targets"—whites and Asians—and would get angry "if you tried to patrol subway stations in predominately white or Asian neighborhoods."[2]

Tsachas was about as subtle as a bullhorn. When he arrived, he categorized all the enforcement numbers by race. If the arrestee or respondent to the summons wasn't Black or Hispanic, the officer usually had to go into his office and explain why he took action. Everyone was complaining about it, mostly to Gentry Smith, our union delegate. Tsachas was a poster boy for the numbers culture, the racial profiling, and the kind of cops it rewarded and produced. And, as I learned from Sergeant Campbell, he had his sights set on me.

On a scorching August afternoon in the back parking lot of the command, Campbell met me and Gentry before we went out on patrol. I had the recorder on.

"What'd he say?" I asked.

"He wants to know what happened to your 2014 annual [evaluation] because he never seen it on there," Campbell said. "They want me to do one over now. And he's just reminding me it has to reflect whatever the interim was." In order to get me on performance monitoring, and ultimately out of the force, Tsachas needed a paper trail on me. He and his third in command, Operations Coordinator Lieutenant Reid,* pressed Sergeant Campbell to redo my annual evaluation from the year before and to add another interim evaluation that rated me below 3.0.

"Here's the next thing," Campbell said, slightly lowering his voice. "I was already convinced that they didn't want you to get promoted. You know that, right?"

I nodded.

"Well, it's clearer to me right now. It's explained to me the things they want me to do. They called me over the weekend about it . . ." Campbell was visibly flustered. "I ain't got no time for this," he continued, shaking his head. "This is not for me, bro. This shit right here is not for fucking me, kid."

He wasn't just complaining about the pressure from Tsachas and Reid; I could read between the lines: *I support you but not like that. This fight isn't worth my job.*

"I mean, this shit's not going away. I don't know what the fuck's going on, man. I'm just praying that the list is gonna drop."

Promotions were coming, and Campbell was trying to run out the clock, hoping that I'd be promoted immediately, which would make this all moot. But Tsachas was trying to ruin me before that happened. And he was gaining ground.

Campbell told me what my new evaluation was going to be—2.5— and what it was going to say, what Tsachas demanded it say. He said he was being pressured to write it up that day. While I was frustrated with Campbell for perpetuating the very problem he claimed to be against, it was tough to blame him; he was a pawn in a much larger game.

Another of Captain Tsachas's ways of punishing me was through retaliatory posts. That's how it's been done in the police force since time immemorial. He ordered Campbell to assign me to the omega booth at

---

* This is the same Lieutenant Reid who had seduced me into Truancy a few years back but ended up getting on me about numbers and throwing me out after our conflict over his attempt to arrest a teenage girl for spitting out a bird feather.

Clark Street, the 24/7 surveillance booth in subway stations nicknamed "The Box," in reference to solitary confinement in prison. A tiny bullet- and bombproof toll booth–sized square painted in NYPD blue and white, it was meant to serve as a counterterrorism measure by preventing unauthorized people from entering the tunnels. But Tsachas had actu- ally been using the funds earmarked for counterterrorism to pay over- time for cops who were doing nothing at all related to terrorism, just the bread-and-butter overpolicing of Blacks and Hispanics.

At Clark Street, the omega booth was placed right at the end of the platform in order to watch anyone who might try to descend onto the tracks underneath the river and set off an explosion. By orders of Tsachas, I was to be at the Clark Street booth until further notice for "not re- sponding to talks." An officer couldn't leave that post without relief, and there'd be times when supervisors delayed on purpose or altogether failed to send relief for me. I'd be forced to hold my urine, suffered mi- graines from hunger, and went a little crazy from the ten-plus hours of isolation.

IN SEPTEMBER 2015, I sat across from Tsachas, in his office, accompa- nied by union delegate Gentry Smith and Lieutenant Shand (the integrity control officer) to adjudicate a command discipline (CD) I'd received. It was a trumped-up charge I got months earlier for submitting my documentation for vacation a few days late. But really it was just an excuse to get more paper on me.

Captain Tsachas's office was a large space at the back of the com- mand, with a big wooden desk that bisected the room immediately at the entrance, and a marked-up calendar and framed accolades on the wall to his left.

"What's going on, anything?" Tsachas asked me as we settled into our chairs, my recorder running in my inside shirt pocket.

I mentioned I'd been at the Clark Street omega booth for most of the month.

"I told you before," he said, "if you're not going to do anything, I might as well put you at Clark Street."

"I never not do anything, sir," I said calmly, accustomed to the condescension by now.

"The union came here back in August to defend you," he said. "What have you done since?"

"I've been at work. I've been at Clark Street."

"What have you done, every day?" he asked, agitated. He then shifted the conversation, struggling to explain what my CD was about.

"This is for putting in the twenty-eight* for his vacation on his way out the door," Shand jumped in. "Because of that, his spot that he was notified for the Puerto Rican Day Parade couldn't be filled. You're supposed to hand in the twenty-eight five days in advance. It was done on the very last day, on his way out the door."

"So, like intentionally you did it," Tsachas said.

"Never, sir," I said.

The 28 was not what notified your superior you were going on vacation. That was set up long in advance and penciled in a diary. "I put in my twenty-eight," I explained, "and [Campbell] said, 'Have fun in Haiti, bring me a souvenir.' Honestly, I was really shocked when I got back when I heard that this caused such an uproar."

"Of course it does," Tsachas said, "because you're supposed to hand in your twenty-eight."

Plenty of cops didn't hand in a twenty-eight at all, and he knew that. "You know," I said, "these things have to be done impartially across the board, and it's disheartening to watch—"

---

* Leave-of-absence form.

"What's disheartening is your entire performance this year," Tsachas said, never passing up a chance to swipe at me. "*That's* disheartening."

I didn't take the bait, and after docking one day of my vacation time, we got to the real reason for our meeting.

"And how's the performance?" Tsachas asked. "I want to listen to you as to why you worked and then you stopped."

"I've never stopped working, sir," I responded, monotone like an army private. I didn't want to fight with Tsachas, but he was constantly making these blanket accusations. I explained that back when I was in Conditions, I hid in those transit rooms with everyone else, so I got the numbers. The drop in numbers just came from the growth of my own common sense.

"How many TABs* have you got this year?" he asked.

"I've never kept a numeric count going."

Tsachas shook his head and then looked down at a chart in front of him. He ticked off my activity numbers, how many arrests and summonses. Then he pushed me on my need to stop theft of service (TOS), Transit's bread and butter. The two-dollar crime of the century. Cops had to plan elaborate stakeouts to catch TOS while missing every other crime not viewable through those vents. It was absurd. I tried to make my case but he cut me off.

"Don't play games with me 'cause I've heard the speeches before," Tsachas said. "I've been CO for almost five years, and I've heard these things. How 'standing around is fantastic, nothing happens when I'm on post.'"

Our back-and-forth grew tense as I defended myself, advocating the merits of preventing crime by remaining visible.

"I don't know what your agenda is," he added.

"There is no agenda, sir."

---

* Summonses.

"But let me tell you," Tsachas said, leaning forward, "your union came to me. There's no reason for me not to send those evals down. And you're on the list to become a sergeant, and how are you going to lead if there is a crime condition in your command?"

I explained what I would do if I got a command before he turned back to my numbers.

"All right," he said, the exasperation coming off him like smoke. "I'm ordering you to go hide and get me TOS arrests for people who have not qualified for a TAB, who are transit recidivists. How does that sound?"

"So, you want me to hide in a room," I said, surprised.

"No, not—I want you to do . . ." He caught himself; supervisors avoided saying this directly. "Stay—how do I put it?—hard to see."

All the talk-arounds and obfuscations were maddening.

"Go make a difference," Tsachas added, gesturing out the window.

"I'm out here making a difference in many ways," I said. "My oath does not end with my tour. Outside of this job and while I'm in uniform, I'm out there and I'm making a difference. You can ask around."

"If you're making a difference outside the job, that's fantastic. But while you're getting paid by the City of New York, you're here in Transit. I need you to be proactive."

I was shuffling in my seat now, agitated at the circles we were going in.

"If you want me to go to a room," I added after a while, "that's all somebody has to say. If you tell me to go in a room, I'll go in a room right now." I wanted it on the record that I was not disobeying a direct order. "Do you want me to go into a room?"

"Yeah," Tsachas said. "We're allowed to go into the rooms, there's no order against it."

"If you say that's policing, it's not a problem."

As he tried to wrap up, I took the opportunity to call out the hypocrisy of the entire meeting. I handed out a couple of photocopied pages from Bratton's Reengineering initiative the previous year, including quotes from the police commissioner, Transit Chief Fox, and George Kelling (who coined "broken windows" and was now a consultant) about how they cared about "quality not quantity" of arrests, wanting police "present and visible," with less emphasis on numbers than on impact, the power of police discretion, and how wrongheaded cops think it's just about the numbers.

Tsachas sat there annoyed as I read to him, even asking at one point, "Who said that?" He was dismissive, thinking of these quotes as just smoke and mirrors, the show put on for the public to hide what was really going on. He made a few half-hearted attempts to quote Bratton saying the opposite. When I was done, he held up the papers with the quotes. "Do you want me to keep this or did you say you want it back?"

"That's yours," I said.

I was never again going to hide in the transit rooms. That practice represented everything I hated about policing. But colleagues who cared about me said, "Raymond, play the game, please. Just two months, man; once you get promoted you don't have to do this no more. You worked so hard for this; don't let them take it away from you."

I asked myself again if what was right and what was smart were no longer the same thing. But if I gave in when things got harder, there was no point to the fight.

The issue was, how much more of this would I have to take? How much more could I take?

Twenty-One

The Brass

October 2015

Paper. In the department, all that mattered was what was on paper. Paper was real; everything else was just smoke. Captain Tsachas had told me himself, "If it doesn't make it on paper, my friend, I can't help you."

The night before the appeal of my annual evaluation, the 2.5 that could sink my career, I stayed up late. I was playing in my head what I'd say to Captain Tsachas, anticipating how he'd respond, what defenses I'd offer. "Boss fighting" was frowned upon in the department, so I would focus on the logic and reasoning of my argument. I gamed out possibilities until the morning light pushed through my blinds.

We were again in Tsachas's office, this time with Lieutenant Reid, the third in command, and Sergeant Campbell, my direct supervisor. Gentry, my union delegate, was there once more, bringing in an extra seat and closing the door behind him. My iPhone was again recording in my pocket.

"All right. We're here for the 2014 evaluation . . ." Tsachas turned to

Campbell, lying right off the bat: "You weren't influenced in any kind of way to make any kind of changes?"

"No," Campbell said, contradicting every conversation I'd had with him.

"Okay, so I'm here as the mediator," Tsachas said. "You're allowed to appeal factual errors, raise misinterpretations on instruction, bias, or prejudice on the part of the rater . . . So, go ahead."

"This numerical system . . . ," I began. "If I'm truly being assessed objectively, then these numbers don't fit. For instance, community interaction, that's a three. I don't mean to sound arrogant, but I definitely deserve a five there. My work in the community speaks for itself." I began to go through my scores in the other categories—including comprehension, communication, reasoning—and systematically explained how the 2s and 3s were inaccurate.

Tsachas exhaled. "Are you going to go through each one?"

"I mean, that's the purpose of— Yes, sir."

"Mr. Campbell," Tsachas said, annoyed. "Do you feel that the scores you gave are a representation of his performance?"

"Uh, referring to . . . ," Campbell said.

"Look at the whole thing," Tsachas said. "Do you feel what you gave him is appropriate?"

"I mean, the community interaction and the physical fitness," Campbell said, "uniform and appearance . . . um." Campbell stared at the eval and dissembled, starting and stopping various explanations. He got caught in a circle talking about quarterly points, the previous evaluations under the last captain, while Tsachas tried to lead him to say the "right things." The CO was demanding that he explain what he was forced to give. It was an impossible needle to thread.

"Start with number sixteen, reasoning ability," I said. "What about my performance shows I lack reasoning ability?" The room was silent as Campbell stared at the eval.

"Go ahead, Mr. Campbell," Tsachas said. "A lot of this is . . . based on your drive. Being proactive."

"The reasoning ability comes from . . . ," Campbell started to say, half-heartedly. "Basically from the enforcement."

"There's nothing about enforcement," I said. "It says I 'lack the ability to form logical conclusions from events.'"

"I know why you got this," Tsachas said, frustrated. "And from speaking to Sergeant Campbell, your enforcement performance is way below average. He has to speak to you often, and now you come in here and you're fighting with words for me. Like you're gonna take each word apart."

"Well, that's what's written here," I said, holding out the eval.

"We know why you're here," Tsachas said.

"Overall," Lieutenant Reid said, leaning forward, "how do you feel you perform as a police officer?"

"I think I'm a *great* police officer," I said.

"Okay, but overall," Reid continued, "where do you think you rank with the rest of your platoon? You got to be honest with yourself. Are you addressing your conditions?"

"Mr. Raymond *was* addressing his conditions years back," Tsachas cut in. "He just had a change of heart or change of mind. Something happened. This is intentional because nobody changes that drastically."

"Okay, to answer your question—" I started.

"You want us to write it more simple?" Tsachas asked. "You're still gonna get the two point five according to Sergeant Campbell."

"Let me ask you something, Sarge," Gentry jumped in. "You think he cannot apply rules? Has Raymond ever broke a rule?"

"No, no," Campbell said, shaking his head. "He never broke a rule, no."

"This is what you wrote as reasoning ability, if you wrote this sentence," Gentry said, slipping in what we all knew to be true. "Why did you write it?"

"Is it . . . basically like . . . ," Reid interrupted, trying to save Campbell. "Your enforcement."

"But it's got nothing to do with enforcement," Gentry said.

"When you don't hide," I said, "that's what the numbers look like. While I'm trying to deter something major, I will enforce something minor, but it's probably less likely to happen. But at the same time, I'm at the service of the people who pay taxes for me to be there."

Reid and I went back and forth, slightly heated, until he took a different tack: "Arrests isn't the only thing that makes a good police officer."

"That's the point I'm trying to make!" I said, baffled. It was like he got turned around inside his own reasoning. "We're in here because of that!"

"The room is the way you get your activity," Reid said. "In Transit, we don't get those type of radio runs. We don't have domestics down here."

"So just get something for the sake of getting something?" I asked. "Captain, the last time I was here, you told me to go into the rooms."

"Yeah, be proactive," Tsachas said. "And what's happened since?"

"Honestly, I haven't gone in the room."

He was taken aback. "So you refuse to take that step forward?"

"But I've made two arrests since we've last met in this place. And one, thank god I wasn't in the room, because if I was in the room at Pennsylvania [Avenue], that would have never happened."

Tsachas knew all about that arrest. Two young Black females approached me and pointed out a creepy white dude who had been trailing them daily after school. I had probable cause to arrest him for stalking. "If I was in the room, she wasn't going to knock on the door in the room and say, 'Officer!' She wouldn't even know I was in there. That's the point I'm trying to make."

"So how many other days were you out there visible and how many collars?" Tsachas asked.

"So is it just about collars? Because Lieutenant just said—"

"You're making the fact that you were there visible to prove to me that this is a great thing to do. How many other times—because you were standing there?"

"The lack of crimes happening *while I'm there*," I said. "That's a number. It is just as important as what you're tallying." Just because they wouldn't measure it did not mean it didn't exist. That number—crimes prevented—if it were on paper somewhere, would be much more reflective of a cop's performance.

Gentry agreed. In his booming preacher's voice, he dove in. "As far as being out there in uniform, in the public's eye, how many people just went past you—a thousand, two thousand? How many people pass you every hour when you're at those stations in uniform and nothing goes down? *Sight.* Being in sight. Stop considering everything as a number. When you consider everything as a number, *stuff* happens. No one in this room and up top want to admit that mistakes happen when you chase a number hard. Shootings, those are mistakes that happen when you chase a number hard."

"I don't understand," Tsachas said. This was at a time when video of police killing unarmed Black people was all over the news.

"Of course you're not going to understand," Gentry said, "'cause you don't want to understand it."

"To try to hurt my career like this," I said, "it's unfortunate. To congratulate me for being on the [sergeant] list but at the same time, throw this at me, that's unbelievable."

Eventually, Tsachas floated the opportunity for me to appeal to the next level. But I'd be appealing up the same chain that sent down the 2.5. Tsachas *created* the eval; he was the orchestrator in the guise of the mediator. It was unwinnable, which was why I was taping these meetings. I wanted to get it on the record that Campbell was forced in this direction.

"So, Sergeant Campbell," I said, "you stand by this?" He hesitated. "You stand by this," I repeated, more as a statement.

He shifted uncomfortably in his seat, then gestured to the printout. "I have to stand by it," he said weakly.

"He has to," Tsachas said. "The 2015 interim eval on appeal is floating around, correct? I can kill it if you show me a little . . . if you are proactive in 2015. I'll make it go away," Tsachas said, holding out a stick disguised as a carrot.

"So what about my promotion?" I asked.

"I don't know what's going to happen to it," Tsachas said.

"Technically, it should be coming probably next month," I said.

"I'll tell you what's gonna happen," Reid said. "You're gonna have to go in front of CARB."*

"Why? I've never been collared. But why? Because of *arrests*?"

"It's not about arrests," Reid said. Everyone was talking over one another at this point. "When you go in front of the chiefs, you gotta explain your activity to them. I think if you did a little more work—" Reid said.

"Oh, I work."

"A little bit more work."

"So I should just go lock up anyone real quick," I said.

"Just do your job," Reid said.

"Just lock up a few people and we wouldn't even be here," I said. "Keep the numbers coming in." My adrenaline was spiking. "I could do *none* of this right . . . get two or three collars and be out of sight *completely*, I wouldn't even be looked for."

Gentry interjected: "You gotta make sure it's the right people, the right collars. Because it was told to me from this command that if you collar the wrong individual you come in this room." Gentry had heard

---

* Career Advancement Review Board, a panel of three-star chiefs whom red-flagged officers need to meet with regarding their promotion.

from a slew of officers that Tsachas was making them justify their arrests of people who weren't Black or Brown.

Tsachas nodded, as though Gentry was saying this was proper. "If you come in with some stuff—let's say, female, Asian, forty-two, no ID, I locked her up for TOS," Tsachas said. "That's not gonna fly."

"Why not?" I asked, dumbfounded. "Why not? You have to be impartial. Wait a minute, the Fourteenth Amendment says we have to be impartial . . . Why wouldn't that fly?" Gentry and I were shocked that the CO would say something so explicitly racially biased.

"If you make it a habit of bringing in the no ID . . . ," Tsachas said, catching himself. He was sweating by now.

"Oh my god," I blurted out. "And I'm seen as the problem and this is what we're doing as a police department. You wouldn't want your kids up against this, a cop on overtime, to lock them up. You keep your kids far on Long Island or upstate. You would not want your kids up against that."

"Why?" Tsachas asked. "This is a lovely city, safe city."

"If you're not Black," Gentry said. "That's what you just said. Asian, same criteria that we locked up Hispanics, Black kid, you wouldn't have. That right there I have a problem with. Don't say that to me, Cap."

"That comment did not come out the way it was supposed to," Tsachas backtracked.

As things calmed down, I told Tsachas and Reid, "This is coming from up there," I pointed to the ceiling, "and you're only assessed based on these numbers. All they care about is what they can see on paper. So I get that part makes it out of your hands, but this, this part is in your hands. This is on you. If I miss out on my promotion for this, it's an injustice."

"You know what you might need?" Reid said. "I know people down at Employee Management. They'll tell you exactly what would happen if you're not performing. You can get fired if it goes down to level three."

"If I have to get fired for properly policing," I said, my voice now fully raised, "then so be it."

I walked out of there with my heart pounding, dizzy from the way everything had been turned upside down on me. After the meeting, Campbell and I debriefed in the juvenile room. He tried to explain himself, saying what was being forced on him. He clearly felt guilty for not speaking up, but I had never expected him to go into battle with me. It made more sense to him to avoid the risk: that was the whole point.

"He's going to hold this against you now," Campbell said, referring to the CO. "He wants to see you this month, you're gonna have two collars. If you don't know, Raymond, it's numbers. They don't give a shit about all that stuff, they don't care about your policing. Because you go before the board, they don't give a fuck about all that. They're asking you about your fucking numbers. You can beat around the bush so much, you can word it so much, they don't give a fuck. What's your arrests? What's your TABs? 'You don't agree with it?'" he said, imitating them. "'Fuck you, get out of there, you don't get promoted.'"

"Why are they trying to make it seem so official in there?" I asked. "Because they have to?"

"Because they're not gonna say . . . I was just shocked when he said, 'Go in the rooms.' Don't matter how the job comes and how you see it, you know what it is. The Reengineering stuff, when I look at it in a nutshell, it's a bunch of caca!"

Campbell reiterated Tsachas's ultimatum: If I played the game, the CO would kill the 2.5s and save my promotion, and by extension, my job. All I had to do was agree to meet the quotas for a couple of months. It was like the devil's temptation.

I can't say I even considered it, because what would have been the point? My whole fight was never about me, never about my promotion. If the arrests occurred organically, then fine, but I wasn't going to hunt to get numbers. If I did what was asked of me to save my job, I wouldn't be able to look at myself in the mirror. It would've made me part of the same problem.

THE SERGEANT LIST came out the next month, and I wasn't on it. I had the eighth-highest score and wasn't among the first group of forty-four promoted.* I was red-flagged, skipped, and given a date for a CARB meeting with a panel of three-star chiefs.

On a cold December morning, I went over to the Risk Mitigation Division, which was essentially a prep session on how to handle your CARB meeting, scheduled for later in the day.

The building was near Chinatown, off Canal Street, with a seating area alongside the wall of an office with cubicles, a windowed conference room on the side. I sat there and waited, too nervous to have eaten, too restless to have slept, alongside three other red-flagged officers. We were called in one by one. There was downtime between sessions, so the other officers told me what to expect. The sergeants in there would ask what you were there for and listen to you defend yourself. Then they'd say, "Okay, at CARB, don't do that. It is not the place to argue what got you here. What they want to see is you being apologetic, saying that you've moved on, that you're ready." It was similar to a parole hearing—just say you did it and you're sorry.

When I went in, I sat down in the conference room across from the two sergeants, my entire file opened in front of them. I had brought copies of my letters of recommendations from Sergeant Stapleton, a previous lieutenant, mentors like Oliver Pu-Folkes, Council Member Jumaane Williams, and other political and community allies.

I explained I was there because I policed the way the department's leaders were publicly saying they wanted all officers to police. I explained

---

* Among the promoted group was one of the officers who had killed Amadou Diallo in 1999.

about the Transit rooms, about how I remained visible as a deterrent and that I enforced what I saw, but my numbers were lower. "I'm here because I didn't police with enforcement numbers in mind," I said. "I did my job properly by being at service to the public."

I sat there waiting for the sergeants to tell me what they told the others, that I had to accept responsibility, apologize, explain that I'd moved on. There was an awkward pause as the two sergeants looked at each other across the table, perplexed.

"What are you doing here?" the female sergeant said. "You don't belong here. I've been doing this a long time and the formula is to die on your sword. This is going to be the first time I tell someone there's no sword for you to die on. You did nothing wrong. You go in there and explain to those men exactly what you said here." She turned to the other sergeant, an Asian gentleman, with a look on her face like, *Right?*

"Shit, yeah," he said, "this is a unique situation. He does not belong here."

"Looking at these evaluations," the female sergeant said, "I expected a very arrogant, lazy person. But I got to be honest: the person I expected to meet with is not here."

I was surprised to get that kind of vindication and walked out of there with some hope. I'd heard from a captain that even if you were initially skipped for the promotion, they could still include you in that same promotion group based on how you did at CARB. When the sergeants told me to go to the chiefs and tell the truth, I thought maybe I still had a chance.

AT FIRST, it didn't even occur to me to record the chiefs. It had been ingrained in me that these were the brass, and the idea was unthinkable. But I reconsidered. The crux of my situation was that I was being told to do illegal things, the opposite of what the commissioner himself said he wanted, and then was being punished for not doing them. I also knew the lawsuit could use such a recording when the time came: it would show how high up these problems really went.

So I went into CARB, nervously hiding my iPhone in my breast pocket, the recording app running. When they called me, I took a deep breath and straightened my back. Getting my lieutenants and sergeants, even my CO, on the record was one thing. Getting the brass on the record was something else. There'd be no coming back.

Michael Julian, the deputy commissioner of personnel, was a permanent member of CARB, while the other two slots were occupied by a rotating group of three-star bureau chiefs. In a large, windowless conference room on the twelfth floor of One Police Plaza, I sat at a glossy, expensive wooden table, under fluorescent lights. The power imbalance was profound; I sat all the way at one end while the chiefs sat at the opposite end.

Chief Julian, one of most liberal people in the department, was an affable guy with thinning wavy gray hair and a politician's diction. Chief Galati was a no-nonsense, TV detective type with a mustache and hooded eyes. Chief Secreto, who ran Housing, was a large, bald Black man with a deep voice. Secreto was the highest-ranking Black member of the department. They began by giving me the floor.

"Good afternoon, I'm Officer Raymond. I joined the department on July eighth, 2008, and the main reason would be to serve my community. It's usually said as a talking point but it's truly something very dear to me. I feel that the community I'm from, East Flatbush, Brooklyn, and the department—unfortunately there's a divide that doesn't need to exist." I nervously bungled some of my syntax. "So, I'm doing my part to mend and bridge that divide. What brings me here today is I had a succession of low evaluations. And this is why I'm here," I said, my voice dropping.

"All right, now, I want to hire a thousand of you," Julian said out of the gate. "We're going out here to do some recruiting next year. I want a thousand Black men hired in the next two years to change the racial makeup of this [department]. All Black men don't think cops are the bad guys. Plenty of them want to do good. We need more of it."

I was thrown off balance, not expecting this at all. Then he looked over my paperwork: "You don't get sick. You don't get CCRBs.* There's a lot of good about you." He talked about an officer's need for discretion and how he had worked with Oliver Pu-Folkes on the Reengineering slides regarding that issue.

Then Julian shifted to my numbers, specifically my low number of felony arrests. "The felonies bother me because there are criminals out there and we got to arrest them and I want to know whether you're a conscientious objector—'I'm not doing nothing, I don't believe in arrests'—or you're truly trying to change the community. But you got terrible evaluations. The kind of evaluations where you're not right now ready to be a sergeant. We need to learn about you. How do you view felons, people who are hurting their communities? You said you joined to stop them? Tell us about that," Julian said in his genial tone, gesturing across the table.

"Absolutely," I said. "So, again, coming from a very tough community, high crime, being born and raised during the crack era, I unfortunately witnessed horrible acts, and these people need to be locked up, and we need to use whatever resources we can get to do so . . . I don't have many felonies, but this is the truth for Transit."

I told them the story of arresting a man with AIDS who was sexually assaulting an unconscious narcoleptic woman on the train. "Thankfully, I was there to effect that arrest. One of the things about Transit, unfortunately, is seventy percent of the crimes happen on the train but most of the arrests happen at the mezzanine. So, if you're on the train,

---

* Civilian complaints.

you'll deter many crimes and you'll be there to effect the arrest when one does happen. But this doesn't produce a steady stream of activity." I was more fidgety than normal, cautiously choosing my words. To have the audience of just one three-star chief was a rare occurrence; speaking to three simultaneously made me nervous.

"Can we just back up for one second?" Galati interjected. His high voice didn't match his TV cop face. "Before we talk about the arrests, tell me why your evaluations are continually poor."

I hesitated. "Honestly, I hope . . . that this process allows Sergeant Campbell to be interviewed. Because you'll learn the truth to that. He wasn't comfortable with those evaluations."

Secreto: "You're saying that he was told to give you a certain type of evaluation."

Galati: "Is it a personal thing between you and him?"

"I have a great relationship with Sergeant Campbell," I said.

Galati: "So it's his boss—"

"You don't have the numbers," Julian interjected.

"The . . . the numbers?" I asked. Trying to get it on the record more bluntly.

"You don't have the numbers," Julian continued, casually admitting the thing that the department swore up and down didn't exist. "So the commander says, 'You gotta put him down low initiative, no drive, passive.' You don't seem like a passive guy to me. You look like the guy I would want walking through the train when I'm on the train."

"Thank you, I appreciate that," I said. "I'm at service to the public at all times."

"It says here 'respectful,' 'well-mannered,' 'performs his duties with integrity.' You don't go sick."

"Never," I said.

"You're not taking advantage of anybody."

"That's not my character at all, sir."

"Let me ask," Secreto jumped in with his bass voice, "you were in a school team at one point. What happened?"

"I was in a school team where I thrived," I responded, talking about my six-week stint in Truancy. "Once Officer Raymond comes, the pants go up, the noise level goes down. I had a good rapport with the youngsters. But it doesn't produce . . . arrests. And, uh . . . it doesn't produce arrests when you have rapport. That group that wants to fight, if Officer Raymond's there, they're not gonna fight."

Galati eventually cut that discussion off and again went back to the evals, which is all he seemed to care about. *Paper.* He started listing my different scores. "I'm having a hard time getting over these evaluations. You've got three separate people that rated you poorly. Two point five is, that's like borderline dismissal," Galati said. "If you're on probation and get a two point five, you're basically getting dismissed . . . It's hard to say, 'Okay, we'll make you a sergeant.' If your activity is low, then what does that mean, that my whole entire platoon is going to be low?"

"I understand completely," I responded. "When the situation presents itself for me to effect an arrest, that's never an issue. I go on patrol to be proactive, which is an ambiguous term. There are many ways in which you can be proactive. Arrests, summonses. Smart Policing* shows there are other ways to take action to address a condition. The current metrics might not be able to measure it, but it is very effective."

"I'm going to give you a comment I say at CompStat all the time," Galati said. "The one thing the chief of department, Jimmy O'Neill, and his predecessor before him, and his predecessor before them, always said: 'We don't care about the activity, the activity means nothing. As long as your crime is down too.'"

I didn't directly respond, but this was demonstrably false. No doubt the chief of department had repeatedly said this, but there was zero

---

* An offshoot of Reengineering 2014.

chance it was true. My every day on the job—and that of every cop I knew—disproved it. It was too large a thing to even debate, a sky-is-green moment. I remembered where I was and whom I was talking to, so I kept my mouth shut.

As sirens passed outside, I again said, "If it's possible to speak to the raters, you'll learn the truth. You'll learn the truth about me. I go out and do my best and try my best to go above and beyond in many ways." I recounted the conversations I'd had with Tsachas where he demanded his TOS collars, upending the whole idea that the department didn't care about numbers.

Secreto then got me talking about my desire to be an executive, my extensive reading, my leadership courses at John Jay, my desire to bridge the gap between the police and the community.

"The reason I asked that is that I see here on the evaluations . . . on community, they gave you a three, that doesn't seem to match what I'm seeing here," he said, gesturing to me. "Communication skills, reasoning ability, threes, twos—if nothing else, you've been in here for a half hour debating and communicating, I don't know why that's so low." Secreto was clearly trying to show his counterparts that the evals were inaccurate, but Julian and Galati wouldn't engage.

"Let me tell you where I'm at with this," Julian said. "By the way, you will be a sergeant one day, whether it's the next class or whatever. You're a good person. You're a good *cop*. But we cannot disregard a series of evaluations that say you're not showing the initiative that they require . . . Ninety percent of the cops are *not* doing the other side of it that you're doing—the customer service side—so I appreciate that. So you're a guy that I'd love to have work for me. But I'd have to get you to do some more—I'd love to work with you to make that happen. I'm going to give that job to somebody else. I think you'll reach your goal to be a chief on this job, and would like you to get started sooner or later, but we have to respect also the recommendation, all right?"

WHEN I STEPPED OUT onto the street in front of One Police Plaza, everything started to tunnel in on me. Though I'd gone in with some hope, it was mostly the outcome I'd expected. But experiencing it did a number on me. A few days after the meeting, when my promotion was officially denied, I would feel like I'd fallen off a cliff.

I was being outright punished for policing the way the department claimed it wanted. As Campbell said, "The one thing you never want to go to CARB for is activity." There was an officer who pushed his wife out of a moving car; he went to CARB and got promoted. But to not feed the machine, not feed the system—that was unforgivable.

They were taking something away from me that I had rightfully earned. I would have to explain to family, friends, colleagues why I hadn't been promoted. They all knew I had aced the test. It was devastating, embarrassing, a low point. I had clawed my way out of poverty, out of hunger, and made it. Now, because I wouldn't hunt my people, I was being punished.

Years later, I found out it didn't matter what I might have said at CARB. I could've brought the chiefs to tears or stomped on the table, the result would've been the same. Tsachas had written an official department letter to the chiefs, stating that in no way was I to be promoted.

The one thing that kept me sane was sitting in my pocket. After the CARB meeting, I braced myself against that harsh New York wind whipping down the block and walked away from One Police Plaza. When I got far enough away, I leaned up against a brick wall and dialed.

"Saki," I said.

"What's up, brother?"

"You will not believe what I just got on tape."

Twenty-Two

Noise

Spring 2015

Soon after I joined the NYPD 12 lawsuit the previous spring, I began talking to an award-winning investigative journalist named Saki Knafo. After the group's press conference about the lawsuit in front of One Police Plaza, he met with the lawyers about scheduling interviews with different plaintiffs. "You don't need to talk to anyone else," Emeka told him. "Just Raymond."

The first thing that stood out was his presence: well over six feet tall in round glasses and a newsboy cap with a pensive look on his face. Slim with dark hair and a rich bass voice, Saki was the kind of guy who made reporting seem heroic. He had been planning a feature story about the issues with the police, what the lawsuit was aiming to do, and my own experiences as an outcast in the department.

I understood that publicity was just a form of public pressure. And historically, things don't change until they have to. Until people make them. Though I was slow to open up to him, Saki eventually became my rock during a difficult time. Friends and family didn't fully understand the nuances of what was happening and what I was dealing with. At a time when it felt like the world was closing in on me, our talks gave me space to breathe. Over the months, I began playing him the recordings of private conversations with supervisors that stood in clear contradiction to the department's public claims.

Our conversations deepened and grew throughout that year, especially after the arrival of Captain Tsachas, who was so blatant and overt about things that most supervisors bent over backward not to say explicitly. But I remained reluctant to give Saki full possession of the recordings. I wasn't yet sure about making them public. It was a point of no return, and I wanted to be fortified before I crossed into that territory.

As the NYPD 12 case wound its way through the courts, it made not a dent in my workday. Until the media gets involved, those kinds of things are siloed within the walls of the city's Law Department. None of my supervisors at Transit District 32 knew that I was part of a lawsuit over the very things they were forcing on me and punishing me for resisting.

In September, a few days after my CD adjudication for turning in my vacation form late, I got news that would send this whole thing into the public arena. While I was at work in front of the United Nations, a giant flat building that hovers over the East River like a monolith, I got a call from Saki.

"Hey, Edwin, what's up?"

"All good, all good," I said. "I'm actually working that UN General Assembly detail. Leaders from everywhere, and the pope and the president are in town, so it's been crazy."

"I could imagine. So, listen . . ." He took a beat. "I just got some amazing news, man."

"What's up?

"*The New York Times* . . . they want our story for their magazine."

"What?"

"The big time, buddy."

"Wow, that's insane."

"It's going to be on the *cover*. Huge." It was far bigger than what I'd expected. "But, Edwin, listen, I need the recordings. They're shocked that it's even real. I told them all of this is proven with secret audio recordings."

"Yeah, I don't know. Let me speak to the attorneys."

"Okay," Saki said. "Let me know ASAP. The *Times* won't do it without the recordings."

When I hung up the phone, my heart beat furiously, like it was going to break out of my chest. Saki's piece was going to be a bombshell. The *Times* remained the paper of record, was read all over the world, and stood as one of the few remaining media outlets that could single-handedly make an immediate impact. They first released the Pentagon Papers about U.S. involvement in Vietnam, reported on Abu Ghraib abuses in Iraq before anyone would touch it, and lifted the lid off NYPD corruption in 1970 thanks to Frank Serpico. It was the story about him on the front page of the paper that finally got the mayor to call for a commission to look into rampant police corruption.

These people wanted paper: I'd show them paper.

I called Emeka and asked him if it would be okay to give Saki the transcripts and recordings.

"Yes, absolutely," he said in his crisp accent. "This is exactly the momentum we need, Edwin. Definitely give him the recordings."

"Okay. Which ones?"

"All of them."

THERE COULD BE no silent protest. No quiet moral example. It was time to fight. Jim's words echoed in my mind. "You were born for this, bro." He was right: I could use my pain for something larger than myself, as my mentors had, as my best teachers taught, as my father had once hoped.

That December, when I walked out of my CARB meeting with a recording of three-star chiefs confirming the quotas and pressure, among other things, I knew the story was going to be even more explosive. But I had to move wisely. An institution like the NYPD would kick into high gear once threatened. Everyone knew what the department's leaders did to those cops they branded "rats" and "snitches." They were smeared in the press, made to seem insubordinate, incompetent, crazy.

In the same way the gang member feels comfortable pulling the trigger among his people because he knows no one will talk to police, the department itself—right on the other side of that line—has the same culture. The same unspoken insularity. The police department's leadership has methods of crushing those who break that blue wall. It's a type of insurance to protect the institution itself, akin to the way a criminal organization operates. It'd be ironic if it wasn't so sickening.

To make myself and my argument harder to ignore, I decided to open up another front in the fight. In studying other police whistleblowers—from Schoolcraft to Polanco, even going back to Serpico himself—the one thing I noticed missing was community support. There was nothing in the department's playbook for how to deal with a cop who had the strength of the people behind him. If I could gain the backing of activists, organizations, and community leaders, I'd be much more difficult to dismiss.

When I went to DC with Jim, there was a woman on the dais who stood out among even the most impressive people there. Carmen Perez was a young Mexican American woman who had cofounded the Justice League NYC, a powerful organization of social justice warriors, educators, artists, and community activists. Her group was an arm of the Gathering for Justice, Harry Belafonte's organization. I knew Belafonte was a civil rights icon but didn't realize that he was still doing the work in his late eighties, passing the torch to the next generation.

Carmen spoke like people I knew, not like a bureaucrat. She was urban and young—around my age—a marked difference from the Al
Sharpton types I'd grown up with. Plus, her group had real force, having
already gotten an audience with New York City's mayor and the state's
attorney general. Carmen talked about broken windows and stop and
frisk, so she understood systemic issues, but she stopped short of talking
about the fuel of it all: the quotas. I could offer the missing piece of the
puzzle.

A few weeks after my promotion was denied, I was on a panel discussing safety in New York City schools with another cofounder of the
Justice League NYC, Angelo Pinto. A young Black attorney with sharp
eyes and a square jawline, Angelo impressed me with his knowledge
about the systemic issues. I met up with Angelo in Chinatown, where I
told him about the suit and Saki's upcoming *Times Magazine* cover
story. We sat in my car with the heat blasting as I played my recordings
for him on my phone. "This is going to be the story of the year," he said,
insisting we bring it to the rest of the group, including Tamika Mallory.
Tamika was as plugged in as they came. In her midthirties, she was already one of the country's leading social justice activists, a voice who
could organize and activate all corners of the movement.*

Tamika agreed to meet with me, alongside Angelo and Carmen
Perez, at Harry Belafonte's Gathering for Justice offices in a Midtown
high-rise. With long straight hair, bright eyes, and a big smile, Tamika
was a Harlem girl who was as passionate about the issues as she was connected. I got the distinct impression that she was skeptical, not of me but
the idea of a cop-activist, which was new. But as we spoke, I watched her
open up and see beyond my uniform. By the end of the meeting, she was

---

* The next year, Tamika, along with Carmen Perez and Linda Sarsour, would organize the Women's March in DC, held
the day after Donald Trump's inauguration. She would go on to make *Time* magazine's list of the 100 Most Influential
People in the world.

on board. "Let's wait for the article and then make our move," she said. Until then, things were out of my hands. I just had to be patient.

NEW YORK CITY WEATHER has a way of mirroring your interior self. In the spring, as the world comes back to life, you just might believe in yourself again. In the deep, late summer, when everyone's on edge, problems hang there like the stagnant heat. And in the winter, when you're tucked tightly into yourself, the cold penetrates as far as you go. That January was brutal, with the kind of cold that sticks sharp in your throat, digs deep in your bones.

With each passing week, I waited to hear from Saki that the *Times* article was coming out. It was painful, like holding a stress position longer than my body was able, my muscles aching from the effort and exhaustion. I had trouble concentrating and sleeping, lost weight, and developed a fierce loneliness. Each delay made me more concerned. It was painful going to work every day staying silent, knowing the whole machine just churned on unimpeded.

After having completed his mission of killing my promotion, Tsachas—along with some machinations from the chiefs—got me kicked out of Transit at the start of the new year, 2016. I was transferred to Patrol at the Seventy-Seventh Precinct, my first time topside. Although the transfer left me feeling anxious about my future, patrolling actually became a blessing in disguise. People weren't passing through from point A to point B in chaotic and transient subway stations. I was meeting them in their homes, in front of their buildings, on their own blocks, which gave our interactions a different dynamic. It reminded me why I had gotten into this job.

I was also lucky to have a commanding officer, Deputy Inspector Eddie Lott, who took me under his wing. A dark-skinned man with a shaved head and wide smile, DI Lott would address roll call like a coach and leave the platoon feeling positive and motivated. He often thanked us for coming to work in a job that could seem thankless. "Brother," he once said to me, putting his hands on my shoulders like a parent, "my job is to get you to walk across that stage," meaning getting my sergeant's promotion. He took the initiative to walk me through the responsibilities I'd face when I became a supervisor, bolstering me when I was at my lowest.

Weeks passed. I'd get dressed for work every day and go on patrol while this dark cloud hovered above my head. One afternoon, my car had broken down, so I was walking on Utica Avenue in Crown Heights. Saki called to say the *Times* was going to push it back again. "Sorry, man," he said, "but it looks like it'll be late April, early May."

I snapped, just completely lost it. "No!" I screamed at him. "I cannot wait until April. I'm not going to make it to April!" Pedestrians were eyeing me as I bellowed down the street, my voice rising above the traffic.

"Okay, okay. Edwin," Saki said, trying to calm me down. "I'll try. But explain again so I can tell my editors: Why is coming out now so crucial?"

"Because this sparks everything!" I yelled. "The Justice League is on standby, a lot of activists are on board to finally work with cops. This shows them we're serious! I keep telling Tamika to hold tight and hold tight—they're all going to vanish. I can't wait until April. I'm not going to make it to April!"

I had built this piece up in my mind to such a degree that I worried I might do something stupid if it didn't come out soon. It was like the article was no longer just reporting on what I was going through; it was like it was the truth itself. It justified my struggle, and until it was public, it was like my pain didn't exist. Like my mission didn't exist. Like *I* didn't exist.

A week or so later, Saki called back. He'd pushed his editors and made it happen. "Okay, it's done. Coming out this week." I wouldn't let myself exhale until I saw it with my own eyes. On a Friday in mid-February,

I got a text from a high school friend: *Edwin, I'm in tears. I'm so proud of you.*

Yeah, any minute, it's going to come out, I replied.

What do you mean? I just read it!

I got online and found it, a picture of me patrolling in uniform with the headline "A Black Police Officer's Fight Against the NYPD."*

After dropping my friend off at work at Macy's in Herald Square, I parked on the side of the street and read the whole thing on my phone. When I finished, neck stiff and eyes teary, I finally let myself breathe. The article was as direct and forceful as I could've hoped. Saki had incorporated the recordings, the retaliation, the hypocrisy. It was all there.

Even though I had been living with this every day of my life, seeing it in the *Times* made it real. I read through the comments, some praising, others insulting, and watched as it spread throughout social media. There was now undisputed proof that no one could ever take away, no matter what they said about me. *Paper.* We'd done it.

WHEN I WENT INTO WORK the next day, I didn't know what I was going to face. Early that morning in the locker room, a young Black cop came up to me. "I just want to thank you," he said. "Finally, somebody said something." I did not expect that, even from a cop of color. There were also some funny looks in there, stares, a few whispers. Around eleven a.m. a radio call came through telling me to 10-2, report back to base.

I didn't know why they'd called me back, but I sensed it was connected to the article. At the desk, I was told, "The CO wants to see you in his office." *Here we go,* I thought. I went into DI Lott's office and saw

* The cover of the print magazine had a picture of me sitting in my car in street clothes.

the XO, the second in command, sitting there as well. I rarely saw him, as he worked the evening shift.

"Close the door," Lott said, his face unreadable. He and the XO stood up and waved me into another back room, a smaller type of locker room that the two shared. I was nervous and clueless, as flashes of mob hits played in my mind. When the back-room door was closed, Lott took a beat, looked at the XO, then at me. Then he gave me a gigantic bear hug, nearly lifting me off the ground. "I'm so proud of you," he said. "I'm not going to say I agree with everything, but man, what an article."

"Great shit, man," the XO said.

"It's very brave what you're doing," Lott continued. "I printed it out and am leaving it at the desk for everyone to read, if they choose to."

As we came back out into his main office, he called me over. "Raymond, come here. I want to show you something." He brought me over to the wall map, which covered all of Brooklyn, with a perimeter drawn around the Seventy-Seventh, his command. "Anywhere in here, you're safe. Nothing can happen to you without going through me. But outside of here"—he pointed to the rest of the borough, into Queens, Manhattan, the Bronx—"you have to be very careful, because there's nothing I can do for you. But as long as you're here, I got you."

"Thank you, sir," I said, choking up a bit. Honestly, I was stunned. It was the first time in eight years that a commanding officer had offered unbridled support like that, and he did it the day after I had blown the whistle in the most public way possible, admitting to recording other COs and even chiefs. But Lott didn't care about any of that. He was a true leader, willing to stick his neck out for me. I had been wondering if there were any of those left.

For the rest of the day, through the weekend, my phone was going off constantly: calls and messages from colleagues, friends, acquaintances, people whom I hadn't talked to in years, who I didn't even know had my number. Sergeant Campbell called to say how moved he was. "As a father of Black sons," he said, "I thank you for what you're doing." There were so many things I wanted to say, but I didn't challenge him. *Why aren't you standing up for your sons?* I thought, but I let it pass. He didn't invent the wheel; he just helped to keep it spinning.

I had a similar conversation with Lieutenant Hayden, and I got calls from mentors like Nickson, who was one of the reasons I became a cop. "I'm so proud of you, big guy," he said. "That took a lot of guts. Everybody knows it's true." I could tell by the way he spoke that I had woken something up in him that had lain dormant. He had put those thoughts asleep twenty years before in order to just get through the day.

The supportive calls, congratulations, and confessions reminded me of a book I'd read by Frantz Fanon called *Black Skin, White Masks*, about the way Black people feel they have to construct two selves to survive. We have to engage in doubling, where we present one self to the public at large in order to navigate white-dominated society and another in our private spaces.

What was even more shocking were the calls from high-ranking officials, including Captain Griffith, who had kicked me out of Truancy. "I'm so proud of you, young Black man," he said. "I don't know how you found the courage, and I hope to see a lot more from you." It was confusing at first. I had long been under the impression that none of the COs said anything about the racial quotas because they believed in the system. But it was clear they just did what was required. None of them had signed up for a mission; they had just signed up for a job.

I heard from those who were at One Police Plaza on the day the article dropped that it was like an earthquake had shaken the building. The brass were caught totally unprepared and were forced to switch into emergency damage-control mode. Commissioner Bratton and Mayor de Blasio were so enraged that they declared no one was allowed to take the day off.

At a press conference a few days later, Bratton was asked directly about the *Times* article and my claims about quotas. "What is your response to his claim and are you concerned—"

"*Bullshit,*" he said, cutting off the question. "Bullshit is my response to that." Jaws hit the floor. Bratton always bragged about never swearing. "If any of our cops out there still think we're pushing for the summonses, et cetera, I'm sorry, we're pushing to reduce crime. For that officer, one of thirty-six thousand, that may be his impression," Bratton said. "He's entitled to that impression, but those are not the practices, policies, procedures that I'm putting into this organization."

My impression. It was the kind of bald-faced lie that allowed Bratton to pretend he cared about the communities he was responsible for policing.

"How could he say it's just you? We all know what it is on this job," one officer told me.

Honestly, I expected nothing less from the commissioner, but what most angered me was silence from the mayor. De Blasio was a self-proclaimed progressive who had not a word to say on the biggest police story in many years. Twelve active New York City officers had filed a lawsuit and were now providing documented proof of systemic oppression of citizens of color by his police department. It dropped in his lap and he didn't do a thing: no investigation, no commission, nothing. I have no doubt Bratton assured the mayor that our accusations were unfounded, which made it even worse. The mayor ignored people on the ground, instead taking the word of the top brass. And we had the evidence.

The mayor was already in self-protection mode after cops turned their back on him for saying he spoke to his Black son about being careful around police, something virtually every parent of a Black child has done. But he paid for it, and maybe he didn't want to pay anymore. His cowardice was disheartening; I was done with him after that. Though precedents had been set for over a century with the Mollen Commission (1992), the Knapp Commission (1970), and the Lexow Committee

(1894), after explosive revelations inside the department, de Blasio failed to use them as guidance. He opted to stay on the wrong side of history.

The very next day was the annual Black History Celebration at One Police Plaza. I almost didn't go, but I understood the days of lying low had come to an end. When I got there, people I didn't know kept pulling me aside saying things like, "Listen, man, thank you. We're all tired of this CompStat shit. This isn't why I became a cop."

"You got some fucking balls that you're here," one lieutenant told me. "That's impressive. You're not even made. The bottom of the totem pole and you show up. You got elephant balls, man."

I got some of the other kind of response too. I ran into Chief Secreto, the Black Housing chief who was at my CARB meeting, and he refused to shake my hand, clearly angry about being recorded. I was hurt, though I understood his side—he had been the only one trying to defend me, and I wanted to tell him I didn't do it to nail him. I just had to have evidence of what was being illegally demanded of me.

When Bratton got up to the podium to speak, the previous day's outburst on everyone's mind, he gave a little smile. "I'll behave . . . ," he said. Incredibly, Bratton had the gall to make a speech about how it wasn't enough for Black cops to join the ranks; they needed to rise to leadership positions. He completely excised his own role in the matter. The previous year, Bratton claimed the police department couldn't hire as many Black male officers as they'd like because so many Black men "have spent time in jail,"[1] ignoring his role as architect of the very policies that put them there. "You are now part of an organization," he continued, "you are now part of a profession that can make profound change for everybody. We open the doors to many more from your communities, to your family or friends, and to do that we need to ensure that those opportunities are there."

The hypocrisy was colossal. Had I not been used to Bratton's double-speak, I would've been baffled. But it was just more smoke and mirrors.

I'd heard it all before. A year earlier, during Black History Month, Bratton said at a Black church, "Many of the worst parts of Black history would have been impossible without police."[2] Bratton knew when and where to say the right things, but he failed to acknowledge his own complicity.

My days as an anonymous rank-and-file cop were over. I was no longer a private citizen. I became a recognizable face on the street—there were very few dark-skinned cops with long dreadlocks—and a target of both support and retaliation. I was no longer just me; I was the face of this larger thing, with all the positive and negative exposure that came with it.

I got mocked, insulted, threatened; called a rat, a snitch, and a traitor, especially on cop message boards like Thee RANT and in corners of Facebook. I got dirty looks at work and had a palpable sense that other cops were whispering about me, avoiding me, talking about me behind my back.

After my sergeant put me behind the desk in order to get experience as a supervisor, an officer said to him, "Why do you have a rat behind the desk?"

There was also a snowball effect, among politicians, activists, and media. I was connected to other organizations, contacted for panels and documentaries, and solicited for media interviews. The Justice League NYC did a press conference, and NBC News reached out to interview me.

A month after I appeared on NBC News, reporter Sarah Wallace called me to come back in for a follow-up piece, this time with most of my fellow NYPD 12 plaintiffs. Before they taped the interview, ten of us got together to meet at a small Irish pub near NBC's Rockefeller Center offices. We pushed tables together and planned to talk strategy for the interview. But we also got to know one another. Even though we'd been experiencing this huge thing that had carved up so much of our lives, we had never really sat down together.

Adhyl Polanco was there, a genial guy, excited to see that others had finally joined him. So was Pedro Serrano, a large bald Hispanic man, who tried to lighten the mood with comedy. I met Sandy Gonzalez, one of the first to join, soft-spoken with a slight stammer, relieved to see our ranks grow; Ritchie Baez, a studious-looking Patrol cop out of the Bronx, who was disciplined and religious; and Derick Waller, the only detective in the group. I also got to know the lone female, Felicia Whitely. A Housing cop in her tenth year, Felicia was a newly divorced mother of two daughters. She had a lot to lose, maybe more than most of us, so she was cautious, opting to read the room before socializing. Like a few of the NYPD 12, she would develop health problems from the stress of the retaliation. Everyone traded stories on how they'd been singled out, punished, taken out of their sector cars, placed on retaliatory posts, put on performance monitoring, thrown on midnights, sent pictures of rats, and gotten written up for minor or invented infractions.

As we spoke, I had a brief flashback to the high school lunch table with friends from other parts of the city, all sharing the same police harassment stories. Now here I was fifteen years later, talking about the same racial-based harassment, this time from inside the police ranks.

"Isn't it crazy," I said, "that we all work the three different bureaus, different boroughs, and we all have the same experiences? If that's not the definition of systemic, I don't know what is."

I told them about Tsachas's reign of terror, and they shared stories of commanders who treated policing Black and Brown citizens like a video game, all in the name of "public safety." Ritchie Baez told us about Captain McCormick, who said at roll call, "If you're searching somebody and your fingers don't smell like shit afterward, you're doing it wrong." When we sat down to speak on camera, there was this buzz in the air. It was rare that this many active cops would come together to say anything against the department. It simply hadn't been done before. The NBC segment would go on to be viewed 100 million times.

There's a pervasive myth that you should first rise quietly so you can get some power and then speak out to effect change. I heard that so many times, from well-meaning people thinking they were offering guidance. But it doesn't work. I've never seen it work. It's a delusion that keeps people getting out of bed and putting on the uniform.

There are people in the upper echelons, Black cops especially, who believe that they will one day push to change things. And that's how it remains, one hypothetical day in the future. So far, they have done little to upend the status quo, but they still like to look in the mirror and tell themselves they will, once they get powerful enough. What they fail to understand is that with this logic, they will never be able to push the button; there will always be a higher position to ascend to. As a sergeant, if you're too loud, good luck getting to lieutenant, where you can be more influential. If you're too loud as a lieutenant, you'll never get your own command as a captain. They will bury you in a dusty corner far from Patrol, like Applicant Processing or the Ballistic Vest Unit.* If you lie low as captain and make it to deputy inspector and then try to fight things, good luck getting to chief. If you make it to one-star chief and blow that whistle, good luck getting to assistant chief, and never mind bureau chief. There's one chief of department, and you'll never get that fourth star if you're too loud. And if you get near the top and make noise, you'll never get selected to be commissioner. If you're waiting, it's never going to be the right time.

The right time is always now. Start now so you can keep your integrity intact.

It might take some time, but I knew they were going to come for me.

---

* NYPD is one of the few police departments that randomly selects vests and shoots them to make sure they still work.

At a planning meeting with Tamika and other activists, I explained how a mother can't spank a misbehaving child at the supermarket. She waits until they get to the privacy of their own home. "Right now, we're in the supermarket," I said, regarding the press attention. But they would wait until the cameras and lights went away and then they would spank us. I was as sure of it as anything in my life.

"They're going to set us up," I predicted. "They don't have to follow the law. Who are we going to call? Them?"

Twenty-Three

Public Enemy

June 2016

I s this conversation being recorded?"

The chief of personnel sat across from me, flanked by two familiar faces: Chief Galati and Chief Secreto. I was again on the twelfth floor of NYPD headquarters battling for my sergeant promotion at CARB, but a lot had changed in six months. I was no longer the individual cop sitting alone at the other end of the long table. I felt like I had an army behind me now. Not just other cops, but activists, organizations, journalists, political leaders, and average citizens.

My article had sparked a firestorm, put me on TV, in magazines, on news programs, panels, conferences. Requests for my expertise and perspective exploded. It was extremely rare to have an active officer willing to tell the truth. The response was shock in some quarters, relief in others.

There was a thick tension in the room at CARB, because all the chiefs knew that I had recorded them in the last meeting. I'd broken an unwritten rule, which was now a written one. All over the building were signs: "No Recording Allowed." Deputy Commissioner Julian had retired, so the new chief of personnel, Raymond Spinella, led the meeting. He was an affable guy with a thick mustache and a shock of white hair. Though the other slots were supposedly filled by random selection, there was zero chance it was a coincidence: Galati and Secreto were there again.

This time they sat directly across from me in the middle of the table. It balanced the power dynamic, putting us on a more equal footing. I could speak more naturally and read every movement of their eyes, every detail in their faces. When Chief Spinella asked if I was taping, I was relieved to answer.

"I'm glad you opened up that way," I said. "No, this conversation is not being recorded. And let me just say about that: I had nothing personal against anyone here. I was being asked to do something that I knew was unlawful, and I had to protect myself."

"We weren't trying to hurt you either," Galati replied in his high voice. "It seemed like your commander was busting your balls and we wanted to see how you carried yourself outside of Transit. Looks like you did well. We just wanted to be sure you understood why enforcement is necessary."

"With all due respect, sir, I never said that enforcement isn't necessary," I replied. "I don't think that. I just don't believe that we should burn the entire village in the name of keeping it safe. Broken windows and quotas end up victimizing the very people we claim we're trying to protect from crime."

Secreto chimed in: "Every time I read in the paper that someone jumps the turnstile and is found with a gun, I think about you. I think, 'What would Raymond say about this, since he thinks these collars are meaningless?'"

"I don't think they're meaningless. I just think everything in Transit is done with an eye toward the needle in the haystack. Every time one of these arrests occurs it gets blasted at roll calls as an example of why aggressive TOS enforcement is essential. But I've checked the actual numbers. Do you know how many guns Transit recovered last year from searches incidental to an arrest?"

"No," Secreto said.

"Eight."

"Well, eight percent is—" Galati started to say.

"No, not eight percent, sir." I said. "Eight *guns*. Out of thousands of these arrests."[1]

They all looked at one another. I didn't add that the reason you read about every gun found on a turnstile jumper in the paper is because the department makes sure to publicize it. It is an essential part of the charade, justifying the practice.

"From the first time you were here," Galati said, "we all felt that you would definitely be promoted at some point in the future. But the concern was would you, as supervisor, be able to hold your cops' feet to the fire? We were just making sure . . . before you got your stripes."

"It was taken from me, though. Everyone told me the most important promotion was to sergeant, because it puts you in a different category where you're no longer one of the guys but now a leader. And that was taken from me."

Galati dropped his eyes, and Spinella nodded slightly, as though he was trying to figure me out. A three-star chief is used to little more than "Yes, sir." But it felt as though there was no rank in that moment: just four men having a conversation.

Once I had made everything public, they had no leg to stand on to deny my promotion. But I still walked out of there unsure. I was ready for them to move the goalposts yet again.

Incredibly, Tsachas was on the promotion list that summer to become a deputy inspector. It was purely discretionary—there's no test above captain—which meant he was explicitly promoted by Bratton.

Tsachas had already been outed as a bigot, both by me and by fellow whistleblower Michael Birch. Promoting him sent a clear message to other commanders that the department has their back and they should carry on as usual. If anything punitive had happened to Tsachas, the captain's union would have had the commanders shut down, as it had after Mayor de Blasio's comments about his Black son, and the leadership couldn't have that.

Upon learning this news, I was so shocked that I wrote an op-ed in the *Daily News* blasting his promotion. I wrote about his systemic campaign to target only people of color for minor infractions, quoted his comments from our private meetings, and referred to conversations that Birch recorded of Tsachas specifically telling him to "target male Blacks."

"What does the department decide to do with Tsachas," I wrote, "who encourages officers under his command to engage in so-called 'reasonable racism,' something you'd expect to hear from the mouths of David Duke or Jared Taylor? PROMOTE HIM TO DEPUTY INSPECTOR!"[2]

I pointed out that Tsachas's rise was a prime example of how this toxic behavior spreads. Those who push the quotas the hardest are elevated, which puts more personnel under them, multiplying the number of cops who are forced to engage in harassment policing in order to sustain their careers.

My peers told me I was crazy for publicly attacking a former CO when my own promotion was about to come through. In their minds I was a shoo-in: *Why poke the bear?* But how could I stay silent on something I'd seen with my own eyes, heard with my own ears?

Bratton defended his decision to make Tsachas a deputy inspector, saying, "It's unfortunate I have some conscientious objectors in the organization who don't want to do police work," not so subtly calling me out. It was an insulting comment to make to an officer who was out there every day. Why would I spend my life in a job that I refused to do? It was nonsensical, a gross oversimplification of my argument. It just showed how they had no more reasonable arguments left.

Why would I risk my life for something I didn't believe in?

THE SUMMER OF 2016 triggered another wave of Black Lives Matter protests after police killed Alton Sterling in Baton Rouge and Philando Castile in Minneapolis–St. Paul. Both incidents were captured on camera, sickening to witness, horrifying to watch.* Castile's death came from a broken-windows-type offense—supposedly a broken taillight— though really it was just a pretext to search him. The officer thought he had the same "wide-set nose" as a robbery suspect. Castile, a registered gun owner, calmly told the officer he had a gun, which triggered the panicked officer's shots. Of course, the pro-gun community and Second Amendment warriors didn't say a word. It was a sad distillation of an American truth: Black people are not afforded the same rights as white Americans. Our skin color alone makes us suspicious.

Then, the unthinkable happened: During BLM protests in Dallas, five police officers were ambushed and killed. The next week in Baton Rouge, three more. Both shooters were former military guys, operating as vigilantes. Tensions were high, and everyone was scared. There was a genuine war going on in America, and as a police officer, I was caught in the middle of it.

Giving an interview with Hot 97's Nessa a week later, I made it clear where we should point our energy: "The cops are just following bad policy . . . anything that's going to bring real change, you got to focus at the top." I wanted to drive home the idea that the individual cop is just caught in a system he can't control or even question. "Right now, the mayor should not be able to stand in front of any podium and not be

---

* Castile's murder was actually live streamed on Facebook by his girlfriend while her four-year-old sat in the back seat of the car.

questioned about what's going on with policing. He shouldn't be able to pass the question off to the commissioner."

While we were talking, I saw someone I recognized watching us on the other side of the glass. He was a tall, light-skinned Black dude with broad shoulders, hair in a short-picked Afro. He was wearing sweatpants and sneakers, and a black T-shirt with a photo of Malcolm X.

Oh shit, I thought, *that's that quarterback.*

In July 2016 Colin Kaepernick's name was not yet a lightning rod—he was a rising NFL star who had taken San Francisco to the Super Bowl a few years before. He was dating Nessa and had tagged along to watch the interview. Afterward, he came up to me in the green room and introduced himself, his giant hands dwarfing mine.

"Wow, man, that was very impressive," he said. "Eye-opening. It's a relief that there are cops who get it, because too often they don't." The distrust of police and the system had made so many people cynical. In the eyes of many activists, police were just oppressors, which doesn't lead anywhere but to demonization.

"Yeah," I said. "People are just trying to pay their bills. They don't see the larger thing that they are a part of." I used the assembly-line metaphor. In law enforcement cops are also completing a repetitive task, but they don't see the bigger picture. If they do, they see it only through the company line: *we're stopping crime.* They don't see the detriments. And they're stuck in an echo chamber: they hang out with other cops, buy the department's PR, and follow media and politicians that are blindly pro-cop.

"But there are a lot more of us," I told Kaepernick. "A *lot.* They're just afraid to speak out. It's career suicide."

"Right."

Kaepernick talked about how he was reading books by political thinkers like Angela Davis, expanding his mind and perspective on the treatment of people of African descent. I didn't know what had elevated his consciousness; it happens to Black men for various reasons. It could've begun with Ferguson and the BLM movement or its resurgence that summer in the wake of the Sterling and Castile shootings. It could have been things he saw traveling around the country with his team. It could have been because he was light-skinned and witness to racist behavior from people who didn't realize he was Black.

"Okay, man, keep in touch," he said as we traded numbers. "Let me know if I can be of help. In any way."

I had no idea what he was thinking about doing, or if the plan was still forming in his head. A few weeks later, the puzzle pieces fell into place when Kaepernick knelt during the national anthem before a game.* He was explicit that he was protesting against police killings of unarmed African Americans, and it started a nationwide firestorm.

"I am not going to stand up to show pride in a flag for a country that oppresses Black people and people of color," he said. "I'm going to continue to stand with the people that are being oppressed . . . When there's significant change and I feel that flag represents what it's supposed to represent, and this country is representing people the way that it's supposed to, I'll stand."

The way people went after him, you would've thought Kaepernick blew up a U.S. barracks. The main attack was that Kap was insulting the troops, a baseless argument. The kneeling had nothing to do with the troops. In fact, by using the national anthem as a forum, he was challenging the kind of performative patriotism that has nothing to do with love of country. Implicit in his kneeling was a basic question: How can we venerate a place where innocent people of color are killed by those sworn to protect them?

It was a brilliant move on his part. Protests rarely infiltrate the world of the people who need to hear them most. Often, protesters march on

---

* Kap initially sat down, but a veteran told him that kneeling would be a more effective way to communicate the point that he was not disrespecting the troops.

predetermined corners among fellow believers, with routes and destinations that don't disrupt the general population. People won't even hear your truth unless you shove it in front of their faces, take it directly to their front door, to a place where they're definitely paying attention. NFL games were America's backyard barbecue. People had no choice but to see it.

"If they take football away, my endorsements from me," he said, "I know that I stood up for what is right."[3] Kaepernick knew what he was risking, and he did it anyway. The very definition of heroic. I immediately started thinking about ways I could support him, not fully realizing it would put me in the crosshairs as well.

AT THE SAME TIME, in August 2016, nearly three years after I placed eighth out of six thousand test takers, I was finally promoted to sergeant. It happened to be the anniversary of my mother's death, bringing some light to a day that had always been draped in darkness. Billy's mother, Mommy Florise, who got me Christmas presents and fed me when I had nothing, was there. So was my brother Ronald, mentors like Nickson and Oliver, friends from the NYPD 12, activists like Tamika, and supportive colleagues. When my name was called, it was the loudest cheering at any ceremony—or so I was told.*

I tried to soak in the moment, embrace it all: the new shield, gold nameplate, the widening on the braid on my trousers, the chevrons added to my sleeves. These were not just symbols, but tangible proof that I had earned my place. That I belonged where I stood. That's really all I ever wanted for myself. I thought of my mother, who never got to know me, and my father, who made me who I was.

Because of my high score, I got my pick of where I wanted to go. I

---

* It was Bratton's last ceremony. A few weeks later, he resigned after a tumultuous tenure at the NYPD, clashing with the mayor, the rank and file, and the community.

specifically chose PSA 2, the Housing Bureau command that covers all NYCHA* developments within three precincts: Seventy-Third, Seventy-Fifth, Seventy-Seventh. These are some of the most impoverished and dangerous neighborhoods in the city, possibly even in the country, including Brownsville and East New York.

"What are you doing?" a fellow new sergeant asked me. "You waste your top pick on PSA Two?"

"I don't see it as a waste," I said.

And I didn't. I saw it as an *opportunity*.

Knowing eyes were on me, I wanted to make sure my argument could stand on its own two feet. If I was going to criticize the system, and make progress in dismantling and rebuilding it, I could not go where it was easy. The notion that we don't have to overpolice certain communities in the name of public safety *had* to be demonstrated in the most crime-ridden neighborhoods. If I could prove it was unnecessary there, it wasn't necessary anywhere.

I also chose to work evenings, the shift with the worst incidents: shootings, homicides, sexual assault, child abuse, murder-suicides. It was heavy stuff, and no matter how many of those scenes you work, it never rolls off you. I took leadership on an early call in which two people were shot on opposite corners of Howard Avenue in Brownsville. One guy was cracking jokes after getting shot in the groin, while the other one lay on his back unconscious, blood seeping from his body. Back at base, I learned that the unconscious man lived, while the laughing one had died.

A few weeks later a guy came to buy weed to sell back in Staten Island and it was a setup, a robbery. He turned his head right at the last second, so the bullet entered through his neck and exited through the jaw, missing all of his important plumbing, sparing his life. Those

---

* New York City Housing Authority.

incidents followed me home at the end of the day. The way that life is this thing of inches. Saved by accident, taken in an instant.

Many of the calls in Housing were EDPs, emotionally disturbed persons. We dealt with some in Transit, but never in this capacity—people in their homes, off their meds, having disputes with family members, with knives and blunt objects around. Many of these incidents went above and beyond police. These people needed help at a level that we weren't equipped to give. I saw people caught in the vortex of poverty, of the misery and hopelessness that came with it, of the violence and ugliness that came down on them with the regularity of the setting sun.

I remember once hearing Bratton say that Black areas call 911 the most, which made no sense to me. In the hood, I'd always assumed people did not call the cops. No one wants to summon the same people who had been violating them. But he was right, and I saw the evidence. In these heated disputes, some people just want to get the other person in trouble. Calling the cops in these situations weaponizes the system against loved ones, like a more serious version of tattling to the teacher. At those times, once the emotions faded, they almost always regretted it and would bring food to the prisoner at the precinct. Then they'd drop the charges and things would cool before something new happened and it started up again.

On morning shifts, parents would call us because their kids didn't want to go to school. I did my best to tap into a rapport I had with young folks, working to get them to cooperate. I reached much deeper than my training and I walked away thinking that with another cop, with a different temperament, it would've turned into a disaster. The cop is not a positive authority figure or even a neutral party in these neighborhoods. A cop's very arrival can exacerbate the problem, and I was conscious of that every time I showed up. Officers would reach out to me when they were having issues with juveniles. Even units that specialized in dealing with young folks needed my assistance from time to time. "You're the only one she listens to, Sergeant Raymond," one Brownsville mother told me. "She started focusing on school and stopped running away after you spoke to her."

Brownsville has a corridor of developments concentrated right on top of one another, which, along with the poverty, gang issues, and structural racism, had triggered so much of the violence. One officer set up a basketball league as a way for these young folks to see the residents of the other buildings differently. After a few months, kids who would've been conditioned to see one another as a threat were instead talking good-hearted trash and even trading compliments on the court. If other services were provided for these kids, the police department wouldn't need to get so involved in their lives.

In every work space I entered, I also had to navigate the stares, the whispers, the not knowing how officers felt about me. I had been in the news pretty regularly for the previous six months, for speaking out against the department, recording chiefs, suing the city. Everything was buried under command structure—"sir" and "boss" all down the line—so it was subtle. I became good at reading body language, tone, suggestive word choice.

As a supervisor, I was very hands-on, out there with my officers. When I filled out their evaluations, I wanted to have a real understanding of what they were like. I remained approachable, never pulled rank, and of course never pushed for activity. But I also didn't point my officers anywhere; I said *follow me*.

Over time, more cops warmed up to me. An officer confided, "Two days before you got here, Sergeant Cerillo shared your article and said, 'Watch what you say around this guy, you got a rat coming into the building.' But I know you now, see that you're about the job." In the locker room, my driver would get bullied, taunted with comments like, "How does it feel to be driving a fucking rat?" He stopped getting invited to the barbecues, to the ball games, to after-work drinks. Just for working with me. There was a price exacted for speaking the truth, for even being associated with the truth, especially in a place where it was in such short supply.

AFTER TWO YEARS OF PROTESTS, starting with the killing of Eric Garner and Mike Brown, then to the death of Freddie Gray in Baltimore, and then Alton Sterling and Philando Castile, I had seen the slow opening up of cops' minds. They were noticing that the image they had of themselves—hero, public servant—was different from much of the public's. And they started to ask why. It happened from the leadership as well. President of the International Association of Chiefs of Police, Terry Cunningham,* addressed that year's international conference by apologizing for police's "historical mistreatment of communities of color" and spoke of "a multigenerational—almost inherited—mistrust between many communities of color and their law enforcement agencies."[4] FBI director James Comey spoke about how white people "have unconscious racial biases and react differently to a white face than a black face."[5] Former NYPD commissioner Bernard Kerik served three years in prison for tax fraud and came out a prisoner's rights advocate.[6] Things were being put out into the open, laid on the table. It made me optimistic.

And then, like hitting a brick wall: Trump. Especially after his election, it all just came to a halt. The open-mindedness stopped and actually started going in reverse. Those cops who might have been opening up were now empowered in their bigotry, in their Blue Lives insularity, in their "law and order" dog whistles, in their racism disguised as public safety.

What was most disturbing was how it transcended traditional color lines. A female officer from my company, a dark-skinned Dominican

---

* San Diego chief of police.

immigrant, was one of the most vocal Trump supporters I knew. She saw the calls for police reform as an attack, even though her very existence was under threat from the people she was supporting. Even though the other side was fighting for her as a Black person, a Latina, a woman, an immigrant, as someone in the middle class—none of that mattered. Her identity as a cop canceled out everything else. Even though it's the one thing that's temporary, that can be taken away, that will one day be no more, that's what she held on to the tightest. That tribalism hardened with Trump and hardened even more in response to being confronted. People like to stick with their own. The sides were dropping down battle lines, firm in their sense of rightness, staying where they felt they belonged.

It became more and more obvious that the space in the middle was no-man's-land. Someone needed to plant a flag there or the sides would dig in even harder.

Twenty-Four

The Men in the Arena

Summer 2017

He walked with a wooden cane, a little slower from the nerve damage and eighty-one years of not taking shit from anyone. Slightly frail, but with strong, sinewy arms, he still had bullet fragments lodged in his cheek from when he was shot and nearly killed in 1971. The past never leaves him because it made him who he is.

I met Frank Serpico through director Steve Maing, who was shooting a documentary about the NYPD 12. After Colin Kaepernick—in his prime and only four seasons removed from leading the 49ers to the Super Bowl—was not signed by a single NFL team, I wanted to offer my help. Kap was blackballed by the entire league for exercising his First Amendment rights and speaking out against police brutality. The defenders of the social order were closing ranks—again.

Kap and I met up that summer. He told me, "So many other players agree behind the scenes, but . . ."

"They're not willing to risk anything publicly," I said.

"Exactly," he said. "It's frustrating."

"Well, a lot of officers have told me to give you the message that they support you."

"That means a lot coming from you, thanks."

"It's not just from me. That's part of the problem. The silence. People hiding so they don't catch any strays."

"Yeah," he said. "No one's willing to stand out front."

"But I have an idea, a way to make them speak up."

I found every voice mail and message of support that colleagues had sent in the last year and a half, since the *Times* article came out. Messages that stated how much they respected me for taking such risks, messages letting me know they were behind Kap, whom I was vocally supporting in public. My idea was to put together a press conference of police support for him. I invited nearly two hundred police and correction officers, telling them the date and the plan, and asking for their shirt sizes. A lot of people said yes, but you never know who will be there standing with you at the moment of truth.

Then I called Steve, throwing the ultimate Hail Mary.

"Listen," I said. "I know you know Serpico. It's a long shot, but any chance he'll come out and join us?"

"Yeah, I don't know, man," he said. "Serpico doesn't come out."

In the decades since he had become the most prominent police whistleblower in history, since Al Pacino made him a household name, people were always asking for Frank Serpico's help.

"Do me a favor," I said, "just ask for permission to give me his number and if it's okay that I call him."

Serpico agreed to hear me out and we spoke briefly on the phone. I told him I understood his reluctance to put himself out there. "But just do me a favor," I said. "Look me up. Then decide." An old-school cat, he went to his local library and did his research. Then he called me back: he was in.

The night before the event, Serpico made the five-hour trip down to Brooklyn from his place upstate. My plan had been to put him up in a hotel with four retired officers rotating shifts guarding his door. But then he asked, "Where do you live?"

"Flatbush," I said.

"You got a couch?"

"Yeah."

"I'll stay with you," he said. And that was that. He was not a man you argued with.

Sporting white hair and beard, tinted glasses, gold hoops in each ear, Serpico carried a simple backpack and wore a gray T-shirt and black beaded necklace with a silver pendant hanging down. When he came in, I immediately showed him a gift I got from my sergeant promotion: a framed copy of his police ID.

"Who is this guy?" he said, pointing at the picture. "I never even met him." It turned out that the photo wasn't of him, but the actor who played him on the television show spun off from the movie. We laughed about it, but it was fitting. Serpico had seeped into the larger culture, had become a separate entity from the man himself.

We broke the ice by trading bios. After learning I was Haitian, he impressed me with some Creole, and even picked up my African drum, playing far better than I ever could have. I learned that he grew up in Brooklyn with immigrant parents who spoke Italian, a father who had a shoe shop in Crown Heights.

As an officer in the sixties, he stood out on the force. Shaggy hair and beard, earrings and bohemian dress, he lived in Greenwich Village, an island of artists and younger counterculture types. His style was unique, and he was open to different cultures (Europe, Latin America) and high art like ballet and opera. Though he stuck out among regular cops, he blended in with *the people*. As Peter Maas wrote in the book that made Serpico famous:

Cops didn't seem to think of themselves as part of the community. Too many of them, Serpico thought, had isolated themselves not only professionally, but socially. They believed they were misunderstood by the "outside world," that there was a general public antagonism toward them, and this notion had fed on itself back and forth, until in fact there *were* "sides" and neither side could relate to the other. If cops talked to people more, instead of just other cops, if they took the initiative in reaching out to them, Serpico was certain they could break down some of these barriers.[1]

In our talk, it struck me how little had changed in fifty-plus years. Everything from the terminology—"four-bys" and the "124 Room"*— to the larger issues in the department that he and I discussed like contemporaries. We both saw the same potential and possibilities, as well as the selfishness and insularity that kept the force from reaching that potential. It's telling that Serpico's testimony to the Knapp Commission could've been written yesterday. Forty-six years earlier, he had addressed the need to evaluate officers beyond arrest numbers and quotas and noted that cops' first duty is to the public, not to one another or the system itself.

"Until the right thing is incentivized," he said, peering at me with his deep, penetrating eyes, "there's going to be another version of you down the line, and it's going to go on and on until we have the leadership who is going to reward the change, *believe* in the change."

It's not often you get to meet your heroes, much less put them up for a night in your home. I was grateful for the opportunity to share with him how much his story, especially the film, had been a touchstone for me. It helped me keep my sanity. Seeing him struggle not just with the system but *with himself* made me feel less lost.

"Well," he said, smiling, with a glint in his eye. "I'm glad the film did

---

* The four p.m. to midnight shift and the admin room in every precinct, respectively.

something good." I could tell he had some misgivings about the movie that made him an icon. Overall, he was equal parts passionate and mischievous, a shit stirrer in the best way.

After we ate sandwiches of avocado and tomato on whole grain bread—we both had plant-based diets—I told him I had prepared the bedroom for him. But stretched out on the couch in his bare feet, he slapped the cushion: "Nah, thanks. I'm good here."

It was the week after white nationalists had marched on Charlottesville, Virginia, so tensions were high across the United States. The country felt explosive, and President Trump purposely amplified the tension. Battle lines had been drawn around race, politics, and policing, and I wanted to stake out some common (and commonsense) ground.

Kaepernick was not anti-cop, and certainly not anti-troops or anti-America; he was *pro-justice*—which is exactly what cops should be about. Isn't that literally what we signed up to protect? I thought it was essential that a group of officers stood up and said so. Were those hating on Kaepernick trying to argue that the murder of unarmed Black people by cops is okay because . . . why? Because you had to support cops no matter what? Because those unarmed Black men and women were actually a threat?

When U.S. sprinters John Carlos and Tommie Smith raised their fists on the podium at the 1968 Olympics in Mexico City, they weren't hating on their country. They were asking for it to be better. They wanted it to live up to its promise. Kap, and the rest of us that day, were asking for the same. As James Baldwin put it, it's his love for America that makes him "criticize her perpetually."[2]

At Brooklyn Bridge Park that morning, I was anxious to see how many cops would attend. I knew a strong showing of law enforcement supporting this man, this cause, with this message would speak volumes. It would contradict the blanket assumptions about police while also pointing out to other cops how much more work we needed to do.

In total, eighty-eight cops (almost all active) showed up that morning.

We handed out black T-shirts with the logo #IMWITHKAP in white lettering and assembled behind a lectern. The media was already there, cameras, tripods, cables arrayed on the boardwalk, the East River and majestic Brooklyn Bridge behind us.

Serpico was feted upon arrival, especially by the older cops and reporters who had grown up hearing his name. As the only white face among us, he later wrote he felt like he stood out, "like a solitary dandelion puff on a newly manicured lawn."[3] Though, of course, he was one of us, in some ways our forefather.

The event was an effort to move past the tribalism and punch through the false narrative about Kap's protest. *We all want justice and safe communities.* A few NYPD 12 cops were there, as was Jim (who changed his name to Kwasi and brought his four-year-old, CJ), activist Shaun King, Detective Weatherspoon, and Council Member Jumaane Williams, who said a few words in a red Kaepernick jersey. The goal was to push the conversations around supporting Kap and good-faith critiques of the police out in the open. Stop with the hiding and self-protection. If you support something, put your body in front of it.

I wasn't naive. I knew there'd be some controversy over the event; it's one of the reasons we did it, to get people talking. But I didn't expect that level of outrage. The firestorm. The blind hatred for this Black athlete who dared speak his mind. Kap was public enemy number one in Copland. Even those who supported my fight against harassment and quotas felt I'd crossed a line by saying anything in support of "that POS" or "that fucking guy." Cops seemed to be caught up on Kap's decision earlier that summer to wear socks that depicted officers as pigs. They completely tuned out the rest of his message, no matter how well he articulated the issues. It was easier for them to simplify and attack, as they tended to do with any criticism.

Later that day, participants in the press conference reported to work and immediately caught the backlash. People had meticulously gone through the photos and videos of the event, circling faces, identifying who was there and where they worked. Many were ostracized, some thrown out of their units. While I was fielding calls from them, I would apologize only to be cut off. "No," one officer said, "let me know when the next one is. I get to tell my kid that I was on the right side of history."

The president was trashing Kaepernick in public, right-wing outlets were painting him as a traitor to his country, and people were writing missives against me online. There were calls to headquarters, racist messages on Facebook, comments on places like Thee RANT and other cop social media sites, even death threats.

> The NYPD used to be the gold standard of policing then you started hiring all these niggers and ruined it. Cops supporting that motherfucker [Kaepernick]. That cocksucker Sgt. Raymond is gonna get what's coming to him.

> You're a fucking disgrace to the uniform. A blanket party* should be held in your honor, asswipe.

A detective from the Intelligence Bureau who was assigned to monitor threats reached out. He told me to inspect my personal vehicle before getting in the car and watch my surroundings. Someone warned me about having heard that if I was in danger on the job, they'd take their time sending backup, or if they could, ignore me altogether. My home was also classified as a sensitive location, meaning any 911 call to my address would require that a supervisor respond right away. My immediate thought was: *But what if the supervisor also sees me as a rat?* It was chilling to think that cops could hate Kaepernick so much that they'd condone the death of one of their own. Though for a while now, they didn't consider me one of their own.

---

* A military gang assault.

I was just another threatening Black man and would be treated accordingly.

THAT SAME MONTH—August 2017—I took the lieutenant's test and again performed in the highest 1 percent (number 26 out of 1,325 who passed). But things were about to be put in motion to stop my career dead in its tracks.

Everything stemmed from an incident that September in Brownsville, about a month after the Kaepernick press conference. I was on my way back to the command for my meal break when a 10-30 (robbery) came over the radio, which as a supervisor I had to respond to. When I got to Rockaway Avenue, my sector—the two officers under me responsible for the area—were already there. One of the officers met me as I got out of my car. "Boss," he said, "it's not a ten-thirty, it's a criminal mischief domestic"—damaging property. I looked over and saw a hefty, muscular Black guy near the curb cursing up a storm. "She broke my shit, man! Look at these fucking mirrors!"

The other officer was talking to a middle-aged woman farther down the block.

"Where's the perp?" I asked.

"She's ninety-Z," he said. *Gone on arrival.*

"So, who's this?" I pointed over to the crying woman.

"That's her mom."

"So, who's the victim?" I asked.

He pointed to the guy in the street who was still screaming about his car. "This fucking bitch!" the guy was yelling, going off about how she had smashed his side mirrors with a baseball bat. "She broke my shit!"

The mother grabbed on to my sleeve, sobbing and begging us not to arrest her daughter. She claimed the couple always went through this. "They fight, they make up, they get pregnant," she pleaded. "That's their pattern."

I then approached the man, who was about twice my size and still pretty heated.

"Listen, man," I said, talking calmly, "you did the right thing by calling nine one one. It'll be handled accordingly. It's good you didn't try to handle this yourself."

Considering his size and temper, it could've easily escalated into something far worse. I knew that positive reinforcement was a powerful tool. Talking to victims and suspects in a certain way can lay the groundwork for preventing further incidents. I saw that as an equal part of my job, though of course I was in the minority on this.

"Ma'am, it's best that you get your daughter to come back here," I told the mother. "Because, if not, it's going to become an open complaint, and she's going to be arrested. Officers can come at any time, and if there's no one there to watch her kids, Child Services will get involved. And you don't want that." I was trying to head off the logistical nightmare that comes with a sudden arrest. The mom's eyes went wide. She immediately got on the phone to get her daughter back.

I told the victim that the mother was contacting her daughter to come back so we could arrest her. He made a face like he was reconsidering it.

"You know what, man, you don't gotta arrest her," he said. "That's my baby mother. She's just mad I moved on. If I get her arrested, who's going to watch my kids?"

"Are you sure?" I asked. "What about your car?"

"I can get this shit fixed. This ain't going to cost a thing."

I signaled to the two officers in code that we wouldn't be arresting the daughter. "He doesn't want her collared anymore," I explained.

"Okay," one of the officers said, a wary look on his face. "But, boss, we actually ran his name before you got here and she has an order of protection against him, so we're just going to lock him up instead."

Lock him up instead.

"What?" I said. "No! This guy was just sitting in his car. The woman busted up his car and we're going to arrest him? He's not in violation. No, no. That's not the right call."

"But we ran his name, and he's been collared over twenty times," one of the officers argued.

"That doesn't change the situation that we're dealing with here," I said. "The circumstances of right now. He didn't do anything here to be arrested. She is the perpetrator. He is the victim. She doesn't own the streets of Brownsville."

Restraining orders were enforced overly technically by officers, which led to unnecessary and sometimes false arrests. The incentive was always to make the arrest no matter the circumstances because it fed the numbers machine. My sector didn't want to give up that arrest, so they just tried to transfer it from one person to another—like people were interchangeable. It was everything wrong with the system.

After making it clear to my officers that we weren't arresting the victim, I went back over to him. "Listen, man, you just told me you had kids. What are you doing getting locked up so many times?"

"You know how it is, my ni**a, growing up in the hood—"

"Listen, I'm from Flatbush, I get it, brother." I tried to replace the N-word with "brother" whenever I could. "You can't keep getting arrested. At what point do you realize you're a father and you gotta be there for your kids?"

"You're right, you're right."

"Brother, you don't belong in jail. You should be free, spending time with your children, making memories with the people you love."

"You right, you right," he repeated, nodding over and over again. He was totally calm by now. "Look, I don't even get in trouble no more. Only time I get arrested is for her."

As we wrapped up, the officers at the scene were looking at me funny, hesitating and talking low out of earshot. That vibe carried back to the command.

For the rest of the month, something wasn't right. Certain officers wouldn't look at me. Those who used to be comfortable around me grew nervous. Those who used to joke with me stopped. I could feel something brewing. After the Kap press conference, I didn't know what was going to happen to jam me up, but I was ready, suspicious that anything I did would be bent and twisted in the service of killing my next promotion.

A couple of months later, I was leaving a community meeting at the Pink Houses in East New York with one of my subordinates. He was looking down at his phone when he stopped and turned to me. "Boss," he said.

"What's up?"

He handed me his phone.

On the screen was a *New York Post* article: "Metro Exclusive: Cop Probed over Claims He Let Domestic Violence Suspect Walk for Being Black."

My stomach dropped and I went dizzy for a few seconds. Then I shook it off and started reading: a month after the incident in the Brownsville Houses, the two responding officers got together with a few other cops and called Internal Affairs claiming that I would not arrest Black people. Nothing in the article made sense. The perpetrator—the ex-girlfriend who had broken the guy's car mirrors—was interviewed as though she was the victim. There was no effort to explain what the call was about, or to get a comment from me or anyone besides their anonymous sources. It was a hit piece, pure and simple, with the backing of people in the department who had it out for me.

As I was reading, notification banners kept popping up from a group chat on my colleague's phone. They were sharing the article and tagging it with comments.

LOL
Scumbag
POS

When I got back to base, it was clear the article had made the rounds. People were either staring right at me or afraid to look at me at all. About an hour later I got a phone call from a female reporter at the *New York Post*.

"Hey," she said, genial and professional. "We're getting ready to release a story, do you have a comment on allegations that—"

"What do you mean?" I asked, cutting her off. "You're getting ready to release a story I just read?"

"Well, yeah, this is to get your comments for the print edition."

"But wait, you want my comments now? Where was the journalistic integrity before you put it out online for millions of people to see? Everyone I know has already read it!"

"We had trouble getting your number—"

"Oh yeah?" I said, agitated. "So why were you so quick to publish? You could've gotten my number from your source. If you're going to smear me, just do your thing. You're now calling me for comments for—"

Her professional tone vanished. "Listen, do you want to make a comment or not?" she said, nasty and curt.

I did not.

A full-page article appeared in the print edition of the *Post* the next day with a headline referring to "reverse racism" and featuring a large picture of me at the Kaepernick press conference. The facts were wildly incorrect, deliberately so. Forget that the man whom I supposedly wouldn't arrest was *the victim* in the incident. Forget that I had regularly arrested

Black people in the course of my job. I had been in public talking about needless arrests of minorities, so they were able to sell a story that fit their confirmation bias. The *Post* had never reported on anything I'd ever done, none of the activism or whistleblowing, but this seemed fit for them to print.

It knocked me off-balance. At work, I was under a microscope. Everyone, above me or below, was watching my every move; anytime I walked into a room it felt like a conversation had just been going on about me. I knew how these things worked; they were going to come for my promotion again.

Months later, my commander took me aside. "You still thinking about that bullshit?" he asked. "Don't even worry about it. It's nothing."

"For any other cop, maybe," I said. "But trust me, this is all they need. They'd been waiting for something like this."

It was the first time that I was in the crosshairs of IAB (Internal Affairs Bureau), though by that point, I knew what that department really was. After I became a whistleblower, a lot of people said things like, "Man, you belong in Internal Affairs." The public has this false picture of IAB as a moralistic anticorruption body; it's yet another thing that has filtered into the real world through the portal of TV cops. Nothing could be further from the truth, from how investigations are conducted, to how officers and supervisors are selected to join, to how effective it is in cracking down on police misconduct.

Commissioner Dermot Shea had the audacity to once say, in a question about the "blue wall of silence" that in "the majority of cases [Internal Affairs] receive, the complaints come from other officers,"[4] implying the wall doesn't exist. He made it seem as if those complaints by cops are out of integrity, but everyone on the force knows they're out of spite. IAB is used for settling scores, not out of any sense of integrity or duty. When cops have personal gripes and want to hurt another cop, they'll use IAB as a tool. No one will call IAB over a cop moving drugs or violating someone's rights, but an officer caught in a work love triangle or lying about his address? Those are IAB calls, often by an enemy on the force who wants to hurt someone's career. Most deep corruption, if uncovered, comes from the Feds and outside agencies and is handed over to IAB.*

Part of the reason that IAB is so ineffectual is that no one wants to be there. All the supervisors in IAB were "drafted" into it. If a supervisor—sergeant or above—wants a transfer, it's called "rolling the dice" because IAB gets first crack at drafting him. If the cop ends up in IAB, he will make a point of always telling other cops he was drafted, lest he get pegged as a rat. Those in the rank of police officer who end up there are trying to get off the hamster wheel of patrol and quotas, hoping to get a detective shield.† IAB is not some moral bastion of the police department: it's the cellar, a career dead end or prison sentence. Internal Affairs is made up of cops forced there, looking after cops stuck there.

AT THE END of the spring of 2018, the first fifty lieutenants were promoted, and I was skipped. That same month *another* fifty were promoted, and I was skipped again. At the time, I couldn't rule out that I was skipped because of a technicality; I didn't have the requisite time in rank (you need two years as a sergeant). I wrote a letter to Commissioner O'Neill noting that my sergeant promotion had been improperly held up and arguing that I shouldn't be punished again for it. I pleaded: Just do the right thing here. Does everything have to be done through the courts and public campaigns? I *earned* this promotion.

---

* In 2011, there was a case of a federal wiretap that caught a white Staten Island cop saying to his girlfriend that he had "fried another ni**er . . . no big deal," admitting to lying on the stand about a Black man resisting arrest. The Feds turned the tape over to IAB, which started an investigation. (Andy Newman, "Officer Faces Civil Rights Charges in Stop-and-Frisk Arrest," *New York Times*, October 17, 2011.)

† I noticed that a disproportionate number of minority cops I knew seemed to be in IAB. When I spoke to them, I found out they all had similar stories. They were tired of getting passed over for the detective shield by their white counterparts, sometimes cops they trained, so they moved to IAB as an alternate route to the shield.

I got no response.

Then I found out the real reason I'd been skipped. I got a notification from the Housing Bureau requiring me to appear for a deposition. It was my first hard evidence that I was under departmental investigation.

I knew I faced a stacked deck. The previous fall, when others were giving depositions for the investigation, a van was supposed to take everyone out to the admin building in Harlem. But when my two drivers and a delegate* tried to get in the van, one of the other delegates wouldn't let them in. Even though the van had more than enough room, they were forced to take another car. Those who would give negative testimony about me all rode together, likely so they could rehearse their testimony, to give it the air of credibility.

In October, I was hit with the official charges, the NYPD's equivalent of a court-martial. The leadership, with the help of a few PBA delegates who had it out for me, pushed forward the investigation because of how perfect it was for them; it didn't come from above. I couldn't claim retaliation because it was from subordinates, just some "good cops reporting corruption."

I could've fought it, and I was willing to. I did a few interviews in the press to get my side of the story out. Activist Shaun King and Justice League NYC were ready to assemble and garner support. Council Member Jumaane Williams held a rally and was pushing for my promotion from behind the scenes. But I was a realist. I'd heard their success rate in these kinds of trials was something like 90 percent, and it didn't require a burden of beyond reasonable doubt, but rather a lower standard called "the preponderance of the evidence." It was a game of "he said, they said," and I was outnumbered. Then it was made clear to me that if I accepted the charges, essentially through a plea bargain, I'd get the lieutenant promotion once the next round came.

---

* The delegate, a Black officer named Wayne Ford, was ostracized for coming to the "I'm with Kap" press conference.

"They're trying to kill your career," a mentor told me. "You have to show them it didn't work. We all know what really happened. If there's an opportunity to be promoted, get that white shirt, walk across the stage, you have to take it. Think about the message it sends."

It was a very difficult decision to accept the charges, though once they removed the "making false statements" charge, I agreed. I felt like I understood why people take plea deals; sometimes to stay standing, that's the only choice.

WHEN I MADE it to lieutenant, got that white shirt and my own platoon, I was proud, but I knew it wasn't really about me. It sent the message that it wasn't automatic career suicide to speak out and push to change things. "Nobody survives what you survived," a captain said. But my hope was that now that I had, others might file in line behind me. I would not be defined by the hits I took, but rather by the fact that I was still standing.

I was now Lieutenant Edwin Raymond, one of only two hundred Black lieutenants out of seventeen hundred on the entire force. A lieutenant is in charge of the entire shift of sergeants and cops. Outranking 94 percent of the department, I was a boss who got to set the tone of his tour.

They called me "The Boy Who Lived."

Twenty-Five

The People

Power concedes nothing without a demand.
It never did and it never will.

—Frederick Douglass

While I waged my own personal fight to save my career, the legal case that I'd put my name on—*Raymond v. The City of New York*—was running into trouble. The NYPD 12 lawsuit was trying to set a new precedent, but the courts don't respond favorably to those who get there first. In fact, the first ones through usually take the most fire.

In June 2018, the city's law department got eight of the twelve NYPD 12 cases dismissed completely.* With them, we also lost the most significant evidence we had regarding the quotas—that it was systemic across five boroughs and all bureaus (Transit, Patrol, Housing). It was a significant blow. For all the attention brought to the 2010 ban on quotas in New York City, the law was written without teeth. It was essentially a labor law, so the only way to remedy its violation was through the union, which would've been futile. There wasn't precedent for the judge to refer

---

* The NYPD 12 did not have class-action status, so all twelve of us had our own separate suits.

to and, like most judges, she wasn't willing to make her own. The other four cases, including mine, had enough constitutional violations that the judge let them continue.*

Year after year, as the city put forth new motions in an attempt to break us, I saw firsthand how the status quo operates. Powerful governmental institutions are immovable because their own strength perpetuates itself; their maintenance and survival are automatic functions of society. We were suing the city on behalf of its citizens for a practice that unjustly harassed, fined, and arrested them, but those very citizens, as taxpayers, were paying to defend it in court.

The NYPD 12 were treated like just another aggrieved party fighting the city, seeking remedy and asking for money. But for us, the money was clearly not the point. If so, we would've quietly done our jobs, gotten our overtime and promotions, eventually collected our nice pensions, and lived comfortably. Anyone accusing us of trying to win the so-called ghetto lottery hadn't been paying attention.

The goal had always been to hold on tight enough and remain standing long enough to get to trial. Whether the court ultimately ruled in our favor was not as important as just getting there. A trial would pull things out of dusty law offices and bureaucratic filings and put them on the front page, above the fold. If we could get testimony on the record, evidence on the books, it would air out the NYPD's racist, self-serving, and corrupt practices. The ugliness would be exposed and citizens would see what was happening in their name.

Of course, this possibility terrified the city, so it put all its money, resources, and size to work to stop us. Their goal was to smother the fire before too many people noticed the smoke. But we were like the embers still burning, refusing to be extinguished, glowing hot.

---

* The others belonged to Ritchie Baez, Sandy Gonzalez, and Pedro Serrano.

ONE ARENA WHERE we were gaining ground was on the screen. That previous winter, in January 2018, Stephen Maing's documentary *Crime + Punishment*, which focused on illegal quotas and unfair retaliation against officers in the NYPD 12, premiered at the Sundance Film Festival, where it won the U.S. Documentary Special Jury Award for Social Impact. It was groundbreaking: the documentation of *active* police officers speaking out against the department and taking their fight to the courts and the media.

The film swept through the department like a tornado. Despite years of denying the existence of quotas, including former commissioner Bratton publicly calling "bullshit" on the accusation, the leadership was forced to implement department-wide training regarding quotas just days after the film's premiere. It was as close as we'd ever get to their admitting that quotas existed. The chief of department, Terence Monahan, its highest-ranking uniformed member, recorded a video that became mandatory viewing, saying that quotas were unlawful and that any supervisor caught requesting quotas, directly or indirectly, would be reprimanded.

"They're too stubborn to ever give you the credit, but you did it," one officer told me. "You actually changed this thing." *For now*, I thought. I knew that whatever changes were made in the wake of *Crime + Punishment* would not be deep-seated or long-lasting unless we made them so. The leaders of the department were following the same playbook they always did after taking bad press: shovel off the negative attention. We had to push to make sure this pressure was permanent, laying the groundwork for a more just police department. It would not be easy. Resisting change was what the department did best.

Screening the film gave me an opportunity to meet and interact with others engaged in the fight. At one screening of the film at the BRIC House in Brooklyn, I met actor, activist, and local icon Michael K.

Williams. In recent years, Mike had been using his platform to bring attention to social justice issues, specifically juvenile ones. Before the film was over, he was in the green room trying to find me to talk about it.

It was clear the film had activated and energized something in him. Actor and activist Malik Yoba, who had invited Mike to the screening, hosted the Q&A afterward and invited Mike to join us on the panel. We stayed in touch, and from that day forward MK and I were brothers. He used his platform to assist in spreading the word about the film and the bigger fight. As he expanded his work in the community, I'd pop up as often as I could.

Crime + Punishment was short-listed for a 2019 Academy Award for Best Documentary and won an Emmy for Outstanding Social Issue Documentary. As one of the main subjects of the film, I became more recognizable, which I saw less as a plaudit than as a tool. I did what I could to take that spotlight and use it to bring attention to this issue that had come to define my life. I learned that from MK: don't stand in the spotlight; be the spotlight itself.

When *Crime + Punishment* began streaming on Hulu, it spread to audiences all over the country, even the world. Officers from England to Australia reached out to me, to ask for guidance, show support, and tell me they were inspired to change things in their own departments. I spoke to officers who were filing their own lawsuits, like the PG13 in Prince George's County, Maryland, who were suing regarding discrimination;* a Louisiana state trooper named Carl Cavalier who had blown the whistle by leaking the files about the killing of an unarmed Black man, Ronald Greene, by police; a retired Richmond officer named Joseph Ested, who connected me with other officers through his organization, Police Brutality Matters, who needed assistance for legal fights throughout the nation. With every successive fight, I felt fortified; we

---

* They won.

were all connected and gaining strength from binding together. Their victories were our victories. I didn't even see them as separate fights. It was all one fight.

This was exactly what my hope had been when I agreed to participate in Steve's film. Mass media can break through in ways that politics and government reform and legal hearings can't. I remember the way Spike Lee's movie on Malcolm X lit up my young mind. The way Serpico himself came to me through a Hollywood film, which brought his story to far more people than news of the Knapp Commission did. If your story hits the public in their emotional core, their heart along with their head, they are more likely to come on board, share with others, or even join the fight. The officers in Prince George's County, in addition to getting a settlement and having their legal fees covered, won a larger victory. Built into the verdict was a series of policy reforms in the police department. That's what I was looking for as well.

I knew that at some point, as part of the legal process, the city was going to offer us money. And I knew I was going to turn it down. I remember discussing my strategy with Anthony Miranda, the retired officer who had advised the NYPD 12, about how I wasn't in this for the money. Miranda, a pragmatist with enough experience under his belt, made sure I understood that money was a symbol and a tool. Money sends a message, hits institutions where they live. It is the language of civil courts. I understood his point, but I still saw victory as getting into a courtroom, not being handed a check before having the chance to air out the systemic bias and the rot of the numbers game in an open setting.

I was a kid who grew up with nothing, collecting bottles in the trash to buy a plate of fried rice. I thought of my mother dying in a city hospital, my father coming to this country as an immigrant and never getting the health services he needed, my friends who thought robbing was the only way they could get things they wanted, Ronald and me lingering at friends' houses in the hopes of getting fed. I fantasized sometimes about taking the city's money, but it was never an actual possibility. Why would I have put up with this if all I wanted was money?

After over four years of delay after bureaucratic delay, motion after motion, the city still couldn't get rid of us. We were still standing. And that meant something.

Spring 2020

No matter how dedicated I am to the fight, I try to keep in mind that we're all connected in ways that may not be obvious behind our separate walls, under our separate roofs. The 2020 coronavirus pandemic stopped the world spinning on its axis while also driving home the very fact of our connectedness. It also highlighted racial disparities that are part of the American fabric—from what minority communities were given for assistance compared to their white counterparts, to the lopsided mortality rates for people of color, to the way Black and Brown people always bear the brunt of public crises.

Police departments, as the enforcers of the racial and social order, did their part. Videos popped up showing NYPD officers using physical force on people, often those of color, for what started as social-distance stops. I even got word at my command that, on my days off, supervisors of other platoons were encouraging my officers to use lack of social distancing as a pretext to stop people. Meanwhile, in the white parts of the city, the police department was handing out masks on the street and in the parks. The pandemic, and the enforcement that came out of it, was a heightened version of the same conflicts that had characterized day-to-day life in neighborhoods like mine.

Then, the powder keg. On May 25, 2020, a Minneapolis police officer knelt on George Floyd's neck for over nine minutes in broad daylight, while three other cops stood by. Floyd's alleged crime: passing a counterfeit twenty-dollar bill. His death, and the jaw-dropping bystander video that caught the murder, led to international protests in what became the second wave of the Black Lives Matter movement. The egregious nature of the incident, along with the unassailable video, sent waves of people into the streets, demanding justice, demanding peace, demanding that the police department sworn to protect and serve account for itself.

The moment was upon us. It was a flash point. What were we going to do with it? Though the outpouring was reminiscent of the Eric Garner and Mike Brown protests in 2014, this was bigger by orders of magnitude. Thousands of people flooded downtown Brooklyn, gathered in Washington Square Park in Manhattan, and marched in the Bronx. In all my life living in this city, I had never seen that many people out and about and gathered at once. And this was during a pandemic and a lockdown.

As an officer working the protests, I got singled out because of my dark skin and white shirt, which indicated leadership. From behind barricades, holding bullhorns or microphones, protesters would point and yell in my face: "How can you wear that uniform? How can you wear your hair like that? You ain't doing shit! Our people are getting killed out here and you're working with *them*!"

The large crowds would repeat protest chants in unison:

How do you spell racist? N-Y-P-D!

No justice . . . no peace! Fuck these racist ass po-lice!

These chants went on for hours upon hours, playing in my head on repeat long after they stopped.

At protests near Barclays Center, we lined up in formation in front of the protesters, to ensure they remained as orderly as possible behind barricades. In uniform, even if you're just standing there, your presence is viewed as a threat. *You* are what they are protesting. As people of my own color called me "house ni**a," "race traitor," or "coon," I mostly just had to take it. I had to listen to dozens of people every day yell directly at me, "Quit your job!" It would ring in my ears when I tried to sleep: *Quit your job!* You can't just shake off something like that.

Sometimes, when I felt like they would listen, I'd try to converse with them. "I care about this community," I'd say. "If I quit, this position doesn't just disappear; it could get filled by someone who doesn't."

At one protest I encountered a young man wearing a Haitian flag around his neck, who was just seething, venting raw emotion. He pointed at me and I walked over. "You should understand, if you're Black!" he was yelling. "We're tired of this!"

"I understand your pain," I said, muffled through my mask, drowned out by the noise. "I connect with you more than you know."

But he was too heated to listen. Those streets were not necessarily a place of debate. People just wanted to be heard. Sometimes, if a protester was amenable to talk, I tried to tell them I understood, that they should look me up. Sometimes they did. But I wore the uniform, so I represented their oppressor.

Like many of my Black brethren in uniform, I was pulled in two directions. Colleagues would call me up in tears because they were having a crisis of faith, uncomfortable with which side of the line they stood on. These cops didn't necessarily deserve the attacks; they had to face the crowds, but they didn't make the decisions. They were just showing up to work, trying to pay their bills, following the policy from the leadership.

Some cops took to social media, *in uniform*, to denounce the actions of police—something I'd never thought I'd live to see. Cop culture exists within a dichotomy: "us versus them." But all of a sudden, those sides were blurry. That in itself was a good thing. It reflected reality. As the protests spread, I felt like I was witnessing the death of the old world, the one where Black cops could carry their double identity so lightly. Whatever barrier they had once put up that allowed them to do this job with a clean conscience came crashing down that summer.

Across racial lines, virtually all cops were outraged by the George

Floyd video, that was a given. But when they realized that the community could not see the difference between them and problematic cops—when people saw little difference between them and Derek Chauvin—some of them wanted out. I was surprised at the number of white officers who were conflicted, too, who reached out to tell me they couldn't take wearing the uniform any longer.

"I can't do this anymore," officers told me. "I'm gonna quit this job."

These cops didn't become police to brutalize citizens or violate their rights. They couldn't tell these crowds that they had children to feed, that some didn't trust the very department that they worked for to do right by those children. I sympathized with all of them, but I also told them to hang on.

"Just the fact that you feel the way you feel is a sign that you belong in this uniform," I'd say. "Because if you were able to just blindly go along, you'd be what they *think* you are. But that's not what you are. They don't see this right here; they don't see the pain you're going through." I was vehement that we could not cede ground to those using the uniform to oppress.

In June 2020, a few weeks after Floyd's death, the CEA, the NYPD captains' union, wrote a letter to Commissioner Shea asking that Comp-Stat, due to the pressure it creates, be done away with.[1] This was a giant vindication of the fight because it showed even the executives were finally admitting publicly that the pressure and incentives from the top were causing the problems at the bottom.

Other things were different this time around. While young activists called for police reform back in 2014, a loud contingent of protesters in 2020 were calling for straight police abolition. During their formative years, they lived through Eric Garner, Mike Brown, Laquan McDonald, Tamir Rice, Akai Gurley, Eric Harris, Walter Scott, Freddie Gray, Sandra Bland, Alton Sterling, Philando Castile, Terence Crutcher, Stephon Clark, Botham Jean, Breonna Taylor, and many more.

The irony was that these young New Yorkers had fewer police encounters than any generation in decades. The stop-and-frisk ruling, the decriminalization of marijuana, and the efforts to suppress enforcement quotas meant the numbers themselves were going down significantly. But that's not what people felt in their hearts, in their guts. The experience of watching one high-profile incident after another—not just reading about it but actually *watching* it happen—shaped their perspectives. Talking points about abolishing or defunding the police became the new axioms. Just a few years prior, such a demand would've been political suicide; now even elected officials had to make clear they were down with the new battle cry.

Getting rid of police or defunding them as a punitive measure is far too dangerous to make sense. If "defund" means channel some dollars to other services, count me in. I know firsthand that police are overburdened in their responsibilities, many of which aren't official. When city agencies go home for the day or close for the weekend, cops take over some of those jobs. If we have to reallocate that funding to create or feed other agencies, I'm all for it. But the police serve a necessary function, and attempts to get rid of them entirely are misguided. My sense from the protests, and the heated aftermath, was that this middle ground either wasn't understood or wasn't embraced. I felt alone out there.

After the death of George Floyd, when I would try to engage with a protester, I sometimes caught the eyes of a nearby captain, clearly annoyed that I was able to talk with "these people." Even with my track record, community efforts, and youth work with PLOT, the top brass wouldn't see me as an asset. I was still the problem cop. If they were too blind to see that I was exactly the kind of cop they needed, I considered that it might be time for me to try to make changes from outside the department.

I thought about how many hurdles I had to go through to get the right elected official to support my efforts, how hard it was to sit down with someone in power who had the guts even to try. Why not *become* that elected official instead of waiting for him to show up? I didn't wait to find the good cop to rise in the ranks; I became him. I didn't wait for someone to speak out against the systemic racism in the department; I became him. Why not become the elected official I was waiting on?

I realized that I could be a rational voice who understood both sides, a rarity. That's one of the biggest challenges of policing: How do we strike the balance between providing adequate public safety and maintaining people's constitutional rights? The people who are having their ideas adopted as practice, policy, and law are usually not in the best position to answer this question. They don't believe in a holistic approach, and the new breed of activists don't trust cops.

In 2021, I ran for the city council seat for District 40, the area of Brooklyn that includes East Flatbush. During the campaign I saw what it was like on the front lines of the political fight. The experience taught me about the practicalities that undergird everyone's ideas and idealism. I saw why progress is so slow and difficult to achieve. Most glaringly, I also saw the way personal agendas get prioritized over public service.

I'd meet with powerful groups, organizations, and unions that seemed far more interested in how much money I'd raised and who had endorsed me than what my values were. This struck me as narrow-minded to the point of counterproductive. Members would reach out, telling me how much they connected with me, but the leadership had already decided which endorsement would be most beneficial to them. It had far more to do with politics and favors than what was best for their members. I saw how individual voices got drowned out by a political process that supposedly existed for their sake. It was the same story: institutions protecting their own survival above all else.

On the other end, consultants were trying to get me to do things that went against my entire identity, actions that would have hollowed out my integrity. They wanted me to pander to unions and political groups to get those endorsements that other groups were asking about. In my meetings with these organizations, I kept my answers true to how I saw things, not what they wanted to hear. Once again, I kept being told to play the game. Advisors didn't understand that the moment I betrayed who I was, I'd lose the whole purpose of my run. Their reaction told me that most people running for office don't push back like that. It's why we have the kind of people we do in charge, like a reverse Darwinism.

Though I didn't win, it was an educational experience. I got a better understanding of the financial aspect of criminal justice, the dollars that fuel the enforcement of broken windows. When the budget is voted on, there are always departments and agencies that miss out. What ends up happening is that there's a gap, and that gap has to be made up in the revenue budget. This is where enforcement comes in. It's not just police. Any agency that could issue a fine, at least under Mayor Bloomberg, was pressured to do so because that's how revenue was raised to fill the gaps. A video went around of a sanitation worker breaking bulbs outside a business, just so he could fine it. It was egregious, and he got caught and disciplined, but no one talks about how he was incentivized to do that.

When you measure people based on a number, they are going to make achieving the number their goal. A friend of mine worked at Macy's and was financially incentivized to get customers to sign up for a store credit card. She would watch her colleagues prey on foreign-language speakers and get them to sign things they couldn't understand. Of course, the coworkers were wrong to do this, but that behavior doesn't happen in a vacuum. Those in charge who create those incentives are far more integral to that problem than the rank and file who are lured by them. Same with cops.

If you find an institution that is harming the public, then you will find instructions from the top that incentivizes it to do so. It's that simple. And that prevalent. What you see in the police department is replicated in virtually all large institutions. It's the status quo that has hardened in place. And the longer it stays there, the harder it is for well-meaning people to chip away at it.

In my thirteen years as a police officer, what I saw from leadership was a disconnect between the policies they encourage and incentivize and the externalities and collateral damage that occur as a result. The crime issue doesn't occupy an island, though it's too often treated that way. It is connected to poverty, housing, health care, family dynamics, education, economics, history, the job market—so many other elements of society. But the leadership doesn't engage in any long-term thinking or foresight. It'd be like if a doctor just focused on an injury or illness without caring how the rest of the body responded. Then the patient came back in a week later with a new problem, and again the doctor just fixed the one issue. They need to look at the whole body.

Cops wonder why they're seen as the community's nemesis, but they're the ones who've laid that groundwork. "Part of the problem stems from a 'warrior mentality,'" writes Alex Vitale in *The End of Policing*. "Police often think of themselves as soldiers in a battle with the public rather than guardians of public safety."[2] This does not start at the rank-and-file level.

The distrust between cops and minority communities runs deep and runs long. I try to do what I can at the individual level. I keep books in the patrol car (especially copies of Michael K. Williams's book, *Scenes from My Life*, and Kwasi's (Jim St. Germain's) memoir, *A Stone of Hope*) and started a drive for children's books by Black authors, about Black leaders. In each book I sign a message in calligraphy, a skill I learned back in my artist days.

It's gratifying to see any impact I've had, even on the one-to-one level. My driver recently thanked me for helping him see himself differently in the uniform. "You know, it used to be that if someone didn't call nine one one, I didn't talk to anyone on my shift," he said. "I didn't even say good morning to people. I never saw myself as part of the community like that. I just came to work. Now I don't."

"See, that's the problem," I said, "and you're a Black cop from immigrant parents. On paper you're everything the police department needs and here you are going with the flow. If we don't incentivize the new flow, it's not going to happen."

Cops often refer to the department as this abstract entity. Even the upper echelon does this, as if they're not the ones in charge. After the *Times* article came out, executives in the department were calling me up, talking about "they" or "the job." It reveals a lack of ownership over decisions, a way to shift blame when things go wrong, frame it as though it's a natural occurrence. We cannot forget that it is always people who make systems real. They can change them. Not overnight, and not without the will to do so, but they have the power.

July 2022

In the summer of 2022, as I was working on this book, we got the news that a federal judge had thrown out the remaining four NYPD 12 discrimination cases.

After seven years of hoping and waiting for justice to prevail, it was soul crushing. The reasons for the cases' dismissal were convoluted. Essentially, the judge reasoned that because our superiors didn't say, "We're retaliating against you because you're an officer of color," we didn't meet the burden of proof to show it was about race. This was frustrating, because of course that's not how things work—anywhere. As we said when we filed the complaint in 2015, the entire system runs on incentives, retaliation, and careful wording. Those in charge know better than to be that obvious and explicit about it, but anyone able to read between the lines understands what's going on.

Another aspect of the judge's reasoning was that, because the disparate treatment in my case started under Black and Brown supervisors, I couldn't claim that racism was behind the low evaluations. This shows a basic lack of understanding of how racism works. Racism can become an institutional fixture, even carried out by people of color, especially when they're in positions of power. Those low evaluations were still part of the system of white supremacy; those cops of color were still feeling heat from the very same system. It's disappointing that people in high positions still think the only kind of racism is the kind that calls you "ni**er" to your face. The ignorance around the true damage caused by racism, both within and without the police department, remains one of my primary targets. Our lawyers have recently filed a lawsuit in state court, so we're going to take another swing. I can only hope that justice and common sense prevail. There is far too much at stake.

A consequence of our federal case being tossed out is that it will be that much harder for the next case that comes along. The police department will be far more prepared next time. What I got on those recordings—you're not going to get that anymore. The brass even refer to *Crime + Punishment* in order to show executives what *not* to say and to teach supervisors to always speak as if they're being recorded. The system has digested our case and is now using it to fortify itself,* making another *Raymond v. The City of New York* that much more unlikely. This ruling now becomes case law not just for the police department but for governmental agencies, companies, and organizations around the country. They can use the federal ruling in *Raymond* to cover for all sorts of systemic racism.

It's painful for me that my name could now be used to perpetuate the very thing hurting my people. I will ensure it is not the legacy I leave behind. I will continue to do what I always have—push my pain forward, plug it into the fight, make sure it means something bigger than myself.

I make a conscious choice to stay living here—just down the road from the grocery store where I worked as a teenager. It helps me to feel

---

* I am sure that the brass will point to declining arrest and summons numbers as proof that there are no quotas or pressure for enforcement. However, that decline in numbers happened only because of collective activism. But the monster is rearing its head again. I'm being contacted weekly by NYPD officers telling me how they're once again facing pressure for overaggressive enforcement and numbers. Those who have risen in the ranks in this current administration and this department are true believers in "quality-of-life" policing theory.

grounded, part of the community, a necessary fixture. I've liked people in the neighborhood seeing me in uniform. *There's Edwin, he used to hand out circulars and now he's a cop.* I know what I saw when I was a kid, how it exposed me to the different pathways of adulthood. I picture a kid on the block seeing me, and who knows, maybe it gives him ideas of what he can be. I will continue what I do with this kid in mind, as well as thousands like him. He's been led to believe that he doesn't matter. Or that he's a problem. Or that he can't do anything about the ills of this world. It is for him, and the next generation, that I'm going to keep up the fight.

But as I've been writing this book, it has become clear to me that I can no longer fight from inside the police department. I can't spend my time in a place that doesn't see me as an asset. With a higher profile has come the opportunity to take on these issues in a larger forum. Out of uniform. And all over this country.

One of the things that triggered this realization was my experience watching Captain Derby St. Fort, a Black captain in the NYPD. As the XO, the second in command at the Seventy-Third Precinct in Browns-ville, Derby had been trying to do things differently: empowering neighborhoods to get involved in community policing, employing violence interrupters (community members who can help the police ease tensions in the street), supporting mentoring programs, bringing in outside organizations to work with kids, and even paying young men and women a stipend to come to group therapy sessions.

Derby is the definition of justice minded, though he wasn't always that way. He evolved over time, after questioning what he was being asked to do. Now, he refuses to tell his officers to focus on the numbers and has them working on addressing the whole person, not just the crime. His goal is to act with the future in mind and catch these young men and women earlier. Instead of the assembly-line mentality perpetuated by the leadership, Derby opts for outside-of-the-box solutions—and he had been seeing results. When Derby was XO, shootings were declining in Brownsville at a time when they were going up across the city.[3] He was building relationships and making inroads. And some of the department's leadership—those who don't believe in achieving public safety in certain neighborhoods outside of harsh enforcement—*hated* him for it. So, in the summer of 2020, Derby was moved out of Brownsville and ultimately to the Sixty-First Precinct in Coney Island. He's still doing his thing and having success, but Coney Island is another world from Brownsville, so his methods are less impactful. Rather than empowering one of the most valuable assets they have, the department's leadership is trying to bury him. It's tragic to me, but it's also instructive.

Derby has been trying to execute a plan that was once my own: rise as high as possible in the ranks (to captain, since everything above that is discretionary) and police in a justice-minded way that isn't subservient to numbers. My thinking was, when my crime numbers went down, I could go in front of CompStat with my head held high and they couldn't say a word.

But Derby has taken this thing as far as it can go. His promotions are being stifled—officers who reached captain after he did are already two ranks above him—and he's been forced to go rogue, speaking out in public and inviting the media to publicize what he's doing. The department's current leadership is never going to embrace him—in fact, they try to smear him in the press—though he continues to make strides.

The key to change is to focus on the leadership. We cannot get caught up in the negative actions of the individual officer because he or she is always operating within a system, incentivized by executives, and laid down in policy. Cops are the most visible and tangible parts of the system, but they're not the system itself. The goals and actions of the police force start much farther upstream than the single cop. We need to put more focus on the headwaters of oppression.

There is a justice-minded movement in this country that the police department is not letting me take part in, so I have to leave. I must leave to help lead it. It's a damning indictment of the institution that they spend time and energy fighting someone like Derby when he is exactly the kind of officer who should be leading them.

Ever since I first spoke up, I've been hearing from officers all over this nation who care about justice: they need help, support, someone to elevate them. I believe I'm uniquely suited to do this, and I can't do it from where I sit.

I'm leaving the department to use my platform to empower others. Thousands have already reached out, looked toward me as a leader, so I'm going to do as Michael K. Williams said: not be the spotlight, but shine it on others. I'm going to work to highlight and empower the right officers across this nation so that leadership, elected officials, activists, and the public know that our police departments have the people who can lead them out of the darkness. Currently, they are not recognized or valued. Putting them in charge takes the guesswork out of finding the right solution. Those justice-minded officers are going to take us into the light.

In 1953, twenty-six-year-old actor and singer Harry Belafonte met the twenty-four-year-old Martin Luther King Jr. in the basement of a church in New York City. He was so impressed with King that he decided to devote more of his time and platform to civil rights, back before the movement even had a name. Belafonte, who passed away as I was finishing this book, was institutional memory made flesh. He had his hands in so much of the work done for our people, from the movement that brought President Obama's father to the country to Carmen Perez and the new generation of activists. From the moment he got involved, he operated with the unborn in mind. At the end of the day, that's what this is about. I work today for those who are not here yet or just being born, hoping they can live in something better.

I carry them with me wherever I go.

Acknowledgments

Though in no way is this list exhaustive, I would like to acknowledge my coauthor Jon, agents Susan and Wendy, Ibrahim and the entire team at Viking, Dad, Mom, Ronald, Abner, Kenny, Winer, Billy, Melissa, Mommy Florise, Kwasi, Bishme, Nikel, Nickson, Sashanna, Michael K. Williams, Malik Yoba, Shani Kulture, Baz, Daniel, Reggie, Jeff, Habby, Carli, Fabrice, Romain, Herby, Freddie, Junior, Cliff, Dooker, Carine, Romzy, Eli, Liana, Kenya, Dia, Vicky, Ludny, John Scola, Emeka Nwokoro, Shaun King, Saki, Sarah, Touré, L'Union Suite, Steve Maing, Scoper, Kai, Muriel, EmpressAK, Jumaane, Rodneyse, Edu, Farah, Diana, Antonio, Jesse, Ray McGuire & Crystal McCrary, Serpico, The NYPD 12, The Gathering for Justice, Until Freedom, Shani Kulture, Kap & Nessa, MiaBelle, Gentlemen's Factory, HALEFO, NLOA, Oliver, Weatherspoon, Aaliyah, Will, Tre, Fred, Mark, Kiko, Black, Corey, Gentry, Andy Dennis, Dwight, Winston, Ryan, Gabriel, Drew, Corinne, Jery, Kaya, Dr. Frédéric-Pierre, Dr. Bornstein, Dr. Williams, Dr. Wilson, Dr. Mitchell, Clai, Benewaa, Jaime, Nicole Bell, Terrence Floyd, GBMNutron, Vic Mensa, IDK, Mike Colter, Micheal Ward, Light Watkins, Shu, Nzingha, Padma Lakshmi, Nikki Reed & Ian

ACKNOWLEDGMENTS

Somerhalder, Katherine Castro, Jessica Seinfeld, Jerry O'Connell, Alaina Huffman, Carl Lentz, Ellen Griesedieck, Ben & Jerry, Jay Upscale, Disney F., Darienne, Miles & Vanessa, Ested, Bohannan, Cavalier, The Prince George's 13, Kayla & Daniel, and all who have supported me on this journey.

Appendix

RECOMMENDATIONS

- *Accountability, from within and without.* State and local governments need to ensure that there's a designated team of justice-minded people from inside and outside the police department assigned to design, implement, and monitor reform. Too often reform is forced on departments, usually after something goes wrong. Then it's the very people who fought against reform who are responsible for implementing changes, sowing a conflict of interest directly into the process. They end up not putting a sincere effort into these tasks and/or sabotaging things entirely. The cycle then repeats.

- *Whistleblower shields.* While other institutions may have protections for whistleblowers, and there are laws on the books, police as a group are hostile to them. The culture of the blue wall has hardened into place, leaving those who speak out as problems that need to be dealt with rather than allies to be supported. The same juvenile "snitches get stitches" maxim that kids honor on the playground is embedded in law enforcement. The only way to change this is by instituting legally binding and enforced safe havens for whistleblowers in police departments. State and local governments need to develop investigative bodies that convene and look into any claims made by whistleblowers. People who are courageous enough to expose wrongdoing need to be supported and protected. Once they are safe and encouraged to speak out, the cultural paradigm can shift.

- *Incentive structure.* The police department needs to ensure that any changes brought to policing are incentivized. Promote those who take initiative in implementing changes in policy and reprimand those who refuse to get on board. This sends a clear message that there are real teeth behind new reform measures, and it's not just more boilerplate changes announced to pacify the public. Over time, officers grow wary of any departmental changes, referring to them as "smoke and mirrors"—as in not real. And they're right.

- *Address implicit bias from a policy perspective.* If there is ever a focus on correcting bias, it is almost always directed at individual officers during encounters with the public. What's never considered is how biases—implicit and systemic—make their way into *policy design*. The same officer who thinks it's okay to pull over a car full of young Black men because crime stats show that there's an overrepresentation of Black men in gun crimes (despite it being far less than 1 percent of the demographic) one day becomes the chief who creates policy that reflects those biases. This then gets forced on their thirty thousand subordinates, who carry it out. When things inevitably go wrong, the cops involved become demonized and forced to face discipline. But the upper echelon, who are often responsible for the policy in the first place, remain unscathed. New and existing policies have to be assessed and reassessed for racial biases to ensure that they're built on an empirical foundation. All new policies should go through a series of checks to ensure they are scrubbed for these types of biases. Demographics aren't destiny and should not be used as excuses to profile or rationalizations before the fact. Only when we get rid of racist policies will we ever change what a cop thinks his or her job is and how to do that job.

- *External investigators for more extreme cases.* Despite the majority of issues stemming from policy, practices, and culture, there are more extreme cases when the individual officer is problematic. Those cases should be investigated by independent agencies in order to maximize validity and efficiency.

- *Replace Internal Affairs.* One of things I was going to fight for if elected to city council was getting rid of the Internal Affairs Bureau. IAB has long been an ineffectual and weak body, filled with officers who don't want to be there and are sworn never to hurt other cops. The Department of Investigations (DOI), a city agency under the mayor that operates separately from the police department, is capable of doing all internal investigations. The IAB need not exist at all, and DOI taking over removes a thick layer of bias.

All oversight should have a good mix of people with actual law-enforcement experience, though. There is too much nuance to these issues. Former or current officers can offer that balance to those who only see what is written in the guidelines.

- *Encourage justice-minded candidates to join police forces.* It has become fashionable on the Left to bash the very existence of police. But this blanket condemnation is counterproductive. The best way to change the police is for justice-minded people to join the force. The battle cries of "abolish" and "defund" deter those same people who would make the best officers from putting on the uniform. Police departments are ultimately made of people, and demonizing the entire force will surely keep the right kind of people away.

- *Seek input from all levels.* Rather than the top-down management style that plagues many departments, input from lower-ranking members should be taken and assessed (especially from those who come from demographics and areas that have historically had contentious relationships with law enforcement). Biannually, the leadership should provide platforms for any member to make recommendations on how to improve the department. Recommendations would then be reviewed and considered by an oversight panel consisting of those both inside and outside the department.

- *Implement a system of "informed discretion."* Broken-windows supporters have consistently demonized those on the other side of the argument by painting them as against enforcing the law. This is a ridiculous claim that clouds the reality: broken windows, as it is practiced, is unfair because it has always been heavily prejudiced against people of color.

  In addition, the quota system that keeps broken windows running has created a police force that forgoes discretion—which is the officer's right—in the name of getting the numbers. "Informed discretion" would be a system that allows officers to record official warnings for minor infractions in a searchable database that would be queried whenever someone is stopped for something minor.

If the database shows that someone hasn't been warned before, then discretion would be appropriate. If it shows that someone has been stopped multiple times for the same behavior, then it becomes clear that warnings are insufficient, and the officer can move on to enforcement. Giving the officer discretion and keeping track of various other police responses besides enforcement will serve both the public and the police department.

- *Immersion should precede criticism.* Law enforcement is a technical job that requires significant exposure and experience. In order to minimize impractical recommendations and legislation proposed by advocates and officials (some of which stem from fictitious depictions of police), programs such as ride-alongs and citizen police academies should be implemented at the local level.

- *Seek out and appoint the right leadership to pivotal positions.* Reform will remain impossible without leaders who can properly frame the issues, who actually believe that things can be rectified, and who are willing to do the work to get it done. Without the right leadership, indifference, stalling, and sabotage will stymie progress. With the justice-minded in place, we have the chance to revolutionize policing as we know it.

Notes

Chapter Three: The Academy
1. Peter Maas, *Serpico* (New York: Harper Perennial, 2005), 28.
2. Isabel Wilkerson, *Caste: The Origins of Our Discontents* (New York: Random House, 2020), 69.
3. Lou Canon, *Official Negligence* (Boulder, CO: Westview Press, 1999), 489.

Chapter Five: Immaculate Perception
1. Kristin Henning, "Boys to Men," in *Policing the Black Man: Arrest, Prosecution, and Imprisonment*, ed. Angela J. Davis (New York: Pantheon, 2017), 83.
2. Renée McDonald Hutchins, "Racial Profiling: The Law, the Policy, and the Practice," in *Policing the Black Man*, 98.

Chapter Six: Black Boys
1. Brian Broome, *Punch Me Up to the Gods* (New York: Mariner Books, 2021), 36.

Chapter Seven: Racist Math
1. George L. Kelling and James Q. Wilson, "Broken Windows," *Atlantic*, March 1982.
2. Rosa Brooks, *Tangled Up in Blue* (New York: Penguin Press, 2021), 269.
3. Henning, "Boys to Men," 58.
4. Tara Boyle et al., "How a Theory of Crime and Policing Was Born, and Went Terribly Wrong," NPR, May 29, 2017, www.npr.org/2017/05/29/530192364/how-a-theory-of-crime-and-policing-was-born-and-went-terribly-wrong.

Chapter Eight: The Invisible Line
1. Mike McAlary, "The Frightful Whisperings from a Coney Island Hospital Bed," *Daily News*, August 9, 2007.

Chapter Ten: Being Seen
1. *The Autobiography of Malcolm X* (New York: Ballantine Books, 1965), 91.
2. *Autobiography of Malcolm X*, 371.

Chapter Eleven: Conditions

1. Al Baker, "New York Minorities More Likely to Be Frisked," *New York Times*, May 12, 2010.
2. Kate Taylor, "Stop-and-Frisk Policy 'Saves Lives,' Mayor Tells Black Congregation," *New York Times*, June 10, 2012.
3. Leah Libresco, "It Takes a Lot of Stop-and-Frisks to Find One Gun," FiveThirtyEight, June 3, 2015, fivethirtyeight.com/features/it-takes-a-lot-of-stop-and-frisks-to-find-one-gun.
4. New York Civil Liberties Union, "Analysis Finds Racial Disparities, Ineffectiveness in NYPD Stop-and-Frisk Program; Links Tactic to Soaring Marijuana Arrest Rate," May 22, 2013, www.nyclu.org/en/press-releases/analysis-finds-racial-disparities-ineffectiveness-nypd-stop-and-frisk-program-links.
5. Chris Glorioso and Evan Stulberger, "I-Team: Many Knife Arrests in New York City, Few Convictions," NBC News New York, May 29, 2015.
6. "Number of Mass Shootings in the United States Between 1982 and November 2022, by Shooter's Race or Ethnicity," www.statista.com/statistics/476456/mass-shootings-in-the-us-by-shooter-s-race/; Michel Martin and Emma Bowman, "Why Nearly All Mass Shooters Are Men," NPR, March 27, 2021, www.npr.org/2021/03/27/981803154/why-nearly-all-mass-shooters-are-men.

Chapter Twelve: Problem Cop

1. Angela J. Davis, "Introduction," in *Policing the Black Man*, xvi.

Chapter Thirteen: Pushing Through

1. Graham Rayman, *The NYPD Tapes: The Shocking Story of Cops, Cover-Ups, and Courage* (New York: St. Martin's Press, 2013), 25.
2. Wendy Ruderman, "Crime Report Manipulation Is Common Among New York Police, Study Finds," *New York Times*, June 28, 2012.
3. Leonard Levitt, *NYPD Confidential: Power and Corruption in the Country's Greatest Police Force* (New York: Thomas Dunne Books, 2009), 254.

Chapter Fourteen: Officer Lil Wayne

1. Nicole Gonzalez Van Cleve, *Crook County: Racism and Injustice in America's Largest Criminal Court* (Stanford, CA: Stanford Law Books, 2016), 2.
2. Davis, "Introduction," xv.
3. Henning, "Boys to Men," 62.
4. Claudia Rankine, *Just Us: An American Conversation* (Minneapolis: Graywolf Press, 2020), 264.
5. Kristin Henning, *The Rage of Innocence: How America Criminalizes Black Youth* (New York: Knopf, 2021), 141.

Chapter Fifteen: Hardheaded

1. New York Civil Liberties Union, "Stop and Frisk Data," www.nyclu.org/en/stop-and-frisk-data.
2. Ryan Devereaux, "NYPD Commissioner Ray Kelly 'Wanted to Instil Fear' in Black and Latino Men," *Guardian*, April 1, 2013, www.theguardian.com/world/2013/apr/01/nypd-ray-kelly-instil-fear.
3. *Floyd v. City of New* York, https://ccrjustice.org/files/Floyd-Liability-Opinion-8-12-13.pdf.
4. Ashley Southall and Michael Gold, "Why 'Stop-and-Frisk' Inflamed Black and Hispanic Neighborhoods," *New York Times*, November 17, 2019.
5. New York Civil Liberties Union, "Stop and Frisk Data."

Chapter Seventeen: The Unheard

1. Alex Vitale, *The End of Policing* (Brooklyn, NY: Verso, 2017), 7.
2. New York Civil Liberties Union, "Stop and Frisk Data."
3. For Bloomberg's comments, see Jennifer Fermino, "Mayor Bloomberg on Stop-and-Frisk: It Can Be Argued 'We Disproportionately Stop Whites Too Much. And Minorities Too Little,'" *Daily News*, June 28, 2013.
4. Harry Enten, "Americans See Martin Luther King Jr. as a Hero Now, But That Wasn't the Case During His Lifetime," CNN, January 17, 2022, www.cnn.com/2022/01/17/politics/mlk-polling-analysis/index.html.

Chapter Eighteen: Front Lines

1. Alex Altman, "Why New York Cops Turned Their Backs on Mayor de Blasio," *Time*, December 22, 2014.
2. Dara Lind, "The NYPD 'Slowdown' That's Cut Arrests in New York by Half, Explained," *Vox*, January 6, 2015.
3. Carla Murphy, "NYPD Officers Do Less; City's Young Black Men Exhale," *Color Lines*, January 9, 2015, www.colorlines.com/articles/nypd-officers-do-less-citys-young-black-men-exhale.

Chapter Twenty: Raymond v. The City of New York

1. George Vlahakis-Indiana, "Black Officers Face Discipline More Often Than White Police," *Futurity*, October 13, 2020, www.futurity.org/black-police-officers-discipline-2454472-2; "Black Police Officers Disciplined Disproportionately for Misconduct, IU Research Finds," *News at IU*, October 12, 2020, news.iu.edu/live/news/27199-black-police-officers-disciplined.
2. These quotes all come from sworn affidavits in the NYPD 12 lawsuit. See Joseph Goldstein and Ashley Southall, "'I Got Tired of Hunting Black and Hispanic People,'" *New York Times*, December 6, 2019.

Chapter Twenty-Two: Noise

1. Lauren Gambino, "NYPD Chief Bratton Says Hiring Black Officers Is Difficult: 'So Many Have Spent Time in Jail,'" *Guardian*, June 9, 2015, amp.theguardian.com/us-news/2015/jun/09/bratton-hiring-black-nypd-officers-criminal-records.
2. Christina Sterbenz, "NYPD Commissioner: 'Many of the Worst Parts of Black History Would Have Been Impossible Without Police,'" *Insider*, February 24, 2015, www.businessinsider.com/nypd-commissioner-many-of-the-worst-parts-of-black-history-would-have-been-impossible-without-police-2015-2.

Chapter Twenty-Three: Public Enemy

1. I discovered this through internal crime statistics regarding stop, question, and frisks on TOS suspects.
2. Edwin Raymond, "The Racist NYPD Captain Who Ruined My Career for Not Targeting Enough Blacks and Hispanics Got Promoted," *Daily News*, June 23, 2016, www.nydailynews.com/new-york/joins-class-action-suit-nypd-article-1.2685918.
3. Steve Wyche, "Colin Kaepernick Explains Why He Sat During the National Anthem," NFL.com, August 27, 2016.
4. Merrit Kennedy, "Head of Police Chiefs Group Apologizes for 'Historical Mistreatment' of Minorities," NPR, October 18, 2016.

5. James Comey, "Hard Truths: Law Enforcement and Race," Georgetown University, February 12, 2015.

6. Ben McGrath, "Bernie Knows Best," *New Yorker*, April 27, 2015.

Chapter Twenty-Four: The Men in the Arena

1. Maas, *Serpico,* 115–16.

2. James Baldwin, *Notes of a Native Son* (Boston: Beacon Press, 1984), 9.

3. Frank Serpico, "Kap, Cops, and Confederate Statues: A Better World Without Double Standards," *Counterpunch*, September 25, 2017.

4. Michael Gannon, "NYPD Outreach at Allen AME Cathedral," *Queens Chronicle*, October 22, 2020.

Chapter Twenty-Five: The People

1. Graham Rayman, "NYPD Captains Unit: End CompStat Now," *Daily News*, June 24, 2020, www.nydailynews.com/new-york/nyc-crime/ny-captain-letter-mayor-compstat-2020 0624-amzjt7fisffs7aqkhdb2sba6tq-story.html.

2. Vitale, *The End of Policing*, 3.

3. Saki Knafo, "Bridging the Divide Between the Police and the Policed," *New Yorker*, April 28, 2021.